MORE BOOKS ON THE TABLE

MORE BOOKS
ON THE TABLE

BY

SIR EDMUND WILLIAM GOSSE

Essay Index Reprint Series

 BOOKS FOR LIBRARIES PRESS
FREEPORT, NEW YORK

First Published 1923
Reprinted 1969

STANDARD BOOK NUMBER:
8369-1410-4

LIBRARY OF CONGRESS CATALOG CARD NUMBER:
71-93340

PRINTED IN THE UNITED STATES OF AMERICA

TO
HENRY NEWBOLT
IN ADMIRATION AND ATTACHMENT

PREFACE

AN earlier series of little essays selected from *The Sunday Times* was so kindly received by the critics and so widely encouraged by the public that I am emboldened to collect a second budget from among the sermons which I preach from that secular pulpit every week. Books continue to be heaped upon my table, and they are flowers that tempt into the sunshine bees, which I call memories, hived in the course of nearly sixty years of indiscriminate and insatiate reading. The Young Anacharsis placed his trust in books, and we are told that he was disappointed. The fault must have lain, I think, in himself and not in literature. I have forgotten who Lucas de Penna was, but I love him for saying that books were to him " the light of the heart, the mirror of the body, the myrrh-pot of eloquence." So they are to me, and more so the older I grow. When the infinite variety and charm of them fail to enchant me, it will be time for me to " cease upon the midnight with no pain."

Perhaps I owe a word of apology to the authors and editors of the books which have started me on my brief excursions and independent reflections. These little essays are not, save in a few instances, to be regarded as " reviews " of the books which inspired them. They do not pretend to give an adequate, though I hope always so far as it goes an honest and candid, account of the contents of each book. My object is not to teach, but, if I may be fortunate enough to do so, to pass on to others the pleasure which I have experienced. If the poet is allowed to create his sonnet out of the emotions awakened by a sunset or a statue, of which he is not bound to supply scientific description, may I not dare a swallow-flight in prose without being called upon to give an architectural plan of the roof from which I start ?

E. G.

February, 1923.

CONTENTS

QUEEN VICTORIA

M.B.T.

QUEEN VICTORIA

MORE than twenty years divide us from an event which was calculated to disturb the balance of judgment in a very unusual degree. In spite of all the excitements which have crowded upon us since, no one can forget the emotion of emerging into the cold night of January 22, 1901, and seeing the newspaper boys, for once discreetly silent, hurrying hither and thither with a huge announcement that the Queen was dead. In the Ciceronian phrase, she had completed a voyage that was long and rough, and now she had sighted land and had entered port. But although this is the common lot of man, the world had ceased to be convinced that Victoria would undergo it. Logically, no one was foolish enough to conceive that she would live for ever, but sentimentally she had come to seem sempiternal, a portion of the order of things, a being without whose continuance future history must be impossible. She was the keystone of Europe.

It is easy to smile at this superstition, which was instinctive. But it existed, tucked away at the back of everybody's brain, and it deeply affected the mode in which, immediately after her departure, everybody spoke of her. Her phantom took divine proportions ; she was clothed with the most extravagant and the most incongruous attributes, and any one who endeavoured, in however respectful and even affectionate terms, to separate the fabulous from the historic elements, and reduce the vast idol to human proportions, was regarded as libellous and " cruel."

There was an orgy of eulogy, which was perfectly genuine, extremely respectable, and curiously silly.

What would have been the fate of Mr. Lytton Strachey if he had published his monograph in April, 1901, I shudder to imagine! He would have been pursued to the reading-room of the British Museum and there scraped to death with oyster-shells. He would have been told that he was not merely rude but criminal, not merely " cruel " but infamous. And yet from one end of his book to the other there is not a touch, or hardly a touch, of unkindness.

If I may hazard a conjecture, I think that Mr. Strachey has fallen in love with Victoria as he studied her career, and that what he started to make a satire has turned in his fingers to an appreciation. But he has emancipated himself from the last strands of that web of legend which had woven itself around her memory. He is the earliest of her biographers to insist that even a cat, and still more a careful student of the whimsicalities of life, may look steadily at a queen.

Mr. Strachey is widely known by his extremely sprightly essays on *Eminent Victorians*. It might easily be supposed that when he came to treat of the fountain-head of Victorianism his sarcasms, which had given some alarm, and his irony, which had awakened a certain scandal, would be accentuated. This does not prove to be the case. *Queen Victoria* is a riper, a more finely-balanced, a more reasonable study than its predecessors. In my opinion, it could hardly have been written in a form or in a tone which would have better justified our hopes in the future of a very remarkable young writer.

The reader of this volume must not expect to find in it a contribution to the political history of England, or even of the Throne, in the nineteenth century. The author keeps very consistently to what is his selected subject, the personal character of the monarch. This was greatly, though

innocently, obscured by the fondness of those who surrounded her, and there were some, pre-eminently among
them Theodore Martin, who carried the fable to an
extremity.

The *Queen Victoria as I Knew Her* of 1908 must be treated
by historians with the greatest caution ; it might almost be
renamed *Victoria as Martin Failed to See Her*. For thirty-
five years Theodore Martin had been the devoted and
romantic slave of royalty. He had excellent qualities of
heart, but he was, or became, the very type of a " gold-
perched singer on the wrists of kings." He had gazed at
monarchy until his dazzlement had become a part of his
religion, and affected all he said and wrote. His portrait of
Prince Albert was composed under Queen Victoria's eye ;
it bears the stamp of her trenchant resolve, and the almost
hysterical violence of her infatuation.

So, when at last the Sovereign herself passed away, it
was impossible for Sir Theodore Martin to regard her in any
other light than that which had become to him a second
nature, and he produced a waxwork image more baffling to
the historian than even a caricature would be. The caricature, however spiteful, at all events indicates a gesture or
an attitude of life ; the waxen bust indicates nothing
at all.

Victoria added to the embarrassment of her ultimate
biographers by the unbending determination of her
emotions. Her judgment of other persons had no light or
shade ; she was either enchanted with everything they
were, did, and said, or she cast them into the dark background of her invincible dislike. She could admit nothing
but the categorically absolute, and the result was that she
rendered those about her, and herself most of all, unin-
teresting to posterity by her emphasis.

The great instance of this is Prince Albert, whose fault-
less legend of beauty and wisdom and moral perfection not

even her prestige could make generally accepted in the
Queen's lifetime, and who since her death has suffered " a
sea-change " of the most deplorable kind. He has come to
be treated as a subject for neglect, and almost as an object
of ridicule. No part of Mr. Strachey's book is more valuable
than that in which he analyses the character of Albert, and
dwells on his painstaking reasonableness, his devotion to
principle, and his patience, which was amazing. His treatment of the minor disagreements which diversified their
lives until the question " Was he the wife and she the husband ? " was ultimately settled by her will melting into
unison with his, is very subtle ; and it is no small feather
in Mr. Strachey's cap that he has contrived to make the
Prince Consort interesting and a man.

In 1875, ten years after the death of Charles Greville,
who had been clerk to the Privy Council, the first series of
his private diary was published by Henry Reeve, and caused
a sensation, as breaches of reticence invariably do. The
Queen was " horrified and indignant " at all he revealed,
and the tone in which Greville " speaks of royalty " particularly scandalised her. She desired " this abominable
book " to be withdrawn from circulation ; but Henry Reeve
was a stubborn man, and would not budge. The *Greville
Memoirs*, which extend until near the diarist's death in
1865, continued to appear, and each instalment gave the
Queen a fresh vexation.

She was probably not aware, for she did not approach
Reeve in a manner which encouraged confidences, that
what he had printed was nothing in comparison with what
he had suppressed. But the MS. was deposited in the
British Museum, and what are most novel in Mr. Strachey's
book are the passages which the Trustees have allowed him
to copy and to publish. Greville had no respect for persons ; he is like Tallemant des Réaux in the seventeenth
century—he neither blames nor praises, but records the

strange things that crossed his eyes and ears with chill impartiality. He is the unseen witness of an indiscretion, and he noiselessly retires, but not until he has taken it in all its features.

Some of the new passages are really important. The cause of Victoria's coldness to her mother is more closely than before identified with the conduct of Sir John Conroy. The story of her solitary quarrel with Lord Melbourne, about the after-dinner drunkenness of the gentlemen of her Court, appears to be new. Some fresh light is thrown on the miserable affair of Lady Flora, and on the Queen's attitude to the Tories after her marriage. The revelation of the manner in which Mr. Gladstone read her letters to his Cabinet is astounding. But it cannot be too plainly stated that addition to matters of fact is not Mr. Strachey's design, but a clear-sighted differentiation of the characters not merely of Victoria, but of the principal figures which surrounded her.

The author is unflinching in his insistence on the mediocrity of the Queen's mental habits. After the publication of *Leaves from the Highlands*—which was a wise and proper, but hardly an æsthetic action—the artful Disraeli might expatiate about " we writers, Ma'am," but no claim could possibly be made for Victoria as a serious author. It would have needed the most delicate art to deal with Mrs. P. Farquharson's red flannel petticoat or Mr. McLeod's sermon on Nicodemus, and the Queen was far from being a Cowper.

Still, I think Mr. Strachey is slightly unjust to her adequacy of language, particularly in private conversation. He throws doubt on the genuineness of her saying that Gladstone spoke to her as if she " were a public meeting," as being too epigrammatic, but this story is well accredited. The fact is that she had formed the habit of speaking with so much decision, and of expressing her thought so directly, that her words, unconsciously, took a concentrated form.

Of this I gave some instances more than twenty years ago, in an anonymous study of the Queen's character which I contributed to *The Quarterly Review* of April, 1901. To this monograph Mr. Strachey pays the compliment of frequent quotation. I may give another instance, which is, I think, unpublished. When she received the news " All is over and Khartoum has fallen," she was asked what she did after her interview with Mr. Gladstone. Her stick shook a little in her hand, and then she said grimly, " My usual remedy—I read a chapter of *Guy Mannering.*"

Mr. Strachey's record is so full that I hesitate to suggest additions. But perhaps he might have dealt a little on Victoria's attitude to State as contrasted with private religion. In the latter direction she was purely eighteenth-century ; she suspected zeal, and was repelled by enthusiasm. She had been trained in her childhood to be " a true Christian " of a type, as she put it, " just plain and comprehensible." Mr. Strachey has an admirable phrase where he compares her mind, in its religious convictions, to a small smooth crystal pebble " without a flaw and without a scintillation."

But in State affairs she grew to adopt an attitude which was perhaps of her own invention, but which was certainly both curious and convenient. She found no inconsistency in remaining the head of several religious systems. It annoyed her that any one should challenge her various headships. The professional attitude to religion which she practised for sixty years gave her at last an ease in dealing with all religious bodies which seemed very strange to outsiders. When the Jesuits at Beaumont College offered her at her Jubilee the *Works* of Cardinal Newman she accepted the gift, on the understanding that she was the head of her Catholic subjects. She was the leader of her Buddhist subjects, too, and of her Mohammedans; she accepted all these responsibilities, and found each of them interesting. When some busybody had dared to criticise the Queen's " encouragement " of these Eastern religions, the Queen was indignant. " Does the man suspect me of being a convert to any of these forms of faith? " she asked.

Great will be the error of those who try to protest that Mr. Strachey has written a disloyal or even a sarcastic book. The worst that can in justice be said against it is that it is what Victoria herself, in her favourite phrase, used to call "not very discreet." Irony takes a foremost part in Mr. Strachey's attitude to life, and of course it is not absent here. An exquisite example of it is the picture, painted without comment, of the Queen's domestic felicity as she listened to Prince Albert cracking jokes at the luncheon-table or playing Mendelssohn on the organ, or expatiating on the beautiful pictures of Sir Edwin Landseer—

> " O Halbert, 'appy Prince,
> With children round your knees,
> Hengraving 'andsome prints,
> And taking of your ease,"

as a contemporary ballad of my childhood, not quoted by Mr. Strachey, described him. That the Queen's mind, in certain directions, displayed a lethargic inactivity, is not concealed. But Mr. Strachey, while insisting on that *chiaroscuro* without which biography is a sham, is blind to none of Victoria's merits, nor to her claim upon our sustained admiration and respect. He reveals her inner mind with a surety of touch which none of his more courtly predecessors has approached, and I cannot refrain from quoting a passage in which he illustrates with extreme felicity Victoria's private interests and his own command of the English language. He conjectures that as she passed painlessly away, her fading mind returned to what she had noted most keenly in her past life—

" to the spring woods at Osborne, so full of primroses for ,Lord Beaconsfield, to Lord Palmerston's queer clothes and high demeanour, and Albert's face under the green lamp, and Albert's first stay at Balmoral, and Albert in his blue and silver uniform, and the Baron coming in at a doorway, and Lord M. dreaming at Windsor with the rooks cawing in the elm trees, and the Archbishop of Canterbury on his knees in the dawn, and the old King's turkey-cock ejaculations, and Uncle Leopold's soft voice at Claremont, and Lehzen with the globes, and her mother's feathers sweeping down towards her, and a great old repeater-watch of her father's in its tortoiseshell case, and a yellow rug, and some friendly flounces of sprigged muslin, and the trees and the grass at Kensington."

THE PRINCE OF CRITICS

THE PRINCE OF CRITICS

SINCE the centenary of Sainte-Beuve's birth there has been published far too much gossip about his private relations with his contemporaries, and too many of his individual weaknesses have been exposed. His name has been made extremely unpopular by revelations which have nothing to do with his books, or so little that their evidence is negligible.

Even M. Choisy, whose recent monograph was a protest against the venomous attacks on Sainte-Beuve, could not resist giving three chapters to Victor and Adèle Hugo, but only one to *Port Royal*. The critic's relation to the Hugos is merely curious and obscure, while *Port Royal* is one of the masterpieces of literature. It is high time that we should shake ourselves free from all this cobweb of slander and concentrate our thoughts on the writings.

No doubt the character of Sainte-Beuve was faulty ; no doubt he became a safer guide among the dead than among his contemporaries. The piercing light which has been thrown upon his laborious and painful existence has revealed several features which are subjects of regret. If Sainte-Beuve was jealous and shifty, if he indulged his egotism at the expense of his friends, if the other malignities are true, or partly true, it is very sad. But such revelations do not affect the literary position of Sainte-Beuve, or make him less essentially a writer who must be read whoever is neglected. He had imperfections, prejudices, limitations, but when we have recognised them all, he remains the greatest literary critic that the world has seen.

Although my weak voice fails to reach the bold young men of *The Times Literary Supplement*, I do not cease to repeat that French literature ought not to be described to English readers exactly in the terms which are current in the latest Parisian coterie. Foreign literature must be presented to us from the comparative and selective points of view, with reference to our own parallel masters and with rejection of what is exclusively French in its interest. The study of Sainte-Beuve offers what we may call a classical instance of this.

M. Gustave Michaut, who publishes a new life of Sainte-Beuve, has been a leading expert in the subject for more than twenty years. He ignores most of the chatter which has occupied the memoir-editors, but he necessarily dwells on a great number of religious and moral episodes which are not essential to us English readers. The critic's intercourse with Lamennais and Lacordaire, his political adventures, even the publication of the *Livre d'Amour*, which was the turning-point of his ethical career, are edifying or unedifying, as the case may be, but to us they are not, or should not be, of the first importance.

For an English reader it is the Sainte-Beuve of the *Causeries* and of the *Nouveaux Lundis* that counts. If that reader is himself a writer, or seriousiy wishes to become one, the study of this quintessential Sainte-Beuve is desirable—is, indeed, almost necessary. Other writers may be postponed, but at the threshold of a serious literary life Sainte-Beuve *must* be read.

All the world has read him ; for the last eighty years his influence has spread like a drop of oil on a pavement. His vitality is extraordinary, since, while his most brilliant rivals, such as Jules Janin and Paul de Saint-Victor, have gradually faded away, and are now only known to a few curious readers, the *Causeries de Lundi* are as fresh as when they were composed.

Take the essays on Lafontaine, on Molière, on Mademoiselle Aïssé; these were published seventy years ago, and they are as amusing, as satisfying to our taste and judgment, as though the liveliest of living essayists had produced them yesterday. We may analyse and define, we may argue through pages as to the cause of this perennial charm in Sainte-Beuve; we are thrown back on the conviction that it is something peculiar to himself, something of that arresting individuality which immortalises the greatest writers and defies anatomy.

As he proceeded, the critic's manner broadened out, became less theoretical, concentrated itself more and more completely on the *corpus* of the person criticised, on his circumstances, on his passions, on his exclusive characteristics. Sainte-Beuve, when he reached his beautiful maturity, contrived, as no other critic has done before or since, to fill his page with life and with the love of life.

Although so much has been written, with not a little darkening of counsel, on the work of this wonderful man, there remains something to be said, from an international point of view, as to the sources of his plan. We must not expect the French exponents, who have so much else to occupy their attention, to dwell on Sainte-Beuve's relationship to English literature. Even M. Michaut passes very lightly over this. But to us it is a matter of some importance. Sainte-Beuve in his early youth studied English enthusiastically; he knew Burns and Chatterton; he formed one of a group of Parisian lovers of Wordsworth, and he used his knowledge of him to resist the overweening influence of Byron. He wrote :—

> " Wordsworth peu connu, qui des lacs solitaires
> Sait tous les bleus reflets, les bruits et les mystères,"

at a date when the sage was still hale enough to march, " booing " his verses, over the Cumbrian mountains.

Moreover, Sainte-Beuve had certainly read Wordsworth's

revolutionary preface, with its celebration of the poetical qualities of daily life in its domestic detail, of the painting of humble persons amidst their intimate surroundings. The early poems of Sainte-Beuve testify to his response to the teaching of Wordsworth and Cowper, whom he called his " elder brothers."

But was he acquainted with the English critics of the generation preceding his own ? This is a question to which we have, I think, no documentary reply, but a certain amount of internal evidence presents itself.

In France, we may roughly say, Sainte-Beuve confronted no precursor. There had been many learned men since the days of Boileau, who had written searchingly on the literature of their country, but their method had been formal and systematic. The classical tradition was practically unbroken when Sainte-Beuve began to read and think and write. But England had never been so completely in bondage, and we had had our intellectual revolution in 1798. The real precursors of Sainte-Beuve were Coleridge, Hazlitt, and, in a sense, Charles Lamb. It is exceedingly tantalising not to know how far he was conscious of the existence of these Englishmen, who had rejected, as he was rejecting in 1826, the consecrated models and the musty rules of style.

The famous " novelty " of Sainte-Beuve's method was patent to Frenchman, but Coleridge had already approached literature without the help of traditional routine, and Hazlitt had pierced to the heart of poetry indifferent to the claims of rhetoric. When Sainte-Beuve was twenty-three, in 1827, he wrote his *Tableau de la Poésie Française au XVIe siècle*, into which he admitted an analogy between the young Victor Hugo and the Pléiade, leaping over the classic school with a gesture which is now seen to have been false. But the book was brilliantly new in its aim, and is still exceedingly stimulating.

The point for us is that there had been nothing in past French criticism remotely like it, and that for a parallel we must turn to Charles Lamb's *Specimens of English Dramatic Poets* of 1808. Sainte-Beuve, by the way, was in complete possession of his powers before the deaths of the three great English critics. His possible relation to their writings is a point which I greatly wish that his French commentators would try to elucidate.

The part he took in procuring a welcome for the great generation of French Romantics is much more familiar. Whatever may have been his subsequent petulance, whatever the influence of prejudices and jealousies on his later attitude, nothing can tarnish the splendour of the courage with which he challenged classical opinion in 1830. Heine amusingly said that Sainte-Beuve put the trumpet to his lips and ran in front of Victor Hugo, announcing him to the world as the Buffalo of Poetry. The *Portraits Littéraires* may seem somewhat faded now ; it is not the book to which lovers of its author turn to-day with the keenest appetite, but this is largely because we take it all for granted, and know what happened afterwards.

In 1831 it marked an epoch ; it was the earliest attempt in French to judge contemporary poetry, not by the old rules and regulations, but by the " pure, frank impression, as naïve as possible," which it produced upon an unprejudiced reader. It broke, once and for all, with the dogmatic etiquette of French criticism, and for the first time it neither attributed praise nor blame according to a formula, but tried to discover what were the individual characteristics which united the author to his work ; to combine literature with biography ; and, above all, to let in a stream of living truth upon what the old dogmas had left impenetrable and dead.

What the result of Sainte-Beuve's labours has been in France the whole of French literature during the last

seventy years exhibits. Those who attack his memory
with the greatest virulence reveal, unconsciously, by their
approach to their subject, the supremacy of his method.
His insatiable curiosity, the width of his comprehension,
the wonderful dexterity of his mental processes, have left
their mark on the intellectual scepticism and enthusiasm of
France. We have seen his work continued and advanced
by Anatole France, by Jules Lemaître, by Rémy de Gourmont, by a crowd of brilliant analysts and biographers. But
fresh generations come back with profit and solace to the
enchanting *Lundis*.

In England his fame has been less general with the
public, but hardly less potent with the professional critics.
Matthew Arnold confessed to having discovered, in his
youth, that it was " salutary to extract the honey " from
Sainte-Beuve's " incomparable portraits," and this although
his own bent was less to the individual than to the broader
aspects of literature. Arnold emphatically proclaimed the
" life-giving stimulus " to be found in the reading of the
Causeries de Lundi, and mourned that so little advantage
was taken of it in England. Yet it is suffused over our later
criticism ; the form of Swinburne and Pater, even perhaps
of Morley and Bagehot, would be other than it is if Sainte-
Beuve had never lived.

The volume which has given me an excuse for these
remarks belongs to the series of *Les Grands Ecrivains
Français*, so admirably conducted, now for no fewer than
thirty-four years past, by M. Jusserand. It is soberly and
concisely written, with the authority which M. Michaut's
name commands. The series must now be almost complete, but I would venture to remind M. Jusserand that we
still demand from him a Buffon, and perhaps a Benjamin
Constant.

THE SHROPSHIRE LAD

THE SHROPSHIRE LAD

TWENTY-SIX years ago a slender volume of poems by an unknown hand was cast upon the world. Christians were being murdered in Crete and the Kaiser was congratulating Mr. Kruger on his repulse of the Jameson Raid; so universal was the stagnation of the world that the noise of these events went echoing from pole to pole. The English poetry of the moment was in keeping with the luxury and somnolence of life; it sang of Fleet Street and the music-halls, it was delicately gregarious. The new poet of 1896 wrote in a tone which clashed abruptly with this artificial and ornamented elegance. The little thrilling songs of the Shropshire Lad were severe and bare, not acquainted at all with the gaiety of towns, but concerned exclusively with the meditations of a lonely life, haunted by memories of an extreme instinctive simplicity.

The verse of Mr. A. E. Housman, therefore, belonging to no recognised school, and disdaining every species of extrinsic attraction, was very little noticed at first, was even dismissed by hasty reviewers as creditable " minor verse " of small significance. But clearer-sighted or sharper-eared readers found themselves arrested and then bewitched by its secret beauty, which enslaved the ear as some subterranean music of goblins might do, heard at twilight in a sequestered glade. Its charm, once detected, remained indestructible, and since 1896 all catholic lovers of poetry have known that though new bards in myriads arise and push the old bards into obscurity, there is one pure, small sound that can never be silenced—the flute of the Shropshire Lad piping where

> " Clunton and Clunbury,
> Clungunford and Clun,
> Are the quietest places
> Under the sun."

But the little volume had no successor, and when a quarter of a century had passed over it, leaving it as fresh but as disconcertingly isolated as ever, it might well seem that Mr. A. E. Housman would live among our notable poets on the score of an " output " as scanty as that of Gray or Collins. Suddenly, without any preliminary flourish, there comes to us a second volume, of the same slender dimensions as the first, in which the familiar voice speaks to us again out of the cloud. It is the same voice ; it is a continuation of the old theme, for the tone, which was so clear and personal in 1896, is as individual as ever in 1922.

If there is any change at all, it is in the direction of a completer technical excellence. In the original volume there were, as we may prove by returning to it, one or two pieces in which the metrical skill was a little dubious, where the tune wavered on the instrument. In the new volume I cannot discover any fault of this kind, the mastery of technique having become complete, the music impeccable. But there is no essential difference, and for this my thanks are offered to the Muses. Essentially we wanted an expansion, not a change, in this sensitive, unique, and unrelated thing. We wanted, not another *Shropshire Lad*, but more of the old one, and that is what we have got.

It is well that we hold exactly what we wished for, since we are to receive no more. A sad little foreword says that those pieces are now published because it is not likely that the poet will " ever be impelled to write much more." The word " much " just keeps the door of hope ajar, but we must take it that these poems, most of which were written before 1910, represent the final harvest :—

> " We'll to the woods no more,
> The laurels all are cut,
> The bowers are bare of bay
> That once the Muses wore ;
> The year draws in the day
> And soon will evening shut :
> The laurels all are cut,
> We'll to the woods no more.
> Oh, we'll no more, no more
> To the leafy woods away,
> To the high wild woods of laurel
> And the bowers of bay no more."

There were sixty-three pieces in the original collection, and there are forty-one in the present, so that we may take it that one hundred short lyrics will be Mr. Housman's bequest to posterity. There are many writers of profuse and successful production who might well wish that they could cut down their publications to a century of as much excellence as this.

Mr. Housman is not one of those poets for whom the choice of a subject is needless, and for whom all subjects are equally good. Coleridge, in a whimsical utterance, seems to hold that diversity of theme is the essential characteristic of free poetical genius. There is something to be said for a formula that explains such wide expanses as the work of Browning and Victor Hugo, but intensity may be gained at the expense of breadth. Mr. Housman, at all events, has, as it seems to me, only one subject, which he treats in a hundred ways. He is the poet of *desiderium*, of the unconquerable longing for what is gone for ever, for youth which has vanished, for friends that are dead, for beauty that was a mirage.

This hopeless desire is concentrated on one scene of English landscape, silent and vague hills and solitary fields which certain proper names identify with a particular dis-

trict—namely, with that part of the pastoral county of
Salop which borders westward on the hills of Wales. Mr.
Housman never describes this country, but he indicates its
character in a way which exceeds the impression made by
any topographical survey, however accurate. I have wandered on " the high-hilled plains," needing no guide but one
little olive-coloured book of verses :—

> " And I would climb the beacon
> That looked to Wales away."

For a collection of lyrics at all analogous to *A Shropshire Lad* (as now concluded) I do not know where we can
turn save to the *Buch der Lieder*. The form of Mr. Housman often closely resembles Heine's :—

> " In the morning, in the morning,
> In the happy field of hay,
> Oh, they looked at one another
> By the light of day.

> " In the blue and silver morning,
> On the haycock as they lay,
> Oh, they looked at one another—
> And they looked away."

There the outward resemblance to Heine is complete,
more so than is usual with Mr. Housman, but the essential
character of the work even here is not really Heinesque.
The reflective melancholy, what I have called the *desiderium*
of the Shropshire Lad, is something radically distinct from
the cynicism of the great German lyrist, and is not occupied,
as his was, with anger and repulsion, with irony and
humour. It is a thing much more simple and primitive ;
it is almost passive in its brooding sweetness. Moreover—
and this is perhaps the source of Mr. Housman's intimate
charm—it is always mysterious. Nothing is told right out ;
the emotion is veiled and discreet ; we are left to conjecture what is the exact nature of it. The language which
this poet employs is not merely severe and chaste, it is often
colloquial ; it seems to tell the most natural things in the

simplest speech. But below this quiet surface there is a
ceaseless mystification, an obvious sense that the half is not
told us :—

> " The night is freezing fast,
>   To-morrow comes December ;
>   And winterfalls of old
> Are with me from the past ;
>   And chiefly I remember
>   How Dick would hate the cold.

> " Fall, winter, fall ; for he
>   Prompt hand and headpiece clever,
>   Has woven a winter robe,
> And made of earth and sea
>   His overcoat for ever,
>   And wears the turning globe."

That is all, and it seems enough, told in this austere and
lucid language ; yet how little it explains of all that it is
needless for us to know ! This is the very essence of perfect lyrical writing, to be a polished pebble flung into dark
waters, awaking one circle after another of wonder and
reverie and vague emotion, " infinite longing, and the pain
of finite hearts that yearn," as another poet says.

In the new volume there is perhaps nothing so violent as
The True Lover or *On Moonlit Heath and Lonesome Bank*,
in which Mr. Housman was emphatic in extending his
sympathy even to murderers and suicides if they were the
desperate victims of an unselfish passion. The indulgence
of unupbraiding affection covered, as with a mantle, sin
and even crime. These are sentiments which may be
dangerous in prose, but to verse all things are permitted.
In the new book we have similar tragedies, but expressed,
or hinted at, with less intensity. The poet plucks the blue
blossom that springs at the four cross-ways :—

> " It seemed a herb of healing,
>   A balsam and a sign,
> Flower of a heart whose trouble
>   Must have been worse than mine.

> " Dead clay that did me kindness,
>   I can do none for you,
>   But only wear for breastknot
>   The flower of sinner's rue."

The longest piece in the collection—*Hell Gate*—is certainly the most powerful which Mr. Housman has published, yet can but be ruined by partial quotation. It is a dream of punishment and eternal pain, mitigated only by the enduring love of those for whom error and disgrace veil not a whit the inner beauty of a soul whose sins are misfortunes and whose shame is accidental. The whole philosophy of *A Shropshire Lad* is involved in the tenderness and the horror of this vision, to my mind one of the most extraordinary which the present age has produced. *Hell Gate* gives me a suspicion that if Mr. Housman had chosen to cultivate this sulphurous fury he might have written a new *Inferno*. The vision of the accoutred soldier, all on fire, pacing as a sentinel before the gate of hell, and shining from far off as a spark against the darkness,

> " Trim and burning, to and fro,
>   One for women to admire
>   In his finery of fire,"

who, as the poet approached,

> "turned his head,
>   Looked, and knew me, and was Ned,"

is overwhelming. Throughout this little volume regretful pity and shadowy passion pass and repass like the flaming sentry at the gate of hell, and the poet stands and gazes in a trance of melancholy pain. And hopeless longing is the end of it all :—

> " So here's an end of roaming
>   On eves when autumn nighs ;
>   The ear too fondly listens
>   For summer's parting sighs,
>   And then the heart replies."

GODS AND HEROES

GODS AND HEROES

A STIFF brown chrysalis, giving a slight occasional jerk to show that it is not quite dead, but wrapped in a bright fleece of golden silk, such is the image which the latest contribution to the Loeb Library presents to a candid mind. The chrysalis is the Greek text of *The Library* of Apollodorus ; the silk is the profuse and interwoven English commentary by Sir James Frazer. In the old days, when learned persons spent their days wrangling over the controversy as to whether the Ancients or the Moderns are supreme, the work before me would have afforded a priceless argument in favour of the latter, since the most infatuated worshipper of antiquity would be obliged to admit that Apollodorus is now, and always must have been, the driest of dry sticks, while Sir James Frazer, of *The Golden Bough*, is a consummate master of style and entertainment.

By what strange freak has *The Library* survived ? When a hundred ancient masterpieces of wit and beauty sank under the waters of time, what induced this dreary miscellany to float ? Manifestly, it has survived for no other purpose but that it might form an excuse for Sir James Frazer to chat enchantingly about the annual sacrifices of the Corinthians and the insolence of lyric Amphion.

There is no author in literature about whose life less is known than Apollodorus. We cannot even tell whether he " flourished " before or after the Christian Era. He is called " The Athenian Grammarian," but apparently because he is confounded with another writer so described who lived about 140 B.C. Without going into details, what is conjectured is that a mythologist of nameless origin wrote, about the time of Christ, two books, one called *Bibliotheke*, or *The Library*, the other *On the Gods*. Of these the former alone survives; I should have supposed that the book before us might well be *On the Gods*, but Sir James Frazer is firm in believing that *On the Gods* is completely lost, and that it is useless to conjecture what it may have contained.

We have *The Library*, which is a summary of Greek mythology, set down in sedate succession, story after story, without illustration or comment. It is impossible to conceive of a less-digested production ; it is just an imperfect, lumbering Lemprière. The obscure person who wrote it was evidently a Greek—perhaps a provincial Greek, since there is one extremely curious feature about it. Neither Rome nor the Romans are even remotely alluded to, although the author must have been a Roman citizen. Apollodorus describes the journeys of Hercules through Italy without even a hint of Latium, and contrives to expatiate on the Calabrian wars of Philoctetes after the sack of Troy without once mentioning Æneas. No reasonable theory has been suggested to account for this deliberate and complete omission of Roman legend.

Why Apollodorus called his collection of stories *The Library* may well be asked. But Sir James Frazer thinks that it was an indication that the author compiled it from a great variety of written books which are now lost, just as Diodorus Siculus called his summary *Bibliotheca Historica* for a like reason. This use of the word seems to have escaped Liddell and Scott in their Greek Lexicon, but it deserves notice as a definition of a work of reference gathered out of a series of earlier sources. Perhaps the lost *On the Gods* was a continuation, in which the author turned his attention to Roman legend, which he purposely omitted in his earlier volume, but it must all be guess-work.

Yet, although *The Library*, in an unannotated form, is

insufferably dull, it would be a great mistake to undervalue it as a hard piece of canvas prepared for scholars to embroider upon. Apollodorus had no selective faculty; he set down every story that he met with, and he appears to have implicitly believed them all. When he was confronted by a variant, he mentioned it, without expressing any opinion as to which version was likely to be the more correct. As nobody is known to have quoted him until Photius did so nine hundred years after his probable death, the obscurity as to his intentions and as to the credit he obtained among his own contemporaries is impenetrable. We have to take him as he stands, in his solid dullness.

The value of Apollodorus consists in his faithful record of what the Greeks in general believed about their origin and the early history of the world. Sir James Frazer considers that he mainly founded his report on a long prose work by Pherecydes, about Greek myth and legend, written some five centuries earlier. This, unfortunately, is lost, except a few fragments, which, however, are sufficient to show that it was " a treasure-house of Greek mythical and legendary lore, set forth with that air of simplicity and sincerity which charm us in Herodotus." That would, indeed, be a " find," worth its weight in rubies, and who knows but that it may yet turn up ?

In the meantime, we must make what we can of Apollodorus, who appears to have trodden closely in the steps of Pherecydes, although without his genius. But, besides his repertory of legends, Apollodorus is valuable because he did not disdain the element of folk-lore, which endears him to the modern school. There is not the least indication that he drew any distinction between the historical and the fantastic tales which he repeated. It was all grist that came to his mill, but the modern folk-lorist is grateful to him for suppressing nothing, however incredible and inconceivable, or even repulsive.

The primitive mind works in defiance of logic. It turns an accident into an argument, and invents a story to account for a theory. All its action is topsy-turvy. A strange instance of this is found in the accounts of the Trojan War, a succession of events absorbing in its interest. Why did the Greeks sail from Aulis ? Various reasons of a political and sentimental kind might be adduced, but they do not appeal to the antique historian.. No ; what really happened was this : A serpent darts out from behind the altar of Apollo, and eats seven sparrows which it finds in a nest in a neighbouring plane-tree ; it then devours the mother-bird as well, and, very properly, is turned to stone. Calchas, who had already prophesied when Achilles was only nine years old that he would capture Troy, comes forward with this ridiculous incident of the stone serpent, which his auditors appear to have thought that they witnessed, and he tells the Greeks that this is a sign from Zeus that the conquest of the Trojans will take ten years.

Forthwith, says the chronicle, " they made ready to sail against Troy." Why ? Because logic was still unknown, and because individuals and large bodies of men were still under the sway of magical suggestion. They believed what was impossible without the slightest examination of evidence, and they leaped to a certainty of the sooth-sayer's power of divination. Or, rather, perhaps, they were docile when the soothsayer pretended, after the event, that certain signs had led him to predict it. But what was the prophet's state of mind ? Was he the dupe of his own fables ? These are questions which are not without interest when we examine the surviving superstitions of our own day.

This brings me back to Sir James Frazer, from whom Apollodorus has detained me too long. The present edition derives its entire importance from the impress set upon it by the mind which has so long and so brilliantly illu-

minated the mysteries of magic and religion. We might be
expected to grudge the time and toil which the English
writer has expended on the old Greek gabbler, but it is
impossible to do so when we appreciate what he has grafted
on that hard stock.

The second volume contains what is called an
" Appendix," in which Sir James Frazer supplies thirteen
essays, or short romances, expanding and confirming stories
rudely sketched by Apollodorus. Some of these essays deal
with standard subjects of mythology, such as *The Origin of
Fire* and modes for securing the resurrection of the body.
But most of them are tales in which the famous antique
legend is traced through the superstitions of other various
and remote heathern peoples.

It is admitted that Sir James Frazer has no rival in this
method of parallels. For instance, no ancient story is
better known or has more valuably inspired the poets than
that of Apollo and the herdsman Admetus ; the god, in
gratitude, caused all his master's cows to bear twins. For
Apollodorus this fact, stated in one bald sentence, has no
meaning ; but Sir James Frazer conducts us to British
Columbia, where twins are a sign that salmon will be plenti-
ful ; to Uganda, where they portend an ample harvest ; to
Sumatra, where the impact of the god has become so awful
that the arrival of twins, as of an intolerable privilege, has
grown to be a theme of terror and dismay. These essays,
wound around rough anthropological superstitions, are
fascinating in the extreme.

No doubt it is the recurrence of Greek themes in distant places, such as that of the marriage of Peleus and
Thetis by the Lake of Tanganyika and in the Faroe Islands ;
or of Ulysses and Polyphemus in Esthonia and La Vendée,
which has led theorists to see in all old myths allusions to
natural phenomena, and particularly to those of fire and
sky. Gods and heroes are so hopelessly mixed up in the

irrational tales of primitive peoples, while the same monstrous characteristics are given to them by races which
seem to have no connection with one another, that there
has long been a temptation to class them all together as
misconstructions of the sequence of such phenomena as the
sun and clouds and moving water.

I speak as one ignorant of the science of these things, but
I cannot but rejoice that Sir James Frazer deprecates this
mechanical interpretation. In his commentary I am much
struck by the warning which he gently gives and persis-
tently suggests to mythologists and ritualists not to resolve
all the stories of ancient Greece into myths and rites, but
to leave a little to the element of pure romance. The
savagè is naturally inquisitive and credulous, and his
mythology is the manner in which a mind incapable of
logic tries to account for the world around him and its
permanent phenomena. But he also builds the gods after
his own image, endowing them with reckless action such as
he himself would exercise if his powers were boundless.

It seems that, at the present moment, as often before, a
too-rigid interpretation is likely to obscure the study of
mythology. Armed with the comparative observations of
those of whom Sir James Frazer is the chief, mythologists
and realists are making incursions into all the realms of
fancy and common sense. They are bent on cutting down
everything and everybody they meet with in the most
ruthless manner. Among these incursionists I understand
that the ladies take a foremost place. The Holy Grail and
the Eddas have already fallen victims, and the most familiar creations of the poets are in danger of being explained
away as Tree Goddesses and worshipful ancestral spirits.
I learn that even Penelope has gone the way of all flesh, and
that a man at Oxford has resolved her into a sort of seagull.
There are silly people even among learned anthropologists,
and Sir James Frazer evidently views with alarm the

investigators who mount their hobby-horse in high glee and ride the poor animal to death. His fascinating essay on *The Clashing Rocks* exemplifies the working of pure romantic imagination in a primitive mind, and gives us the analysis of a fairy-tale spun out of nothing more substantial than a picturesque dream. Yet even this Tylor conceived to be simply " a broken-down fancy of solar-myth." From such extravagances Sir James Frazer is preserved by his habit of weighing evidence and by his delicate appreciation of literature. The ancients were not such fools as the ritualists take them to have been.

FREDERIC MYERS' POEMS

FREDERIC MYERS' POEMS

A REPRINT of the verse of a well-known Victorian writer, who died twenty-two years ago, has been received in certain quarters with a severity unusual in these mild times. It is evident that the poetry of Frederic Myers finds little favour in the eyes of the New Criticism, and that the number of his thoughtful admirers has been very seriously curtailed. We cannot do better than to inquire into the causes of this change, and to see how far it is justified by the character of the work and how far it is the result of whim and prejudice.

In contemplating changes of taste, it is often much more illuminating to analyse the lesser than the greater exponents of a bygone school, because individuals of startling genius rise above the conventions of their time, and survive all veerings of fashion. To study Victorian poetry in Tennyson is to meet with personal features which surpass mere temporary fluctuations of taste, and, therefore, what those fluctuations point to is best studied in such a writer as Myers, who was never exalted, even by his most fervent admirers, to the first rank. We have authority to take his best verse as an example of what was generally approved of in 1863, and appears to be generally disapproved of in 1923.

When I came up to London as a lad, the two literary phenomena which earliest impressed me were the death of the Dean of St. Paul's—the "poet-priest Milman" of Byron's epigram, whose biblical *Belshazzar* I had been taught to admire—and the popularity of *St. Paul*, the poem of a young Cambridge man of whose future the highest things were predicted. These features seemed like the end of an old age and the beginning of a new one. Little attention was being given to verse by the reviewers in those days, yet *St. Paul* did not pass unrecognised. In particular, George Meredith dedicated to it an article in the *Fortnightly Review* which was alone enough to make it famous. The previous year had been marked by the unparalleled sensation and scandal of Swinburne's *Poems and Ballads*. Matthew Arnold had recently chastised, in scathing irony, the poverty of English religious verse, and by general consent our poetry was admitted to be inevitably secular and usually Pagan.

What made *St. Paul* instantly notable was the fact that it was not merely orthodox but evangelical, and yet was adorned with the richest results of scholarship and fancy. Wesley asked why the Devil should have all the good tunes, and here was a very young and ardent poet asking why the Devil should have all the elegant metaphors. People whose sensibility shrank from " the roses and raptures of vice " welcomed a lily which was quite Japanese in its floral exuberance.

When *St. Paul* was published in 1867, Frederic Myers was a recently-elected fellow and classical lecturer at Trinity College, Cambridge. He had been sent there, as he says, " far too early," and we have the impression of him as a sublimated schoolboy, pensive, pious and precocious, but quite ignorant of the world. He was steeped in Greek and Latin poetry, and in Tennyson as a continuer of the classic tradition. From the age of fourteen he had shown a facility in writing verses which was marvellous and dangerous. When he was twenty he travelled in Greece, alone ; throughout his life, it seems to me, whether in company or not, Myers was always alone. " Few men can have drunk that departed loveliness into a more passionate heart," and he left Greece " with eyes tear-brimming, and a bitter-sweet passion of regret." He staked his faith on Plato's *Phædo*, and was a solitary Pagan ecstatic.

But he returned to Cambridge, and a fresh element entered his life. He met that remarkable woman, Mrs. Josephine Butler, to whose initials he dedicated *St. Paul,* with a mysterious inscription in Greek, indicating that he owed to her his own soul. She introduced him to Christianity, and in the double fervour of Greece and of the Gospel he wrote *St. Paul*. This intensity of faith lasted but a year or two, and then Myers succumbed to a fit of agnosticism, which was like "nightmare panic amid the glaring dreariness of day," and from which he ultimately escaped by accepting a scientific theory for the phenomena alleged by Spiritualists. He preserved, as a constant moral stimulus, a passionate confidence in personal immortality, of which, to his last hour in Rome, he was striving to attain an absolute certitude.

When we examine *St. Paul*, which is by far the most important of Myers' poetical writings, we must bear in mind the conditions which have just been mentioned. It is the work of a sensuous fancy inflamed by Greek poetry and scenery, and yet humbly accepting the doctrines of the Pauline Epistles. It had a High Church character, accentuated by a broad black cross on the scarlet binding, a cross which gave offence to some tender consciences. I recollect that a spinster Plymouth sister, intensely moved by the poem, gave away a great many copies, but in every case, with a brush of black paint, turned the Puseyite cross into a star before she distributed the books. The citations from the New Testament were so frequent that in some places the poem is almost a cento, and yet it is so luxurious in diction that even infidels were gratified :—

> " So even I, and with a heart more burning,
>   So even I, and with a hope more sweet,
>   Groan for the hour, O Christ ! of thy returning,
>   Faint for the flaming of thine advent feet."

No wonder that ears assailed by this amorous orthodoxy
should be so thrilled as to fail to inquire how far all the
roseate imagination and redundant music represented the
stern spirit of Paul the Apostle.

The melody of the stanzas was, indeed, extraordinary,
and I do not know how criticism, whether of yesterday or
to-day, can omit to acknowledge it. It owed nothing to
Tennyson—though much of the diction of *St. Paul* is
Tennysonian—and still less to the new fiery numbers of
Swinburne. The metre is smooth and swift and nervous ;
and it has a unique peculiarity which has never, I think,
been remarked upon or explained. It is what I may call
ambidextrous ; each line can be treated as one of four feet
or of five, at the choice of the reader :—

> " Then, in the sudden glory of a minute,
>   Airy and excellent, the pröem came ;
> Rending his bosom, for a god was in it.
> Waking the seed, for it had burst in flame."

Read this aloud, and you will find that it goes equally well
in a dactylic gallop or in an iambic trot. Myers kept up
this double movement, on the whole very successfully,
through the entire poem.

There is no doubt that this rapturous measure, so curiously original, translated the twin fervour of Paul and
Plato which coursed through the veins of the young
Cambridge don. It led him into doctrinal extravagances
which the admirers of his own day condoned, and it disguised from them considerable weaknesses. Those admirers
called *St. Paul* a " canticle of ravishing beauty built up of
sweetness and simplicity." It is not quite that, and, in
particular, it is specifically devoid of " simplicity." Yet
it is a poem of too much originality and fervour to be dismissed with a sneer. It will always preserve a certain
niche in the temple of mid-Victorian verse.

The admiration once intensely felt for *St. Paul* has withdrawn from what are called "literary" circles, but is by no means extinct. So lately as 1916, a variorum edition, tenderly and exhaustively annotated by Mr. E. J. Watson, testified to an enduring popularity. But the faults of the composition have been emphasised by time. It is not a logical statement of the convictions of that Hebrew of the Hebrews who was determined to know nothing but Christ, and Him crucified. It is a series of disjointed ejaculations by a converted Greek, who was far from indifferent to the charms of honeyed diction. "My speech and my preaching was not with enticing words," the real Paul told the Corinthians, but Myers expended on a soliloquy put into the mouth of the Apostle every artifice of florid daintiness.

It is an even more serious fault that the poem has no definite object or end, no coherence; its cantos do not progressively build up a poetic structure, but might be shuffled in a bag, and then rearranged with no loss of effect. When we add to these drawbacks a perpetual straining after something transcendent, and a careless use of the most striking rather than the most appropriate word, we are in possession of the reasons why *St. Paul*, like so much mid-Victorian poetry of the second or third class, legitimately excited sympathy and admiration when it was published, but has been unable to retain critical esteem.

However, *St. Paul* was a fine juvenile performance, in its way, and will not be forgotten. Unfortunately, it was the harbinger of a summer that never came. In throwing off some of his faults, Myers resigned his charm as well. During his brief period of Christianity, he supplemented *St. Paul* by a *St. John the Baptist* in blank verse, but this was not impressive; it was correct and sonorous, but it lacked interest. And then, in the subsequent period of his melancholy, and in his ultimate obsession about immortality, he frequently enshrined his dim and yearning emotions in verse. These pieces dealt in landscape and in

what was called The Larger Hope, and they were polished
and highly-coloured exercises, but they lacked character,
and the human touch was absent.

There was something disembodied, something that evaded
reality and repelled sympathy in the intellectual aloofness
of their author.   He seemed to be living in a Leyden jar; he
spoke of being " immersed in thundering chaos, alone amid
the roar of doom," and all his mental actions were forms of
an endless, solitary brooding upon the unknown, the feeding
of an uncertain hope upon vague philosophisings.   This is
not the attitude of a man who writes poetry with effect.
He should have something more definite to impart than the
fact that his longings for what is unrevealed are insatiable.

Of the original verse of Frederic Myers I have been unable
to speak with fervour, and it is that alone which lies before
me to-day.   But I must not leave his admired and respected
memory without a word about his gifts in other spheres.
He was a translator, or transmutor, of classic poetry whose
skill was deserving of the warmest recognition.   If he had
concluded his version of the *Æneid*, with fragments of which
he adorned his essay on Virgil, it would have been the best
in our language.   He was a prose writer of dignity and distinction ; his two short lives of Shelley and of Wordsworth
are as pleasant reading to-day as they were forty years
ago, and are enlivened with occasional touches of humour
which the student of Myers' poetry would not expect.

He was a delicate, if slightly over-subtle, critic, with
incessant references to classical precedent which sometimes
led him into pedantry, as in his over-laboured *Letter on
Tennyson*, where one might be pardoned for supposing that
poet to have belonged to the Neronian age of ancient Rome.
No anthology of nineteenth century prose should omit the
page in his essay on George Eliot, where he describes a walk
with that novelist " on an evening of rainy May."   It
would be perfect—if it were not a little *over*-perfect.

THE COURT OF FAERY

THE COURT OF FAERY

THE little epic poem of Drayton called *Nimphidia* has been a great deal more talked about than read, and a pretty popular edition of it is, therefore, welcome, although this would be more useful if it contained some prefatory information. The poem became prominent in the eighteenth century owing to a strange error of some scholars, who announced that it contained the source of *Midsummer Night's Dream*. This fallacy long prevailed, and critics boldly repeated that "Shakespeare unquestionably borrowed from Drayton's *Nimphidia* to enrich his fairy world." Shakespeare unquestionably did nothing of the sort ; what borrowing there was was done by Drayton ; but the legend gave a fallacious value to the *Nimphidia*, and led to a constant exaggeration of its importance, until Malone, exactly a century ago, settled the question by proving that Shakespeare had the priority by nearly thirty years. The date of the composition of *Midsummer Night's Dream* is uncertain, but it was licensed in 1600, whereas no edition of *Nimphidia* has been discovered earlier than 1627.

At the same time, Malone considered that an expression of Drayton's, calling the contents of the folio of 1627 " These my latest poems," proved that Drayton had just written *Nimphidia*. This does not seem to me to be certain, because the author, then sixty-four years of age might well have introduced a piece of his youth among later poems; We may take it as absolutely fixed that Shakespeare never saw *Nimphidia*, but that Drayton at some time or other had seen or read *Midsummer Night's Dream*.

47

poet described it as a " strange Herculean task," and so it is. *Polyolbion* is the biggest thing, resulting from the sturdiest effort, between *The Faery Queen* and *Paradise Lost*. As most readers know, it is a celebration in alexandrine verse of the wonders of " Albion's glorious isle " ; it is a monument of geographical patriotism, very fascinating to dip into, very difficult to read through steadily. Most persons are glad that it exists, and mean to peruse it, but get through life without having managed to do so. As the flesh is weak, waverers may be recommended to pass right on to the Thirteenth Book, where the landscape and the hunting scenes are very attractive.

As Drayton grew older his touch became lighter. His folio,—containing, among many other things, the famous *Battle of Agincourt*, as well as the *Nimphidia*, of which a reprint lies before me,—was published in 1627, when he was well over sixty years, a great age for an Elizabethan. It shows a springiness, an elastic ardour not to be found in the author's early writings, such as his soporific sonnets and his tedious studies in national history. If Drayton had died at Shakespeare's age his fame would be as permanent, but less brilliant than it is. His mind sparkled out in several directions in which it had hitherto seemed rich but rayless. In particular, he became attracted by the purely English conception of a fairy world, where tiny creatures " fleet the time carelessly " among beautiful natural objects, such as flowers and butterflies. An eighteenth century critic compared the Elizabethan conception of a sphere inhabited by delicate creatures without reflection or conscience, to " an elegant piece of Arabesque." It was frosty, frail, and evanescent ; no breath of the living world of man intruded upon its aerial artificiality. I have called this specially English, although I am well aware of the elfin-world of Germany, and of the fact, exposed by my friend Sir Sidney Lee, that Oberon first breathed " the spiced Indian air" in the French romance of *Huon of Bordeaux*. But I hold, in spite of all this, that a character peculiar to the light Warwickshire woodlands belongs to the fairyland of Shakespeare and of Ben Jonson, of Spenser, and of Drayton. One of its prettiest expressions is to be found in what Mr. Saintsbury has happily styled that "symphony for marionettes," the fantastic and petulant poem of *Nimphidia*.

The queen of the fairies in *Nimphidia* is Mab, and she corresponds with Titania in *Midsummer Night's Dream*. She has an attendant fay, who waits upon her in an aery palace hung under the moon by the arts of necromancy, and this "pretty light fantastick maid," Nimphidia, has made friends with Drayton, and reveals to him the secrets of the Faëry Court. She reports that a faëry knight, named Pigwiggen, has fallen violently in love with Queen Mab, who is not as much displeased as she ought to be. Pigwiggen entreats her Majesty to meet him secretly in the bowl of a cowslip, and this assignation becoming known to King Oberon, awakens in him all the furies of jealousy. Pigwiggen answers to Titania's "lovely boy stolen from an Indian King" in *Midsummer Night's Dream*. Mab does not seek privacy, since she takes with her

> "Hop, and Mop, and Drop so clear,
> Pip, and Trip, and Skip, that were
> To Mab their sovereign ever dear,
> Her special maids of honour ;
> Fil, and Fib, and Pinck, and Pin,
> Tick, and Quick, and Jill, and Jin,
> Tit, and Nit, and Wap, and Win,
> The train that wait upon her."

The whole party scramble up upon a grasshopper, with a cobweb thrown over them all to make them invisible, and start for Pigwiggen's cowslip. Meanwhile Oberon has heard of the expedition, and has become " as mad as any hare." He arms himself with an acorn-cup on a stalk,

fights a wasp (which he takes to be Pigwiggen), lashes a
glowworm for carrying a lamp at her wrong end, ruins a
beehive, and finally flings his leg over the back of an ant,
and gallops in pursuit of the guilty pair. After ignominious
adventures, he meets his faithful servant, Puck, who sends
Hobgoblin to arrest Mab and Pigwiggen. Nimphidia warns
the former just in time, and the ladies all bolt into a hollow
nut. Meanwhile Pigwiggen, greatly daring, starts to challenge Oberon to single fight. But the King sends a fairy
called " Stout Tomalin " to meet him, and each riding
on an earwig, the champions have a sharp encounter. But
Proserpina, the goddess of Fairyland, intervenes and
empties over them a bag (called a " poke ") stuffed with
fogs from Styx. She descends, and, calling all the personages together, including the now stupefied jousters, she
hands round a cup of water of Lethe, which the male
characters sip, with the result that soon

> " King Oberon forgotten had
> That he for jealousy ran mad,
> But of his Queen was wondrous glad,
>   And asked how they came thither ;
> Pigwiggen likewise doth forget
> That he Queen Mab had ever met,
> Or that they were so hard beset,
>   When they were found together."

Mab and her " light maids," however, recall the circumstances perfectly, but are very careful not to allude to them,
and the adventure ends in feasting at the Fairy Court,
" with mickle joy and merriment."

Nimphidia is a poem of fancy, not of imagination.
Shakespeare, while he wrote of fairy revels in the forest
wild, and of the shrewd and knavish spirit of Robin Good-
fellow, believed in all those moonlight wonders, and
observed them in consistent vision. He entered into their
mechanism so deeply that he subordinated all the human
characters in his divinely beautiful play to its fairy per-

sonages, whom he saw before him, dancing and weaving their spells in the perfume of the eglantine. He gave them the shadow of human ambitions and the outline of human passions ; he made them true to themselves and in harmony with those laws of nature which the very conception of them had seemed to outrage. Of Drayton so much cannot be said. He does not believe in his own fairies, but uses them as a basis for building up a structure of graceful and vivid but wholly preposterous fancy. He does not even realise with consistency the size of his creations, and attributes to them nothing equivalent to the infectious laugh of Puck, or the fine agitations of Titania. His machinery is clumsy, where Shakespeare's is always deft and graceful. Nevertheless, *Nimphidia* is a work of abiding merit, eminent in its place and time if we refrain from comparing it too closely with its elders and betters.

A GREAT AMERICAN LIBRARY

A GREAT AMERICAN LIBRARY

WITH careful consideration of the danger of emphasis, I cannot claim less for the five sumptuous volumes of the Catalogue of the late John Henry Wrenn than that they carry the art, or science, of modern bibliography further than it has ever been carried before. The Emperor Julian said that some there were who loved horses, and others birds, others hunting wild beasts, but that, as for him, since he was a little child, he had indulged a wonderful longing to acquire and to possess books. This passion shows no trace of expiring as the world grows old ; more and more collectors expend their money and their cunning in filching away rare volumes from other collectors. It is a recognised and honourable sport, and leaves more material behind it than golf or cricket.

But, as the wish to gather together literary jewels grows on men, the desire increases to learn the exact value and to set down the accurate description of their treasures. The world is full of fakes and pitfalls, and so the literature of bibliography develops and becomes essential ; it becomes fuller of detail and more rigorously technical. The most exact of living bibliographers is Mr. Thos. J. Wise, whose modest and strenuous labours have gradually raised an entirely new standard of what a catalogue of books should be. When I say that the genius of Mr. Wise shines through each of the 1,500 pages of the Wrenn Catalogue I say enough to prove to every lover of books the value of this compilation.

The great library here catalogued is one which few Eng-

lishmen and not all Americans can hope to visit. It is a far
cry to Austin, an inland town in the interior of the State of
Texas, of which it is the jobbing centre. This remote city,
on the borders of Mexico, possesses a university opened
fewer than forty years ago, but richly endowed and full of
honourable ambition. I doubt if John Wrenn had ever
heard of it, and I can imagine the look of mild surprise with
which he would receive the news that his beloved books are
lodged there. Wrenn was a paper-maker of Chicago, born
in 1841. He made a fortune by his typical American energy
in business, and then determined to enjoy himself rationally.
Why he " took up " book-collecting I know not, but about
thirty years ago a very gentle, rather shy, sentimentally
persistent American gentleman began to make an annual
visit to London in search of first editions. He had the good
fortune to secure Mr. Wise's acquaintance, and the wisdom
to avail himself of that expert's unparalleled experience.

Wrenn's name was never in the newspapers, but every
autumn, when he went back to Chicago, the books were in
his baggage. He often talked of a catalogue of his library,
but always postponed it. At last, in 1911, he died suddenly
while he was paying a visit in California, leaving his collection to his son and daughter, who were filled with reverence
for his memory, but lived at a distance from one another,
and had no common convenience for keeping the books
together.

What was to be done ? The vulture auctioneers and the
shark booksellers were already rubbing their hands in glee
at the idea of cutting up so rich a carcass. But Wrenn's
family stood staunch. They reminded each other that their
father had always wished that his books should not be dispersed ; he had called his library " my little monument,"
and they decided that, whatever their pecuniary loss, that
monument should not be shattered. There were important
public reasons for this. Wrenn's library is in certain respects

unique ; in particular it contains not merely a few dozens, but some hundreds of more or less obscure books, of which not a single other copy is known to exist in the United States. Along certain lines of the less hackneyed departments of English literature it is more rich than any other library ; to break it up would have been to destroy a very important record.

Meanwhile, Wrenn's son, under Mr. Wise's direction, began the huge task of cataloguing, which took many years, and involved several visits to England. Still, no decision was come to as to the destination of the books. But in 1918 the problem was solved by the public spirit of a leading inhabitant of Austin, Major George Littlefield. By this time Wrenn's daughter was, unhappily, dead, but her husband, Mr. F. F. Norcross, continued the family traditions. The books were officially valued, and of the very high price named Major Littlefield paid two-thirds, the Wrenn family waiving their claim to the other third, and the whole being then generously presented to the University of Texas. Nor did the beneficence of Major Littlefield cease there ; he built, and gave to the university, a magnificent building, which will for all time attract students of English literature to the modest city of Austin. In the annals of bibliophily I know of no prettier story. Moreover, observe a final touch of delicacy ; the edifice is called The Wrenn Library, not The Littlefield Library.

The importance of the Wrenn Library does not rest on its containing all the popular conventional rarities. The First Folio of Shakespeare is not here, nor any of the early quartos, nor the privately printed edition of George Herbert's *Temple*, nor Walton's *Compleat Angler* of 1653, nor the Kilmarnock Burns. For these monsters Wrenn had no consuming desire, but what he most set his heart upon is defined by Mr. Wise as " books of real literary value for which the pages of any other catalogue will be searched in vain." He

neglected English literature up to the close of the sixteenth
century ; it is in the seventeenth and eighteenth centuries
that he was so astonishingly rich. In the nineteenth his
taste was a little capricious, but he had a great affection
for Shelley, Wordsworth, Tennyson, D. G. Rossetti, and
Swinburne.

His aim seems to have been generally cumulative ; when
he adopted an author he tried his utmost to make his collection of that author complete ; but he had some isolated
treasures of almost fabulous importance. I propose to
dwell on his broader principles, but I must mention those
instances of extreme interest which have caught my eye as
I turned over the pages. It would almost be worth while to
trapes all the way to Texas to examine the celebrated copy
of Chapman's *All Fools* (1605), which that strange bandit
John Payne Collier used to convey his forgery, and by
which he took in all the learned world. Here is Shelley's
Victor and Cazire of 1810, long believed to be unique, with
its interesting history ; and here is *Deborah and Barak*
(1705), the only copy yet discovered of the satirical poem
by William Penn.

The Commonwealth was a period which simply pullulated
with pamphlets in prose and verse. Most of these are
anonymous, but many were signed by, or can safely be
attributed to, famous or at least notorious names. Bibliography has neglected this class of literature, to which Wrenn
gave particular attention. James Barlow is ignored by the
Dictionary of National Biography, but did not evade the
notice of Wrenn, who collected a large number of the
fantastic tracts which Barlow published during the Civil
War. Barlow was a fervent Royalist, and one of his poems
bears the pleasant title of *The Faery Leveller, or King Charles*.
John Cleveland was by far the most popular of English poets
during the lifetime of Milton, and his eccentric writings
afford the Wrenn Catalogue fourteen interesting entries.

But it is in that darling of the salerooms, John Taylor the Water-Poet, that the Wrenn Library particularly excels. For some reason which I do not fathom, the original issues of this vivacious but rather vulgar poetaster command prices at the present moment which are simply preposterous. During the Civil War the printing-presses groaned under the effusions of the Water-Poet, which bore such titles as *A Dialogue, or rather a Parley between Prince Rupert's Dog whose name is Puddle, and Tobie's Dog whose name is Pepper.* Of these, Wrenn, who had a positive passion for Taylor, contrived to amass no fewer than forty-five. But I do not think he secured that which contains a woodcut which is supposed to be a portrait of Shakespeare. However, what he did collect would represent a little fortune in the open market.

A remarkable department in the Wrenn Library deals with what Mr. Whibley has called the Underworld of Letters at the close of the seventeenth century. These insolent satirists and pamphleteers have hitherto defied the researches of the bibliographer, and their curious publications have neither been collected nor examined. Wrenn took a singular interest in them, and he possessed no fewer than twenty-three of the pamphlets of Tom Brown, whose publisher advertised him as " not inferior in satyrical Prose or Verse to Petronius, Martial, or any other of the witty ancients."

Of Ned Ward here are still more examples ; forty-two of the Hudibrastic squibs which he sent forth from his " genteel punch-shop " in Fullwood Rents. Here are thirty of the preposterous vivacities of Tom Durfey. The burlesques of Charles Cotton, who wrote the mock-Virgil, and of John Dennis, the old enemy of Pope, are not less amply represented ; nor is Peter Motteaux, who wrote *A Poem on Tea*, translated Molière, and died a disgusting death. Only I do not find Captain John Stevens, who translated so many Spanish

romances of low life.   It was extremely intelligent of Wrenn
to be the first to penetrate this Alsatia of letters, this queer,
crowded world of the coffee-houses and of Grub Street,
where never a book-collector had ventured far before him.
His reward was that it led him on to Defoe and Swift and
Mandeville, where he outran all competitors.   His first
editions of Swift are 121 in number ; of Mandeville twenty-
nine ; of Defoe 119.   Who, in future, will dare to edit a
Queen Anne worthy without making a preliminary journey
to Austin, Texas ?

It is in the eighteenth century that the Wrenn Library
pre-eminently shines.   Never was seen before such a
galaxy of Addison and Prior and Gay, of Fielding and
Goldsmith and Smollett.   I cannot imagine where Wrenn
contrived to pick up the less famous and therefore much
rarer writers—twelve separate first editions of Tickell,
twenty-six of Savage, fifty-one of Garrick.   It is enough
to make the Bodleian fling itself into the arms of the British
Museum and sink there in a swoon.   The Popes, too, are
wonderful, and nearly one hundred in number.   Prodigious ! as Dominie Sampson would say.   But I observe,
with a gleam of malice, that the rarest and best of the
Dunciads, the B of Thom's list, is absent.

When we come down to the nineteenth century I find
Mr. Wrenn's selection to have been a little uncertain.   He
confined himself to the greatest names, and he was poor
in De Quincey, in Leigh Hunt, and particularly in Hazlitt.
The few publications of Beddoes are very rare, but what
was rarity to Wrenn ?   I am surprised to find Crabbe
neglected.   On the other hand, Byron, Shelley, and Keats
are redundant in splendour.   A copy of *Endymion*, in the
original drab boards, with the white paper label intact,
and some lines of verse in the poet's handwriting, is enough
to render an envious bibliophil unwell.   Let him calm
himself.   No other collector shall ever boast of this

treasure. It dwells secure at Austin, Texas, till the crack of doom.

The manufacture of these five volumes is beyond praise. It was impossible to chronicle such a multitude of volumes without sacrificing something to brevity, and therefore the attributions are sometimes too summary. This could not be helped, but the student must be warned to take many of them with caution. The exactitude of the descriptions, on the other hand, is something quite extraordinary. Searching with a jealous care, I have "spotted" but a single misprint—Heywood's *Gunaikeion* appears as *Tunaikeion*. The books are printed on fine Whatman hand-made paper, and bound in primrose-yellow buckram. At a moment of acute national self-depreciation we may cheer ourselves by noting that these beautiful volumes were made by a London, not an American firm, namely, by Messrs. Heron & Co., of Tottenham Court Road.

THE DANIEL PRESS

THE DANIEL PRESS

In the winter of 1836, when the Princess Victoria, destined to be Queen of England a few months later, happened to visit Wareham, in Dorset, there was presented to her a baby in long clothes who was the eldest and then only son of the perpetual curate of Trinity Church, Frome-Selwood. That was the far-away year of the Irish Tithe Bill in the Lords and the publication of *Sketches by Boz;* Newman was defining to a bewildered laity the theory of the Oxford Movement. But the infant throve, and outlived his monarch and most of their contemporaries, and had reached his eighty-fifth year when he passed away in peace. His early youth was spent in rural Somersetshire, but when he was seventeen he was elected to a scholarship in Worcester College, of which he ultimately rose to be the beloved and respected Provost. His life was so intimately bound to the University that it is difficult to think of Oxford without him, without the familiar figure, tall beyond the common stature of man, venerable in a long white beard, and crowned by a smile, that was always friendly and calm, and perhaps a little fantastic. A host of friends, old and middle-aged and young, mourned the disappearance of Charles Henry Olive Daniel, who had claimed so little and had been to his associates so much.

Mere personal charm, however, cannot long preserve the memory of a name. Daniel was not a writer, nor a pre-eminent scholar, nor the revolutionary Head of a House. He will live in the recollection of what long seemed to be a whim, the mere innocent vagary of a life otherwise

seriously occupied. He was born to be famous as a printer,
and he was only nine years of age, at his home in Frome-
Selwood, when he persuaded his parents to give him a
toy-press. His earliest productions have not been preserved, but in May 1846 he printed a four-page letter,
in which he thanked his friends for having " employed his
types and his thumb " in the past, which shows that they
had already been active. Mr. Madan, in his work on
The Daniel Press, with all the professional sobriety of the
bibliographer, tells us that this treasure " was set up in a
composing-stick, arranged in short lines, not more than
three, tied together with string, inked with the thumb and
pressed on the paper." This is very technical, and sounds
primitive. But the child persisted with ceaseless tenacity,
improving steadily as he went on. The productions of the
Frome Press are of excessive rarity, and it cannot be
truthfully said that they are very attractive. I am the
proud possessor of one of them, *Sir Richard's Daughter :
A Christmas Tale of the Olden Times*, printed in 1852 and
issued in blue paper wrappers. This was a poem by W. C.
Cruttwell, an uncle of the printer, and bears on its title-page
the stirring words : " Excudebat H. Daniel : Trinity
Parsonage, Frome."

The Frome Press, however, is a mere forecast or herald
of Daniel's real work, and its effusions are not regarded
seriously by collectors. The typographical mania seemed
to have ceased when Henry Daniel took his degree in 1858.
He had other fish to fry ; he had to take charge of the strange
and ephemeral paintings which Rossetti, Morris, and Burne
Jones painted upon the ceiling of the Union Debating
Hall ; and he presently went up to London for a few years
to be Classical Lecturer in King's College. Even when a
fellowship at Worcester College called him back to Oxford,
ten more years passed before the old passion seized him,
and before he brought the Frome hand-press to his college

rooms. He started again, and his earliest production was the *Notes from a Catalogue of Pamphlets in Worcester College Library,* of which only twenty-five copies were struck off in 1874. To this followed *A New Sermon of the Newest Fashion,* an oddity of the seventeenth century, and a set of two Colloquies of Erasmus, issued with the encouragement of Mark Pattison. This last is the earliest publication of the Daniel Press which has any beauty. Pater called it " the most exquisite specimen of printing I have seen," and it was widely admired. The flushed printer felt that he had found his vocation, and prepared for higher things.

By this time, through a happy accident, Henry Daniel had discovered the implement which best suited his delicate craftsmanship. Professor Bartholomew Price, observing his passion for typography, asked him whether he had ever seen the antique type-matrixes which lay abandoned in the Clarendon Press building. They had belonged to the much-maligned John Fell :—

> " I do not like you, Dr. Fell ;
> The reason why I cannot tell—

who was Dean of Christ Church and Bishop of Oxford until his death in 1686, and who built the tower over the gateway of the college, in which he placed the bell, " Great Tom." Dr. Fell " earnestly applied himself to purge Christ Church of all remains of hypocrisy and nonsense," and used to go early in the morning to the chambers of noblemen and gentlemen-commoners " to see what progress they made in their studies." Perhaps this was how, although a " pious, learned, and zealous person," he made himself disliked.

Among other examples of Dr. Fell's zeal, he abounded in editions of the classics, for which he had a special type manufactured. This type had not been used for nearly two hundred years, when Price took Daniel to look at it.

The printer's keen eye instantly recognised the capabilities of this "broken and imperfect fount, a dusty and disused legacy," left by the redoubtable Dr. Fell. "Spurred by its charm," says the President of Magdalen College, in his eloquent memoir, Henry Daniel perceived that it was the very thing he needed to give character and originality to his work. He easily persuaded the Clarendon Press to resign the matrixes to him, and with this fresh instrument "he went on to new enterprises and elaborations, introducing flowers and head-lines, tail-pieces, and borders, miniations by his wife's hand, and a score of dainty devices." He went back to the age of innocence in typography, and the old-fashioned letters of the Fell Press exactly fitted his whimsical and curious taste.

The Daniel Press set forth its most beautiful and, as it has turned out, its most valuable issue in 1881, when the famous *Garland of Rachel* was published. The fascinating history of this casket of ivory and gold has now for the first time been told in any detail. In 1878 Henry Daniel had married, and in 1880 a daughter Rachel was born to him. It was suggested by the Humphry Wards that Rachel's father's friends should celebrate her first birthday by contributing poems to a collection in her honour, which should be printed by Daniel on his Fell types. I believe that it was Mrs. Ward who suggested that the famous *Guirlande de Julie* of the seventeenth century should be taken as the model.

Accordingly, an appeal was made to the poets, and as Daniel knew everybody in the younger world of letters it was made very widely. The young lady to be celebrated was beautiful, with a translucent pallor of complexion and hair that was like spun gold. Nevertheless, it is a delicate and a perilous thing to celebrate the charms of a *belle* who has not yet reached her first birthday. Several of the chosen bards had not sufficient courage to accept the task,

but, surprisingly, no fewer than seventeen faced the music
that they made.

Conjoint efforts of this kind was something of a novelty
forty years ago, and *The Garland of Rachel* was very widely
discussed. It was composed entirely by those of the new
generation who were prominent at that date ; it was almost
a manifesto. Among those who have died since, and who
ingeniously celebrated in verse the printer's little daughter,
were Austin Dobson, Andrew Lang, John Addington
Symonds, Henley, Courthope, and Locker-Lampson. Among
those who are still living was the present Poet Laureate.

The Garland of Rachel was, as Mr. Madan points out, the
earliest " adequate " specimen of the Fell type, and it was
the first into which Daniel introduced important ornament
and coloured miniation. Alfred Parsons specially drew for
it two designs : one of them presented the prophet Daniel,
with the stature and features of the printer, engaged in
prayer while an excessively ill-favoured lion prowled around
his feet ; the other was a frieze of flowers. These were,
in future, to be identified with the Press, but Dr. Fell
would probably have thought them frivolous. Only thirty-
six copies were printed, and each contributor received a
copy bound in stiff white vellum and with a special title-
page, bearing his own name. For example, the title of
mine is : " *The Garland of Rachel,* by Edmund Gosse and
divers kindly hands." Andrew Lang considered the best
contributions to be those of Dobson and Bridges, but there
is much to be said in favour of his own, a ballade, never,
I believe, reprinted, which begins :—

> " 'Tis distance lends, the poet says,
>   Enchantment to the view,
> And this makes possible the praise
>   Which I bestow on you.
>   For babies roseate of hue
> I do not always care,
>   But distance paints the mountains blue,
> And Rachel always fair."

To descend to a vulgar detail, when *The Garland of
Rachel* finds its way, on very rare occasions, to the auction
room, it fetches about forty pounds.

After this great success, the Daniel Press proceeded
merrily. In 1883 the printer began what will always connect his name with the poetical literature of his age, namely,
a desultory publication of new works by Mr. Robert Bridges.
He started with an edition of the drama of *Prometheus the
Fire-Bringer*, issued to sixty subscribers. The present
memoir prints an amusing Hudibrastic by the Poet
Laureate, beginning :—

> " In friendship that began may be
> In eighteen eighty-two or three,
> When Daniel printed my *Prometheus*—
> A thing that others judged beneath use—
> He living then in Worcester House,
> Along with many a rat and mouse."

It was at Mr. Bridges' suggestion that Daniel printed in
1884 a volume of *Odes and Eclogues*, by R. W. Dixon, a
poet of the pre-Raphaelite period to whom justice has never
been done ; and at mine the posthumous verses of Henry
Patmore. But he came back constantly to Bridges, in a
succession of precious quartos, which include *The Feast of
Bacchus* (1889), the *Eton Ode* (1893) and the six volumes
(1893–94) of *Shorter Poems*. All these are of great literary
importance apart from their bibliographical rarity and
curiosity. Other examples of little books which now
command a respect which is far beyond what was anticipated
when they were produced are Walter Pater's *The Child in
the House* (1894), and Mary Coleridge's anonymous *Fancy's
Following* (1896).

When Henry Daniel succeeded to the Provostship of
Worcester College in 1903, he announced, to the consterna-
tion of his friends, that the Fell Press would issue no more
books or leaflets. He carried out this determination so
rigorously that two productions, which were in process of

manufacture, were left unfinished. These were a reprint of Gascoigne's *Queen's Entertainment at Woodstock in* 1585, which Mr. Pollard afterwards completed, and Sir Richard Bacon's *Recreations*, which is still a fragment. Only once was the printer persuaded to break his vow, and that was in the direct service of his college. In 1906, Sir William Hadow and other friends begged him to print a Latin service of *Worcester College Prayers*, and he yielded, only insisting that the copies were not to be sold, nor ever removed from the Chapel. " So ended the Daniel Press, as the Provost must have been well content to end it, with the words, ' Laus Deo.' "

On September 6, 1920, Henry Daniel died, and was buried in Oxford. He lives in the memory of his older friends as Sir Herbert Warren admirably describes him " with his tall, erect figure, his bright and sanguine complexion, his hair and beard of fine and ruddy gold." Younger companions, on the other hand, recall him, as Mr. Masefield does, in the fine poem contributed to the present memoir,

" In wisest age in all its happiest bloom."

The sanguine and auburn turned under the touch of years to parchment and silver. The monument, which is now raised to his memory by the Clarendon Press, is one which would have exquisitely gratified his sense of fitness. To the great printer is dedicated a cenotaph of rich topography. This quarto is the first book that ever was printed within the sacred walls of the Bodleian.

YORICK AND HIS ELIZA

YORICK AND HIS ELIZA

"Amazing Revelations! Letters read in Court!"
Fancy dwells upon the natural disappointment of the editor
of some evening newspaper who discovers that the correspondence of Sterne with Eliza is one hundred and sixty years
old, and therefore of no use to him. What luscious head-
lines, what succulent paragraphs are lost ! *Qualis artifex*, he
murmurs, and bursts into tears. Never was a love affair
more preposterous and noisy, with laughter tottering at the
heels of tragedy. In the account of it given by Messrs.
Wright and Sclater, there is not much, if anything, about
Sterne which is positively new. Indeed, the facts are a
little slurred over, and could have been more fully stated, as
I may be able to point out later on.

Without Sterne, Eliza Draper would possess no particular
interest, and therefore the editors cannot neglect him
altogether ; but they hurry past him. Their real interest is in
the curious pictures of Indian life given in those letters of
Eliza, none of them written to Sterne, which Messrs. Arnold
Wright and William Lutley Sclater print for the first time.
They do not mention that Sir Sidney Lee and others have
already described these documents. I wish that they had
been a little more explicit about the source of what they say
they owe " to the courtesy of the late Lord Basing, amongst
whose family papers they are preserved." Lord Basing was
a Sclater-Booth,. and Eliza was born a Sclater. We might
have further particulars.

Eliza Sclater was a lively creature, tropical and precocious. She was born at Anjengo, in the extreme south of

Hindustan, on April 5, 1744. The editors give a full account of her Anglo-Indian family, which was reputable and extensive. She was married—I presume Messrs. Wright and Sclater are sure of their dates—at the age of thirteen, and was a mother before she was fifteen. Hence, when in 1765 her husband, Daniel Draper, a morose and middle-aged Indian official, brought her to England and left her there, she was a world-worn matron of twenty-one summers. But she was extremely vivacious, slightly hypochondriacal (she called herself " the enthusiastic votary of Health "), and determined to combine the maximum of liberty with the minimum of scandal. She meant to follow " the Dictates of Gallantry," while preserving the laws of respectability.

What happened to her during the first two years is uncertain, except that she paid a round of visits to country friends, and then settled in London in the house of some Anglo-Indians, who afterwards became Sir William and Lady James. The editors are vague in their statement of her first meeting Sterne, and their reader might imagine that it took place in 1765, but this would be a mistake. Other documents show that it must have been in the last week of January, 1767, that Sterne, visiting the Jameses, first beheld Eliza. He fell " half in love " with her at once, and told her so. A month later he was expatiating to his daughter, Lydia, on his intimate friendship with " one of the most amiable and gentlest of beings." The friendship proceeded rapidly and far. He sat by Eliza's bedside when she was unwell, and she dined with him at his house in New Bond Street. She called him her Brahmin, and he called her his Brahmine. He made no secret of his hope that their respective spouses would disappear or be explained away, and that he might carry his Eliza, a bride, to that vicarage in Yorkshire which he had so deplorably neglected. It was all over in ten weeks.

This is a brief outline of the " affair " which has scandalised biographers so much, and which roused Thackeray, in particular, to a paroxysm of prudery. But let us examine it a little more closely, and try to control our blushes. That the queer couple behaved in a very silly way may be admitted at once, but let us consider the circumstances. Sterne had just finished *Tristram Shandy*, which had made him the most talked-about author of the age. He was the spoilt child of literature ; he had been indulged by the clergy, petted by the aristocracy, flattered by all the world to the top of his bent. He was not yet fifty-five, but dissipation and phthisis had added a score to his years. He was now an old man, almost a physical spectre, a worn-out machine kept going by the intellectual fire and whirling activity of his spirit. He was no longer expected to be in any sense an exemplary specimen of a clergyman, although he was just publishing a second series of *Sermons*, which he duly presented to Eliza ; but he was charming, enthralling, and like a capricious fairy.

To understand Sterne we must forget all that solemn moralists have said about him, and think of some volatile figure out of a Gilbert and Sullivan opera. I find it impossible to comprehend the violence which Thackeray displayed in his treatment of this episode. " Wretched old sinner," indeed ! That is no way to speak of Yorick in the last phase of his motley dance through life. It is plain that Eliza was the end of him. She was the flame into which the moth, with its golden wings widely extended, flew and was consumed. But this was nearly a culminating accident ; the hours of the moth were numbered before the flame attracted him.

What was the nature of the attraction ? Messrs. Wright and Sclater help to explain it by means of their record of her life and of her character as displayed in her letters. Eliza possessed a charm which depended more upon her liveliness of sympathetic response, and on the intensity of gaze in her fine eyes, than upon positive beauty. She was

a sentimental, and even a Shandean siren, peculiarly fitted
to lead silly old men on to the rocks. Long after Sterne's
death she played identically the same sport with another
elderly rake, the Abbé Raynal, and it is amusing to compare his ravings with those of his predecessor. It is plain
that Eliza was a past-mistress in the art of exciting a bom-
bastic sort of cerebral passion.

The editors of the new volume scarcely allude to the
Journal to Eliza which Sterne kept after the lady returned
to Bombay. This document accompanies the *Letters to
Eliza* which were published, not without more than a suspicion of blackmail, seven years after Sterne's death. It is
that which most of all awakened the puritanical fury of
Thackeray and other hostile critics. It is a delirious
rhapsody in which " poor sick-headed, sick-hearted Yorick "
tries to make any change of purpose in Eliza impossible.
He is not sure of her : " I cling the closer to the Idea of
you " as the physical presence recedes. Critics have spoken
of the *Journal to Eliza* as an indelicate production. It
depends on what is understood by delicacy. In others of
his writings Sterne is often very indecent, but there is not
a coarse word or innuendo in the *Journal ;* ecstatic raptures
confine themselves to tenderness and regret.

Evidently the solemn head-shakings of preceding biographers have terrified Messrs. Wright and Sclater. They
hardly dare to touch the Yorick episode. They earnestly—
and repeatedly—hope that the relation was not a " guilty "
one. Thackeray exulted in the thought that it was
" guilty," and brought down the sledge-hammer of his
virtuous indignation on the erring pair. But neither he
nor any one else seems to have noticed that Sterne himself
threw on his connection with Eliza all the light that should
be asked for. He wrote, " Not Swift so loved Stella,
Scarron his Maintenon, or Waller his Sacharissa as I will love
thee." These names were not quoted at random. What

may have been Swift's disability is uncertain, but we know that in love he was not as other men are. Scarron was paralytic before he married. The passion of Waller for Sacharissa has always been a bye-word for artificiality. Sterne could hardly have spoken more plainly to his physician than he did to the public in this list of names, yet no one seems to have taken his meaning. He explains that the too-famous *Journal* was " a Diary of the miserable feelings of a Person separated from a Lady for whose Society he languish'd." The sparkling eyes, the ready response, the tender histrionics of Eliza—" Nature design'd me for an actress," she says in one of these new letters— shot a delusive fire through the veins of that " bale of cada- verous goods consigned to Pluto and company," which Sterne described himself to be when she had left him. Moreover, he was collecting impressions for the *Sentimental Journey*.

It was all very absurd and extravagant, and is justly annoying, no doubt, to sober, reserved votaries of Mrs. Grundy, but to call it " guilty " is ridiculous. Those who so speak of it forget that Sterne made no secret of his relations with Mrs. Draper. He showed her letters " to half the literati in town." He gave an account of their friendship to Lord Apsley, and expatiated on the whole affair, while it was going on, to the Archbishop of York " and his Lady and Sister." His friends aided and abetted. Are Mr. Wright and Mr. Sclater sure that he wrote the stanzas on Eliza's indisposition? I think they will find that Hall-Stevenson composed them for his use. Sterne flung his hysterics wide-cast over England, and his lamenta- tions were none the less genuine because he listened with complacency to their melodious echo. He was sadly deficient in the bashfulness which should adorn a clergyman of the Established Church, but when virtue has acknow- ledged that, it may surely moderate its transports.

" Best of God's works, farewell ! " whispered Sterne
through his choking sobs when Eliza, on board the *Earl
of Chatham*, sailed from the Downs to rejoin her husband
in India on April 3, 1767.   At first she wrote to Yorick in
terms " the most interesting and the most endearing that
ever tried the tenderness of man."   But Horace long ago
recorded the dangers of a social voyage when

> " only faith, or triple brass,
> Can help the ' outward-bound ' to pass
> Safe through "

the dangers of equatorial flirtation.   The transit to Bombay
occupied nine months.   There were agreeable gentlemen
on board, and Eliza could not help assuming what she
called " a bagatelle air."   Moreover, she was in love, she
had all along been in love, with her youthful and hearty
cousin, Thomas Lumley Sclater.   She was fond of analysing
her feelings, and she fancied that she perceived a likeness
between herself and St. Paul, the Apostle to the Gentiles,
although here one fails to follow her line of thought.   At all
events, when she landed at last in Bombay, whatever she
may have remembered, she had forgotten poor Yorick.
She received the news of his death with indifference, but
philosophised as follows :—

" I've a world of Romance in my temper, that I love to indulge
because it only leads me to refine upon the best the sweetest affections
of the human heart, not but that this passion for the Tender, Delicate,
and Elegant produces some mortifications, too, as I seldom meet
with Persons that come up to my Ideas of perfection, consequently
am vastly disgusted *toute en semble* with anything ungenerous, Ill-
liberal or unfeeling, which I do, and daily must expect to meet with
in the common Intercourses of Life."

We follow the remainder of her career with abated
curiosity, but it is not without interest.   Mr. Draper was
promptly transferred from Bombay to Tellicherry, the
principal seat of the Company's power on the Malabar
Coast.   Here Eliza found herself by turns the wife of a
merchant, a soldier and an innkeeper, as she described her

husband in his varied functions. She liked Tellicherry ;
she called it the Montpellier of India. Her letters contain
picturesque and curious information regarding life in a
factory towards the close of the eighteenth century. She
was active and happy at Tellicherry, and out of mischief,
but in an evil hour Mr. Draper was moved to Surat, and
then back to Bombay, where society was full of tempta-
tions and where her estrangement with Draper became
complete. The " almost broken-hearted " Eliza fled from
Marine House, letting herself down one night by a rope
fastened to her bedroom window, into a boat which bore
her off to Commodore Sir John Clarke's flag-ship. She was
taken in by her uncle, John Whitehill, who was adminis-
tering Masulipatam, and, gaining her divorce, she began
to look out for a young man, " mild, yet manly," distinguished by " Dignity of Soul not alloy'd by any Mixture
of Ostentation." She came back to England in 1774, bent
on discovering this paragon, but she found instead a copy
of her old Yorick in an infatuated Abbé Raynal, who was
urging her to fly with him in terms closely reminiscent of
Sterne, when Eliza incontinently died at Clifton on August 3,
1778. Her distracted lover celebrated in stilted and
redundant prose her sensibility, and " that almost incom-
patible harmony of voluptuousness and decency, which
diffused itself over all her person and accompanied all her
motions."

IZAAK WALTON'S ADOPTED SON

IZAAK WALTON'S ADOPTED SON

A BRIEF prefatory note to a pleasant selection from the poems of Charles Cotton tells us that Lovat Fraser was "always trying to persuade his friends of the rare qualities" of those poems. But it does not offer so much as a hint who Cotton was, nor when he wrote, nor anything whatever about him. He is not well enough known to be treated in this way, and the indolent reader of the verses, after looking at Lovat Fraser's sparkling vignettes and tail-pieces, may care to be told a little about a poet and prose-writer who once was a favourite of the public, and who, in spite of praise a hundred years ago from Wordsworth, Coleridge, and Lamb, has been completely neglected of late. A strange ill-fortune has attended Charles Cotton, in that he has never, though occasionally and partially popular in the eighteenth century, been collected or edited. No complete, or even adequate, collection of his writings has ever been made, and he is an author whom it is impossible to consult, except piecemeal. He was an angler of high repute, who knew better than any one else (except Walton)—

> "What the best Master's hand can do
> With the most deadly killing fly,"

and in 1676 he published the Second Part of *The Complete Angler*, which is often reprinted. But his other works are scattered, and it needs some diligence even to bring them into focus. Of his best poems—and the best are very good—none were published during his lifetime.

Charles Cotton was a typical country gentleman of the best class of Cavaliers. He was born on April 28, 1630, probably at Elvaston, his mother's home in Derbyshire, although

87

there were other houses belonging to his " ancient and honourable family." It is very difficult to distinguish him at first from his father, who seems to have been identical with him not only in name, but in character, pursuits, and vacillating fortune. The elder Charles Cotton was the friend of Herrick and Suckling, and is the subject of one of Clarendon's careful portraits. It was long supposed that the tributes of the former and the analysis of the latter referred to the poet, but Oldys showed this to be impossible. Father and son had the same politics and the same habits ; each went to France and made an unusual study of French literature, though at different times. Until the elder Charles Cotton died in 1658 it is almost impossible to decide which was which, and I do not feel quite certain that some of the poems attributed by their son and grandson, Beresford Cotton, to the younger were not really written by the elder.

But this is vain conjecture. No life of Cotton exists, but at the time when the great popularity of his burlesques was waning, Oldys, the antiquary, collected what information he could, and prefixed it to the 1760 edition of *The Complete Angler ;* so far as I can discover, this has never been reprinted. I possess a precious interleaved copy of Langbaine's *English Dramatick Poets* of 1691, into which the Rev. Rogers Ruding copied in 1784 biographical notes made by Oldys, which supplement the printed notices. This contains some further gossip about Charles Cotton. But he remains rather shadowy.

The work of Cotton in verse is divided into two sections so diametrically opposed that it is difficult to realise that they proceeded from the same mind. His popularity during his lifetime and for a century after his death depended upon his skill in " vesting Apollo in the jacket of Harlequin." European literature was invaded at the middle of the seventeenth century by a sort of chicken-pox, called

Burlesque, which raged for a few years, and then wore
itself out. When Cotton went to Paris, probably about
1648, he found this disease rampant among the French
poets. Saint-Amant, between whom and Cotton a great
similarity of talent and temperament existed, had introduced it into France with his *Rome Ridicule* of 1643 ; he
had already a swarm of imitators.

Of these, the most thorough-going was Scarron, who
turned all the sentiment and passion of the ancients into
buffoonery. He published a travesty of Virgil, which
Cotton seized upon and imitated in his *Scarronides*, repeating
the narrative of the *Æneid* in rattling comic octosyl-
labics. This fashion of burlesque invaded Paris with a sort
of fury, and for the time being excluded all other forms of
poetry. It dominated literature to such an extent that a
poem was published under the repulsive heading of *The
Passion of our Lord in Burlesque Verses*. This piece was
quite serious and pious, intended for edification, but the
publisher gave it that title because no one would buy
poetry unless it were " burlesque." The passion of parody
was soon exhausted in France, but it lasted longer in England,
where Cotton had many imitators during the next fifty years.

The eighteenth century knew Cotton in verse only as a
writer of burlesque. He turned Virgil into this sort of thing:—

" Have you not seen, upon a river,
A water-dog that is a diver
Bring out his mallard, and eft-soons
Beshake his shaggy pantaloons ?
So Neptune, when he first appears,
Shakes the salt liquor from his ears,
And makes the winds themselves to doubt him,
He throws the water so about him."

It is amusing enough in a short passage, but inconceivably
tedious in the extension of a lengthy epic. Moreover, the
indelicacy of Cotton in *Scarronides* and in *Burlesque Upon
Burlesque* is carried beyond all bounds. The popularity
of these poems, which were incessantly reprinted down to

the reign of George III., is a curious proof of the coarseness
of taste underneath an Addisonian veneer which existed
in England through the end of the seventeenth and beginning of the eighteenth centuries. No indulgence of modern
taste will ever endure a reprint of these disgusting travesties
of Virgil and Lucian. Cotton's original burlesques, *A
Voyage to Ireland* and *The Wonders of the Peak*, are of quite
a different order, and possess considerable merit of a rugged
and boisterous kind. They demand an attention which I
cannot give them here.

But it was not the rattling doggerel of *Virgil Travestie*
and *The Scoffer Scoff'd* which fascinated Lovat Fraser.
By the side of his jocular parodies of the ancients, which
delighted readers by their audacity and realism, Cotton
cultivated a vein of delicate reflective poetry in the spirit
of a previous generation. These lyrics, of an old-fashioned
purity and sweetness, did not amuse the Restoration in the
least, and they passed unnoticed. In one department the
pioneer of a new style, in the other Cotton was the latest
to cultivate the manner of the Jacobean age. During his
lifetime he brought out no collection of his serious poems,
and these were not collected until 1689, two years after his
death, when it was hopeless to find an audience for them.

Since that date they have never been reprinted in full, and
they hardly tempt an editor. They are wanting in con-
centration, for Cotton was a garrulous bard, very natural,
sensuous, and genuine, but too easily pleased with what he
wrote and insufficiently attentive to technique. Hence his
beauties are accidental and rather rare ; the little selection
made by Lovat Fraser gives hopes which the 729 pages of
the original volume do not sustain, the divine liquor being
diluted in such a bucket of doggerel that it loses its aroma.

Cotton's love-poetry is unaffected and apt to become, as
all his best writing does, suddenly personal. His verses to
his wife, Isabella Hutchinson, of Owthorpe, have an odd

touch of reality. Before their marriage, it appears, Isabella was the ruling spirit, but after it the husband rebelled in these surprising terms :—

> " Lord ! how you take upon you still !
> How you crow and domineer !
> How still expect to have your will,
> And carry the dominion clear,
> As you were still the same that once you were."

This must have taught "Chloris" her place, and so must the still clearer statement:—

> " But your six months are now expir'd ;
> 'Tis time I now should reign."

This sounds as though it might lead to trouble, but the poet ends with a recantation :—

> " Though I pretend to wrestle and repine,
> Your beauties, Sweet, are in their height,
> And I must still adore."

He could be much more gallant than this upon occasion, and not Carew, nor Suckling, nor Cotton's old friend Lovelace had written a more charming song than *Celia's Fall*, in which the triviality of the incident described is relieved by the grace of the language and the harmony of the metre :—

> " Celia, my fairest Celia, fell !
> Celia, than the fairest, fairer,—
> Celia (with none I must compare her !)
> That, all alone, is all in all
> Of what we fair and modest call,—
> Celia, white as alabaster,
> Celia, than Diana chaster,—
> This fair, fair Celia, grief to tell !
> This fair, this modest, chaste one—fell !
>
> " My Celia, sweetest Celia, fell !
> As I have seen a snow-white dove
> Decline her bosom from above,
> And down her spotless body fling
> Without the motion of the wing,
> Till she arrest her seeming fall
> Upon some happy pedestal,—
> So soft this sweet, I love so well,
> This sweet, this dove-like Celia fell.'

There is more of this in the 1689 volume, but enough is as good as a feast.

Cotton's principal merit as a serious poet lies, however, in his treatment of natural objects. He preserved longer than any one else in that Restoration, when mankind seemed to have lost the use of its eyes, the habit of keen observation. In his best pieces the landscape of Derbyshire is mirrored with picturesque exactitude, and he is a painter less exclusively in miniature than Herrick, who preceded him. Cotton's *Summer's Day*, in some eighty quatrains, is a masterpiece of nature painting, full of little vignettes like these :—

> " The rail now cracks in fields and meads,
> Toads now forsake the nettle-beds,
> The timorous hare goes to relief,
> And wary men bolt out the thief.

> " The fire new raked and hearth swept clean
> By Madge, the dirty kitchen-quean ;
> The safe is locked, the mouse-trap set,
> The leaven laid and bucking wet."

There was nothing like this in English literature for another fifty years. The author had his eye on the object ; he saw the rail wading among the reeds and " cracking," or clapping, as she went. " Bucking " is clothes being soaked for bleaching. All this is on a small scale, but Cotton had, in addition, a sense of the grandeur of seas in motion and of the grotesque in mountain scenery denied to all his contemporaries. In *Winter* and *The Storm* he approaches the sublimity of a Salvator Rosa.

We must not forget, however, that Cotton was, above all things, a fisherman. A great piscator who followed him in the reign of Anne, James Saunders, wrote that Cotton " was, without doubt, the most laborious trout-catcher, if not the most experienced angler, both for trout and grayling, that England ever had." He haunted the Dove, that swift and limpid stream, where he built a fishing-house, bearing Izaak Walton's initials and his own interwoven in a cipher. This still exists in a lovely bend of the river, and is said to contain the two anglers' portraits and other trophies, but when I paid a visit to Dovedale some years ago in the company of Mr. A. C. Benson, we found it locked up. During the Cromwellian persecution Cotton fled to the rocks and caves of Dove, with her " silver feet in crystal fetters," and here the venerable but adorably cheerful Izaak Walton, his piscatory father, joined him. When the fish would not rise the friends " plied the glass then quick about," for Cotton, among his other proclivities, was a famous Bacchanalian, whose " delight was to toss the can merrily round," and who even, I regret to say, preferred wine to verse in his declining years :—

> " Drink, and stout drinkers, are true joys ;
> Odes, sonnets, and such little toys
> Are exercises fit for boys.

> " Who dares not drink's a wretched wight ;
> Nor can I think that man would fight
> All day, that dares not drink all night."

But what does Mr. Pussyfoot say to that ?

BURLESQUE

BURLESQUE

BURLESQUE is a little province of English literature which historians have neglected, and, I think, misunderstood. It enjoyed a sudden development and brief vogue in the middle of the seventeenth century, and to this we may devote a little attention. First of all, we may turn to the encyclopædias for the broader aspect, and they inform us that the name comes from the Italian, *burla*, a joke ; that the ancients practised the thing, especially in the Homeric *Battle of the Frogs and Mice ;* and that the Italian epic poet Berni excelled in travesty.

But all this, and inquiry into the movement of comic or satiric verse in England before the Commonwealth, is beside our present mark. What was properly known, in English and French, as " burlesque verse " was a form of poetic art, strictly defined, which was cultivated for a few years with extravagant zeal, and then dropped. The effect of this form upon subsequent humorous literature was considerable, but indirect, and I need not analyse that here. I will merely try to give a succinct account of the movements, almost simultaneous, which culminated in *Hudibras* with us and in *Le Virgile Travesti* with the French.

Dryden, wishing at once to pay a compliment to Samuel Butler and to deprecate burlesque, showed his fine critical discrimination by saying : " It is indeed below so great a master to make use of such a little instrument." Dryden recognised that burlesque, as used in *Hudibras*, was not a mere accident of expression, but was " a little instrument " of definite character. It consisted of satire, written in short, rapid verse, daringly modern in its language, and entirely devoted to ridicule of persons and matters hitherto regarded as sacred, or at least stately. It had broken out in France in the middle of the seventeenth century, where it was adopted so suddenly that it is difficult to say who introduced it. The name is attributed to Sarrazin, but there seems to be no instance of it earlier than the *Rome Ridicule* of Saint-Amant, which was written in 1643. This piece, a long diatribe against the antiquities of the Eternal City, such as the "*piètre et barbare Colisée, exécrable reste des Goths,*" is a violent—and rather amusing—diatribe against the fashionable admiration of the ancient Romans and all their surviving works. It is conceived in the spirit of the modern Futurist, who calls upon his fellow-Italians to fling the leprous palaces of Venice into her stinking canals.

Saint-Amant, who wrote, but did not dare to publish, an equally violent attack on England, where he was for some months French ambassador, shows elsewhere the merits of a real poet. In paradox he was soon outdone by Scarron, who was almost wholly a writer of burlesque, and whose verses are to France what Butler's are to England. Scarron was accompanied by Sarrazin, by a host of others, even for a moment by Cyrano de Bergerac. All scribbling France gave itself over to the manufacture of riotous couplets, strung together into more or less shapely " poems," all concerned in ridiculing something or other which had been universally thought reverend or beautiful.

When this fashion was at its height the Jesuit critic Vavasseur tried to stem the tide by declaring that no Greek or Latin writer had ever employed *le genre burlesque,* that there was no mention of it in antiquity, and that Aristotle, Longinus, and Quintilian had ignored it. He was wrong in his facts, and he misunderstood the position. It was because it was recognised as a revolt against the dignity of ancient tradition that burlesque was so ardently cultivated. It was welcomed as an act of defiance, a glove flung by the moderns in the solemn face of antiquity. Tired of the domination of the classics, the Parisian public screamed with delight at seeing Apollo tossed out of his temple and made to rinse pots in the kitchen.

It really marked the beginning of the great Quarrel between the Ancients and the Moderns, which has gone on ever since. The scholastic tyranny of Greek and Latin had reached a point where it could be borne no longer, and Scarron openly declared that classical literature filled him with horror. He started his series of travesties of the sacred books of antiquity, and he was rewarded by a burst of spontaneous merriment. Everybody knew the text of Virgil, which had been considered only a little less inspired than the Holy Scriptures. Scarron therefore started a ridiculous "travesty" of the *Æneid*. The First Book was received with sympathetic laughter, and for the next ten years pedantry, uttering shrieks of pain, was stretched on the rack of octosyllabic verse. Coarse imitations of the classics, of heroic legend, even of the Bible, were the rage throughout Paris.

Scarron, who was a genius on a small scale, had invented something new. The fashion for burlesque became identified in France with the Fronde, as it was in England with the Civil War. In Paris the fury of it lasted ten years ; when Mazarin returned in 1653 the vogue of burlesque sank to nothing. Scarron himself turned to other fields when once the Fronde was over, and the classic spirit, chastened and modernised, came back into favour. But the body of Scarron's odes and travesties and *mazarinades* remained in their astounding volume and vivacity, and were eagerly studied abroad when they had already lost their freshness for Parisian readers. They possessed one quality distinctly attractive to the English mind, namely, their realism. It was part of the system of burlesque to introduce into verse the names of homely objects, to use words hitherto considered beneath the dignity of verse, and to confide to the reader personal details of a kind hitherto never mentioned.

Scarron, bored by the grammarians, irritated by the priests, enraged by the political anarchy of the times, studded his buffooneries with images, allusions, phrases from low life, which gave spice to his improvisations and completed the scandal. He had an amazing gift for poetical autobiography ;. his works, in that age of solemn self-restraint, teem with details about his private doings and the secret life of Paris. The effect was defined by Dryden when he said that burlesque " tickles awkwardly with a kind of pain," but this sort of tickling was already more familiar to the English than to the French habit of mind.

This Scarron fashion of burlesque was discovered in full blast by English Royalists who escaped to Paris during the Fronde. We find that it was accepted by two eminent English writers—by Charles Cotton and by Samuel Butler—to whom we owe its introduction here. But while conditions in France greatly encouraged the immediate production of burlesque, the rule of the Puritans made a delay in its publicity needful in England. Hence—and also because literary life, so minutely recorded in Paris, found hardly an echo in London—we cannot tell exactly when burlesque was brought to us. I have conjectured that Cotton was in Paris about 1648. By that time Scarron had published, tentatively, the First Book of his *Virgile Travesti*. He was not at all sure that it would be well received, but it was, and in course of time he continued his buffoon narrative, prefixing a remarkable epistle to the Chancellor, Seguier.

Cotton appears to have known at first only the earlier publication, and I take this as some faint evidence that his familiarity with it dated from about 1648. I do not know whether it has been observed that Cotton was better acquainted with the contemporary French literature of his youth than any other of the English Royalists. Besides his numerous translations from the *Astrée* of Honoré d'Urfé, which was still extremely popular, he made selected versions of Théophile, Maynard, Racan, and Benserade. The two last he may well have met in person, and it will be noticed that these and others from whom Cotton quotes are the poets whose vogue was at its height before 1650.

The best example of original burlesque which we have in English is, however, the *Hudibras* of Butler, which may have been begun about 1650, but the main structure of which seems to belong to a period after the death of Oliver Cromwell in 1658. What Butler was doing in the long duration of the Rump Parliament is matter of guesswork. If he went to France, as we are told that he did, it must have been before he entered the household of the Puritan scoutmaster, Sir Samuel Luke, under whose shadow Butler hatched in secret his great sectarian satire. Supposing him to be in Paris about 1650, he would find the vogue of burlesque at its height, and Scarron the unquestioned master of it. I confess I cannot agree with those who have ingeniously traced the form of *Hudibras* to Cervantes, to Cleveland, and to the *Satire Menippée*. There is something of the material and colour of all three in *Hudibras*, but the form seems to be entirely Scarron. The essence of burlesque, as we have seen, is the ridicule of matters hitherto held as sacred in short, rhymed verse, which owes its effect to its rapidity and reverberation, and to its daring use of realistic or even vulgar terms in describing matters of solemnity and dignity. The aim of burlesque was to set poetry topsy-turvy, and this was done to perfection by Scarron,

> " Qui d'un style rempli de beautés et de charmes,
> Et par d'incomparables vers,
> Fera rire tout l'univers,"

as La Mothe le Vayer put it.

We have only to stand the work of Butler and of Scarron side by side to see how closely the English poet had studied the manner of the French one. It is impossible not to wonder whether Butler was ever admitted to the brilliant salon of the Hotel de Troyes while all that was witty and desperate in Paris gathered round the little cripple, who, huddled in his famous armchair of grey velvet, defied by his fabulous hilarity the ravages of the worst arthritic rheumatism on record. Such a fancy is useless ; the living Scarron and Butler could not have communicated, but the influence of *La Mazarinade*, I feel sure, quickened into speech the long-silent genius of the author of *Hudibras*. The essence of Butler's burlesques is the diffuse and ample ridicule of things hitherto held sacred. His most famous book treats the whole Puritan scheme of religion, politics, and morals as a matter at which a cat would laugh.

But we may borrow an example less hackneyed than *Hudibras*. The satire on the Royal Society, called *The Elephant in the Moon*, is perhaps the most typical example of burlesque in English. It takes a subject hitherto treated with deserved respect, namely, the spread of scientific research, and pours ridicule upon it in short, vivid couplets with frequent double rhymes. The astronomers gaze through their telescope at the moon, and see an elephant advance into the centre of the luminous orb.   This marvellous discovery leads them to a thousand pedantic speculations, until somebody discovers that it is merely a mouse which is creeping over the lens of the instrument. But the learned men are not convinced :—

> " Some swore, upon a second view,
> That all they'd seen before was true,
> And that they never would recant
> One syllable of th' elephant ;
> Avowed his snout could be no mouse's,
> But a true elephant's proboscis ,

> Others began to doubt and waver,
> Uncertain which o' the two to favour,
> And knew not whether to espouse
> The cause of elephant or mouse."

Apart from direct imitations of *Hudibras*, the vogue of burlesque in England was brief ; it scarcely survived the death of Charles II., to whom was attributed an extreme fondness for this kind of metrical wit. A Puritan divine, the Rev. Robert Wilde, of Aynhoe, cultivated it in strange productions, of which his *Iter Boreale* was the most famous. Wilde approaches very near to the French abandonment, the eager patter of self-betraying rhymes which is so remarkable in Scarron and in Sarrazin :—

> " Cambridge, now I must leave thee ;
>   And follow Fate !
> College hopes do deceive me ;
>   I oft expected
>   To have been elected,
> But desert is reprobate ;
>   Masters of colleges
>   Have no common graces,
> And they that have fellowships
>   Have but common places,
> And those that scholars are
>   Must have handsome faces ;
> Alas ! poor scholar ! whither wilt thou go ? "

The practice of travestying the classics was carried on by Captain Alexander Radcliffe, whose burlesque imitations of Ovid enjoyed a remarkable success. His aim was, frankly, " to blaspheme the best poets " of the classical age, and he bravely declared that, " in his own simple, naked shape," he came nearer to the original than the best of the serious versions. Radcliffe's theory was that " nineteen judicious translators " had not been able to give " the least hint or light into Publius Ovidius Naso's meaning " because of their pomposity and want of humour, and that he was able to do so triumphantly by making the poems homely, colloquial, and modern. Radcliffe, also, we may note in passing, made them very vulgar and indecent, as Cotton made the dialogues of Lucian. *Hudibras* escaped this snare, which lay close the feet of all the other clever and revolutionary versifiers who attempted to destroy the classic tradition, and who for a very brief period succeeded.

SNAP-SHOTS AT SWINBURNE

SNAP-SHOTS AT SWINBURNE

THE collection of anecdotes about the Home Life of Swinburne, to which Mrs. Watts-Dunton has allowed her name to be affixed, bears a like relation to biography that the instantaneous photographs in a daily newspaper bear to serious portraiture. What the poet's dignified ancestors would have said to all this homely gossip does not bear thinking about, but their shudders are of a bygone age, and need not affect us. Literature has to cater for the tastes of what are called " lower middle-class " readers, and if that is done good-humouredly and without malice nobody ought to object.

There is no malice and plenty of good humour, especially of a rollicking order, in the pages of this so-called *Home Life*. But, surely, no great man was ever more completely shorn of the mystery which his admirers loved to weave around him. There is no honey-dew here, and no milk of paradise, but we see the poet " partaking of the biggest, fattest gooseberries I have ever seen." We may miss the laurel and the glory, but Swinburne stands revealed before us, " waving his hand towards the jam and the hock," and " airily saying, ' Shall we have luncheon now ? ' " I am far from despising these details, nor does it shock me to be told that the great poet " braced his trousers too high," or that his locks, once so redundant and so umbrageous, were, in later years, " often cut by the barber." These are the natural results of " snap-shotting," and as, in the parallel case of the daily newspapers, something of reality and nature may be secured which the stately portrait fails to give, so it cannot be denied that this surprising *Home Life* does render aspects of the poet which are fresh and are characteristic. Parts of this little book may always retain a certain value from this photographic point of view.

It is all very innocent and pleasing, but I recur to my amused feeling of amazement at the homeliness and familiarity of the wandering tale. When, in a happy August, a family released from London takes its annual holiday at the seaside, Papa in knickerbockers, Mamma in a large sun-bonnet, and the hilarious children carrying spades and pails, the eldest sister will be discovered proudly conveying her Kodak. With nimble skill she plies the confidential instrument, and when the three joyous weeks are over their adventures are repeated in scenes of Papa paddling, dear little Charles " doing the goose-step," and Euphemia being assisted into a bathing machine. These relics of a bygone happiness, if not perennial, nevertheless last for a very long time, and on winter evenings may produce a plaintive sense of pleasure, enhanced by the often startling verisimilitude of the likenesses.

That, it seems to me, is exactly the nature of the satisfaction with which Mrs. Watts-Dunton's artless pages will be read. But I cannot expel from my mind the contrast between the dignity of the poet's calling and the charming triviality of these anecdotes. " When there came a general pulling of Christmas crackers, Swinburne appeared to be thoroughly in his element." Shades of magnificent Ashburnhams and hard-riding Swinburnes of the Northumbrian border, what do you say to your latest and greatest scion requesting " his old friends Miss Watts and Mrs. Mason for the honour of a ' tug-of-war ' " ? No matter, illustrious shades, what you say or think ! We live in democratic times, and we like to be told that Rossetti, regardless of expense, " had ordered two ducks to be placed on the dish at the same time." *Two* ducks—only think of that, O

Father of all of us, Païan Apollo, destroyer and healer !
Let it not be imagined for a moment that I am reproving
these revelations.   I delight in them, as I delight in the
snap-shots of the newspapers.

There are two very clearly defined " schools of thought "
with regard to Swinburne's career, so completely opposed
to one another that it is hopeless to try to reconcile them.
As everybody knows, the poet began independent life in
a blaze of eccentricity and violence, which led at the age
of forty-two to a complete breakdown of his health.   He
then, in circumstances which are now familiar to every
one, was rescued from the very edge of the grave by
Theodore Watts, who, with not a little courage, undertook
to take him in charge.   It was an experiment which might
have ended disastrously ; in fact, Watts showed both skill
and patience, and it ended successfully.   For thirty years
more the poet, completely subjugated and cured of all his
excesses, lived a contented captive at Putney.

Now, the difference of opinion which exists and divides
all Swinburnians into two irreconcilable camps is founded
on the question : Was the former or the latter of these
sharply defined periods the significant one ?   It is needless
for me to reiterate the arguments which I have often put
forward to prove that the really important phase was the
earlier one ; that, in short, if Swinburne had unhappily
died in 1879 the world would have lost much valuable
prose and verse, but would have lost nothing essential,
would always have had before it the splendid efflorescence
of lyrical and rapturous originality.   On the other hand, I
am free to admit that in my desire to insist on the ineffable
gusto and blaze of the unfettered Swinburne of the earlier
period, I may have undervalued the gentle records of the
long captivity.   The bird in the woods seemed to me so far
more inspiriting than the same bird pecking hempseed in
its Putney cage that I may have undervalued the latter.

If so, no harm is done. For now the reader possesses the
record of Mrs. Watts-Dunton. He becomes aware that
" Swinburne had his boots made of calf leather, while
Walter preferred a soft kid." I am properly reproved ; it
appears that Swinburne was allowed a complete freedom
of choice in at least one direction.

The inconsistencies in Swinburne's character were very
extraordinary, but not incapable of explanation. He was
essentially the divine child that Mr. Clutton-Brock has
defined with exquisite felicity, yet he was also the great
gentleman of Mr. Max Beerbohm's beautiful study. What
he lacked was a hold on the solid facts of life ; there never
hovered above earthly ground so footless a Bird of Paradise.
In his final hermitage he resigned everything, even freedom
itself, in exchange for release from responsibility and apprehension, and he rewarded the care which was taken of him
by an innocent confidence which was infantile and touching.

For this reason, though I can smile at the evidences of
his simplicity, I resent a little the perpetuation of anecdotes
which reveal too grossly his resignation and docility. He
was neither an imbecile nor even a simpleton, and some of
the stories which people at the Pines have repeated stretch
our credulity too far. The preposterous tale of his being
wooed from one kind of alcoholic indulgence to another by
successive appeals to his literary prejudices has been exposed
already, and should not be repeated. I cannot force myself
to believe that he continually played with a terra-cotta
new-born babe emerging from an egg-shell. Gossip is all
very well, but there should be a limit to the permissible
ridicule of one who was a noble poet and a man of com-
manding intellectual gifts. Indeed, we seem to have
reached a point where the poetry and the prose of Swinburne, and not the oddities of his cloistered old age, may
again be recommended to public attention.

The poet has been dead for fifteen years, and it is not

unfair to ask what exact foundation there is for the minute observations and detailed conversations which *Home Life* contains.   How is Mrs. Watts-Dunton able to remember all these words and circumstances with such fullness ?   There is no evidence that she kept a dairy, and she gives no indication at all of the sources of her knowledge.   An anecdote may impress itself so deeply on the memory that it can be clearly rehearsed after the lapse of years, but sustained talk is more easily imagined than repeated when a long period of time has elapsed.   The very minuteness of the record here, dealing as most of it does with highly ephemeral moods and trifling topics, creates in the mind of the reader a faint atmosphere of doubt.   Can it be that, in its detail, this book is a kind of romance, founded, of course, on great familiarity and a habit of disciplined memory ?   We have had presented to us of late years so many biographies which were amalgams of fact and fiction, and more than a few that were not actually written, but dictated or authorised by the nominal author, that we lose our sense of security.

All this is of little real importance ;   what matters is the picture given of the man, and this, though too sentimental, seems on the whole to be accurate.   Of course, the author has had recourse, as she had a perfect right to do, to the recollections of others, and some of these are of permanent value.   The most important is an account by Mme. Tola Dorian, Swinburne's Parisian translator, of the meeting between Victor Hugo and his British adorer in November 1882.   Of the circumstances surrounding this event, caused by the visit of Swinburne to Paris to witness the performance of *Le Roi s'amuse*, there has been a strange diversity of report. Mme. Dorian was present, and her account may be taken as final.   She took Swinburne to dinner at Hugo's house : Watts-Dunton had a toothache and could not come :—

" It was a cold, dreary day, and poor Hugo was feeling very irritable and nervous, full of aches and pains, more than usually

deaf, and in one of his worst moods. . . . Swinburne also was in a
highly nervous condition. . . . Now Swinburne also was deaf, and
I shall never forget the scene that followed. Trembling with agita-
tion, he went off into what sounded like a carefully-prepared speech
full of Eastern hyperbole : Victor Hugo was the great sun round
which the little stars, etc., etc., etc. Hugo sat with his head bent
forward, his hand to his ear, and his efforts to catch the words gave
his face a threatening expression, and his terse ' What does he say ?
What does he say ? ' sounded like a growl. This did nothing to
tranquillise Swinburne, who grew more and more nervous as he
began at the beginning again.''

This was a melancholy climax to the enthusiasm which
had been boiling in the English bard for thirty-five years,
and Mme. Dorian's narrative makes comprehensible the
manifest cooling towards Victor Hugo, as a person, which
began to set in. Yet Swinburne's loyalty to the French
poet forbade the slightest intellectual abatement, and it was
as late as 1886 that he published the monograph in which
he reached his utmost frenzy of Hugolatry.

ROSTAND'S PLAYS

ROSTAND'S PLAYS

THE toil of translating six long plays out of French alexandrines into English heroic couplets strikes me as so intimidating that my first instinctive movement is one of homage to a metrical artisan patient and undaunted and high-spirited enough to be the author of seven hundred pages of translation from Edmond Rostand. It must have cost Mrs. Henderson Daingerfield Norman a real labour of Sisyphus to cope with the terrible burden of the poet's weight rolling back every instant into the arms of the indomitable athlete, who never rested or shirked until the final verse was achieved. Nor, though the result is rather more like Planché or Gilbert than like Rostand, and though the curious perfume of the French romanticist has too often evaporated, is the result other than on the whole satisfactory as well as stupendous. The translator has been no traitor ; her resolution to give the exact meaning of each quip and flourish has been rewarded by success in a very large number of instances, and she has been preserved from falling into the snare of trying to surmount difficulties by adding fancies of her own. In fact, I cannot recollect another instance of a French dramatic poet being so completely and at the same time so faithfully presented to an English reader, who, with no knowledge whatever of the French language, may really, by the help of Mrs. Norman, form a very fair notion in what the poetic talent of Edmond Rostand consists.

The versifier in Mrs. Norman excels the critic. Her admiration for the object of her labours knows no bounds,

She says, in her brief introduction, that until, in December
1918, "he entered into light perpetual, Edmond Rostand
was the poet of light, from the April starlight of *Romantics*
to the full summer sunshine of *Chanticleer*." This marks
the spirit of enthusiasm which, no doubt, supported the
lady through her arduous task. But those who are not
engaged in the momentous business of translation will
hardly, if they are wise, pitch their raptures so high. Mrs.
Norman says that she reached her power of utterance
"through pangs of keen delight." That is just as it
should be, for nothing is worth doing in literature which
is not inspired and sustained by ecstasy.

Yet we cannot quite take the author of *Chanticleer* at
Mrs. Norman's valuation. She speaks of his plays as Shelley
spoke of the "starry" Spanish autos, but Rostand was
hardly Calderon. It is a remarkable fact, to be taken into
consideration in every careful estimate of Rostand, that
his works generally produced a certain dazzlement at their
earliest appearance. The reception of the successive dramas,
although never quite unanimously favourable, was in the
main triumphant. While other poets have had to conquer
the suffrages of unconvinced and tepid audiences, Rostand
always carried the public and the critics and his colleagues
away with him from the first. It was only on reflection
that objections protruded themselves and that the "April
starlight" of Mrs. Norman's hyperbole took something of
a lamp-like character.

The "case" of Edmond Rostand is one of the most
curious in literary history. To this day his exact position
has never been defined, and criticism has been shy of
attempting to place him among the writers of his time. His
career was brief and splendid ; he flared like a comet across
the sky in a blaze which lasted practically for ten years,
and no more. At a moment when French poetry had
become extremely subtle he astonished the world with

his prodigal simplicity. While the Symbolists were occupied
in describing, in veiled and difficult language, their most
secret sufferings, their *minces tristesses*, Rostand shouted,
like the morning star, of the joy of life in numbers intelligible to every one. He had lived by the side of Mallarmé
and Verlaine without, apparently, becoming aware of their
existence ; he went back to an entirely different generation,
to Victor Hugo, to Banville, to the early pure Romantics.
He was welcomed with enthusiasm ; he was played all
over the world ; his success seemed boundless ; he was
elected to the French Academy at an earlier age than any
other modern candidate.

But there was a speck in the fruit and a Mordecai at the
gate. While all the audiences of two hemispheres were
applauding him, the inner circle of his contemporaries
excluded him altogether. He has no place in the *Masques*
of Rémy de Gourmont ; he is not so much as mentioned
in that important repertory, *Poètes d'Aujourd'hui* of Van
Bever and Léautaud, which includes fifty-three French
and Belgian writers. The group of the *Mercure de
France*, so powerful in opinion at the opening of this century, would have none of Rostand. At the moment of the
triumph of *Cyrano de Bergerac*, the *Mercure* pontifically
stated that M. Edmond Rostand excelled in one art, and
one art only—that of writing bad French.

The " case " of Stephen Phillips is the only one which
can be compared with that of Rostand, and the parallel is
very imperfect. The English dramatic poet enjoyed considerable success, both with playgoers and readers, but
Paolo and Francesca was a mild affair by the side of *Cyrano*.
Phillips was the object of scornful attack, but the critics
never disdained him with half the asperity which was
poured out upon Rostand in the cafés of the Boulevard St.
Michel. The supporters of each playwright, but particularly
those of Rostand, declared that the censure was pure

prejudice, and did not scruple to attribute it to envy. No one can doubt that in the case of the author of *L'Aiglon* jealousy had something to do with it. A society which takes literature, and particularly poetical literature, very seriously, could not fail to contain persons who, finding their own ingenious works neglected, and those of a poet whose method was in direct opposition to all that they were admiring and teaching, lifted to the skies—it could not but be that some persons in such a society, being human and so frail, should persuade themselves that this terrible rival was an impostor and a traitor to the art.

There was an element of envy in the designation ; and yet it was not altogether an unrighteous judgment which denied to Rostand the highest honours of poetical creation. It is very difficult indeed to say what it is that leaves upon the unbiassed memory a tinge of disappointment, a slightly bad taste, when we think of the six flamboyant dramas. There comes back to us the old tale of the lunatic, who said that the feasts in the asylum were magnificent and delicious, worthy of Belshazzar, but that, he could not tell why, all the dishes had a damnable smack of water-gruel.

Edmond Rostand, after one or two negligible efforts, took the stage with *Les Romanesques* in 1894. This was a comedy founded on the manner of Shakespeare as seen through the gay little rhymed pieces of Banville. The plot was a sort of intentional burlesque of *Romeo and Juliet*, with touches of *A Midsummer Night's Dream*. The play sparkled with gaiety and absurdity ; the comic element was carefully sustained on a high literary level, with allusions to moonlight among the honeysuckle-bowers of Stratford-on-Avon. The action was rather childish, but very merry and sentimental, and the couplets were rhymed with astonishing richness. (The richness of Rostand's rhyme was his strength and his bane from first to last.)

There followed next, in 1895, *Princess Faraway*, a

coloured pageant of chivalry in the fourteenth century, contrived to display in its apogee the romantic side of Madame Sarah Bernhardt's genius. This was the old story of Rudel and the Lady of Tripoli. Here were shallops and silken sails, amorous crimson roses, a knight in emerald mail, songs—rather long songs—warbled by troubadours kneeling on one knee. It was all delicious, but too sweet ; and the comic vigour of *Les Romanesques* seemed to have retreated a little.

Rostand withdrew for two years, and then returned to the stage with *The Woman of Samaria*. This also was carried by the magic of Madame Bernhardt to a splendour of success, but when we read it in cold blood after a quarter of a century, something seems to have passed out of it. *The Woman of Samaria* is a mystery play, in which the solemn scenes of the Gospel are enacted against a sky which is " gold and pink." It is all very picturesque and lively, the sentiment is tender and evangelical ; the poet essays no audacities, but keeps to the tradition in the story and the dogma. It is a little too brightly coloured, a little too like that variegated dainty, a Neapolitan ice—the story of Jesus as told by a troubadour, who is very skilful and charming and melodious, but essentially not spiritually minded. And then, immediately on the heels of *The Woman of Samaria*, came the prodigy of prodigies, *Cyrano de Bergerac*.

The quarter of a century which has slipped by since *Cyrano de Bergerac* took, not the town only, but the world, by storm, has tarnished a little the splendour of its triumph, but I do not think that time will ever entirely destroy its charm. Rostand has been blamed for falsifying the history and character of the actual Cyrano, who was a romantic Gascon of the seventeenth century, had a very large and disfiguring nose, and wrote plays which were good enough for Molière to steal from. All this does not seem to me to matter in the least ; the famous nose by any other name would be as glowing a carbuncle, the swords and the verses would flash about with no less spirit and audacity. The modern poet had a perfect right to take as much as he wished to take, and no more, from a figure which ought to be highly gratified at being so unexpectedly lifted out of comparative oblivion.

The real point about Rostand's play is that it is an accomplished poem, and yet sustained throughout by the utmost radiance of high spirits. It is a masterpiece of heroic buffoonery, adorned and supported by the art of a masterly metrical artificer. In the earlier dramas there had been an excess of prettiness, an absence of the solid basis of feeling. In *Cyrano*, fantastic as it is, the pathos of the hero's isolation, of the contrast between his generous soul and his disfigured body, has an element of genuine tragedy, while his unselfish loyalty to the stupid Christian is a motive of novel beauty, exhibited in a manner extremely attractive. I need not dwell on this, because few modern dramas are so widely familiar, and every one who has seen or read the play will recollect the culminating scene in which Roxane hangs in agony over the corpse of Christian, kissing what she takes to be his latest letter although it was really Cyrano who had written it. This is an example of much that none but a dramatic poet of a high order could have conceived. The worst that can be said of this melodious tragedy of a clown is that the author's facetious agility is out of keeping with passion. But *Cyrano de Bergerac* is a masterpiece.

The twentieth century opened with a yet greater success. In March 1900 appeared *The Eaglet*, a long tragedy occupied with the character and the fate of the unfortunate son of Napoleon and Marie Louise, the ill-starred Duke of Reichstadt. The tender and somewhat effeminate boy-hero was played by Mme. Sarah Bernhardt, whose triumph in the part is celebrated. I have nothing to do with the theatrical history of this play, although the performance of Guitry (as Séraphin Flambeau) will not soon be forgotten.

As a poem *L'Aiglon* is worthy of close attention. Rostand had begun with the study of Shakespeare in *Romeo and Juliet;* he comes back to it here in *Hamlet* and in *Julius Cæsar.* He is no less rich in his rhymes and agile in his versification than he was before, but he owes little now to mere ornament, and he has ceased to place his confidence in the glitter and reverberation of tirades. In *The Eaglet* love has no place, and there is little variety of intrigue ; all depends on the exposition of character in rapid, appropriate, and brilliant conversation. The figures of Napoleon II., of the Empress Marie Louise, of Metternich, of Flambeau, pass before us in swift alternation, and we hurry to the inevitable tragic dénouement. The famous scene with Metternich at the mirror, which closes the third act, is melodramatic, perhaps, but of the very essence of genuine dramatic poetry.

The career of Rostand, since it was to be so brief, should have ended here. *Chanticleer*, diabolically clever as it is, adds in the long run nothing to his glory. It was an attempt at the impossible, this brilliant tragi-comedy in which, after the manner of La Fontaine, all the characters are birds and beasts. The famous scene in the second act, where Chanticleer explains to the adoring Pheasant that it is he who, by his clarion call, summons the sunrise every morning, is superb. Mrs. Norman has been unusually fortunate in her rendering of this passage, the original of which has, indeed, something almost superhuman in its radiant violence. Yet even here — ? Truly, as I permitted myself to say in the beginning of this little inadequate essay, no " case " in literary history is more curious than that of Rostand. Dowered to excess with almost every gift, was not something essential lacking to him ? What was it ? May it not have been the humility of a contrite spirit in the face of Nature ?

DAUGHTERS OF FIRE

DAUGHTERS OF FIRE

So far as I am able to discover, this is the first time that any attempt has been made to present in English important extracts from the work of Gérard de Nerval, who has been dead for nearly seventy years. In France, although he is but rarely mentioned to-day, and although the essential slightness of his work has caused him to retreat behind the more robust and vociferous of his contemporaries, there has never ceased to survive a quiet enthusiasm for his picturesque, pathetic, and singular personality. Gérard de Nerval is one of the oddest apparitions in literature. His legend is more persistent than his books, and the wealth of anecdote and mystery which it contains is sure to be perennially attractive.

Mr. James Whitall, as he explains in a brief but graceful preface, has always been drawn to the figure of Gérard de Nerval, and has at length yielded to an irresistible impulse in attempting a translation of what is doubtless the most durable of his works, the group of three stories which he published shortly before his suicide, under the title of *Filles du Feu.* Mr. Whitall has been fully aware of the difficulty which lay before him in rendering the delicate, fantastic, and almost diaphanous prose of Gérard into another language. He has surmounted this difficulty with great success. Comparing his text here and there with the original, I find that he slightly paraphrases the latter in order to escape the stiffness of a too-literal version, but reproduces the sense and the grace of Gérard's sentences with remarkable fidelity.

The real name of the French writer was Gérard Labrunie, and he was born in Paris on May 22, 1808. The English reader of his books is often struck by his likeness to Sterne, and there is a whimsical parallel to be found in the way in which the two authors came into the world, each the son of a wandering and unlucky soldier and of a mother who followed her spouse on his incessant campaigns. The infant Gérard was sent to live with a robust grand-uncle, who had a rambling house in that delicious part of the Ile de France, which lies between Senlis and Meaux. This is the country which is described, with a rapture which heightens its picturesque colour, in all Gérard's personal writings. It animates the whole of *Sylvie* in the present volume.

Montagney, where he spent all his childhood, is a remote village of this district, close to Ermenonville, where Rousseau died. The rolling agricultural landscape, as I saw it in 1916, when it was just breathing after the shock of the battle of the Ourcq, has a very English look, and recalls the aspect of the Cotswolds. But round Montagney and Ermenonville, it changes to a wilder character, with moors of heather, little lakes in the forest, "le désert," as it is locally called, edged with pines and strewn with rocks. This is the landscape which Gérard loves to describe, and the reader of *Sylvie* adds to his own enjoyment by realising how faithful, with a little pardonable exaggeration, is the picture.

His poor wandering mother dead in Russia, his father lost for years in the Napoleonic adventure, Gérard grew up a solitary but happy child in the scenes which he depicts. But his grand-uncle possessed a library of books on occultism and magic, in which the precocious infant soaked his imagination at a very incautious age. His biographers have gone so far as to conclude that in this way he caught, as by infection, his positive mental disease. It is true that, to the end of his life, Gérard continued to dabble in theosophy, to call up spirits by the rules of cabbala, and, when he finally became mad, to indulge in the most incoherent acts of exorcism. Paris rang with tales of his excruciating appeals to Lilith, Nahema, and Moloch. But he was naturally eccentric, and perhaps rather drawn to the invisible and the supernatural by an inherent tendency than made crazy by any commerce with Rosicrucian literature.

He came to Paris as a lad, burning to excel in letters, and almost immediately he took his place in the Second Cénacle, formed of romantic youths who had adopted the principles of the new Romanticism as laid down by Victor Hugo. These amiable and preposterous lads astonished the town by their long hair, their Spanish cloaks, and their huge dark sombreros. They took exotic names in the fervour of their faith. Auguste Maquet became Augustus Mac-Keat, Joachim Hounau called himself George Bell, Théophile Dondey was disguised as Philothée O'Neddy. There were also Gaspard de la Nuit and Petrus Borel and Napoléon Tom.

To these hirsute bandits of the pen, such a name as Labrunie seemed an outrage. Gérard changed it, at first, to Lord Pilgrim, but soon abandoned this infelicitous nickname in favour of Gérard de Nerval. I do not know what was the meaning of " Nerval," but I cannot help thinking that it was a dim recollection of the romantic Norval of *Douglas*, whose father fed his flocks upon the Grampian Hills. Among the young men with whom Gérard was early intimate were those more serious and better-grounded Romantics, Maxime du Camp and Théophile Gautier. He dazzled them all by publishing, in his teens, several slim volumes of poems, which enjoyed much temporary success, and are now unreadable.

His eccentricities did not prevent Gérard from being a

most charming person. Gautier says that " good-nature
radiated from him as from a substance naturally luminous,
and it continuously enveloped him in a peculiar atmosphere." But his oddities grew upon him ; he saw visions
and dreamed dreams. He was seized with an imperious
desire for travel, which took him to Germany, to Italy, to
England even, and finally to the East.

Already, in Vienna, in his thirtieth year, he had passed
into a state of rapturous exaltation, and coming back to
Paris in 1841 he lost command of his mental machine. He
had cultivated, from childhood, the habit of identifying all
his emotions, all his memories, all the facts of his existence,
with insubstantial phantoms of the brain, so that he lost
the power to distinguish between life and a dream. He
was now haunted by the spectre of the mysterious and
beloved Aurélia, of whom *Daughters of Fire* speaks so
abundantly. Wherever he went she accompanied him in
her refulgent robes and waving her many-coloured wings.
This enamoured vision was more real to Gérard than reality
itself. He was happy, and he was harmless, but incontestably he was mad. One evening he was found in the garden
of the Palais Royal, dragging a living lobster after him by
a blue riband. He divested himself of all his clothes, and
rushed along the street singing " stellar mysteries " at the
top of his voice. It became necessary to shut him up for
several months, after which he grew calm again and returned
to his friends and to literature.

On New Year's Day, 1843, Gérard de Nerval started for
Egypt—where he adopted the Arab dress—Palestine and
Turkey. He was absent in the East for a year, and his
adventures are detailed in a unique and marvellous volume,
the *Voyage en Orient*, published in 1856, after his death.
In this extraordinary book, which will always attract
lovers of what is strange and charming, Gérard de Nerval
astonishes us by the mixture of what is minutely and

accurately observed with what is obviously unreal and even
delirious. There was about all he wrote this odd inconsistency, as of a very sane intelligence that is at the same time
definitely a little mad. However, for some time after his
return from the East, he remained as normal as he ever was.

But in the early part of 1853 he began once more to lose
sense of the actual, and to yield himself entirely to the
phantoms which attended and excited him. He was shut up
for a short time, and then sent to Reims, with the idea that the
aspect of the cathedral, for which he nourished a passionate
enthusiasm, would calm his nerves. It had that effect, and
he extended his excursions to his old familiar haunts, to
Senlis, to Dammartin, to Montagney. He found his adored
Sylvie again, but greatly changed, and she had married
her friend the pastrycook, Big Curlyhead. The absurdity
of playing Werther to this excellent matron, surrounded by
children and enjoying a peaceful activity at the back of
the shop, seized Gérard, not with despair, but with amusement, and he sat down to tell his own story, becoming,
therefore, a kind of Werther after all.

The first of the third stories which Mr. Whitall has so
gracefully translated, *Sylvie* was written, the biographers
declare, with immense difficulty, almost entirely in pencil,
and on odd scraps of paper. The author scribbled the
sentences as he walked hither and thither in the scenes that
serve as a setting for the story. In these circumstances, it
may be regarded as extraordinary that the style is so
perfect and the arrangement of the workmanship so
admirable. But Gérard had been writing now for thirty-
five years, and he was master of his pen, although scarcely
of his mind. *Sylvie* is by far the most accomplished of his
works, and it is nearly the last. It was published in August
1853, but the excitement caused by its correction for the
Press, again, and this time finally, unhinged the author's
brain.

Eleven days after the appearance of *Sylvie*, Gérard was
once more in the asylum of Emile Blanche. He was contented; and here, if I am not mistaken, he wrote the series
of sonnets, called *Les Chimères*, in which those who are
lucky enough to understand them, have seen a prediction
of Baudelaire. He was so quiet and inoffensive that he was
allowed to leave the asylum, and he added the two shorter
stories of *Emilie* and *Octavie* to *Sylvie*, and published the
three together as *Les Filles du Feu* in 1854. But he was
incapable of self-preservation. After eccentricities of the
most astounding nature, he was found at daybreak, on
January 26, 1855, hanged to a lamp-post in a dark alley
called the Rue de la Vieille Lanterne. He was suspended
by a sort of knitted girdle, which he had been carrying
about with him for some weeks, assuring his friends that it
had been worn, though it appeared to be quite new, by
Madame de Maintenon when *Esther* was played at St. Cyr.

Although Gérard de Nerval was tormented by æsthetic
delusions and bore all the stigmata of madness, his style is
simple and clear, his thoughts are expressed with precision,
and his narrative is more reasonable than that of most of
his fellow-romanticists who enjoyed complete mental
health. We have just been told that Marcel Proust, who
was by no means inclined to indulgence towards his
romantic predecessors, greatly admired both the construction and the style of Gérard's tales. The reader
of *Sylvie* and *Emilie* who knew nothing of the author's
morbid condition would never guess it from the conduct
of those stories; the little tale of *Octavie*, it is true,
shows signs of cerebral disturbance. His friends, and
he enjoyed the confidence of the best spirits of his time,
are unanimous in bearing testimony to the sweetness of
his nature. Even when he was most demented, he continued
loveable and gentle. Heine, who knew him intimately
and who had seen him in some of his worst paroxysms,

said of Gérard after his death : " None of the egotism
of the artist was to be found in him. He was all compact
of infantile candour. He was kindly, he loved every one,
he was jealous of nobody, he never crushed a fly. If a
spaniel bit him he shrugged his shoulders." This sweetness of character illuminates, with a kind of fairy sunset, the
story of *Sylvie,* in which Gérard de Nerval's literary career
culminates and closes, and till nearly the last days of his
life he seems to have been exultantly happy. Even then—

"When one by one, sweet sounds and wandering lights departed,
He wore no less a loving face because so broken-hearted."

THE ART OF PARODY

THE ART OF PARODY

ADDISON, wishing to be kind to John Philips, said, in his grand manner, that *The Splendid Shilling*, in which Philips imitated Milton's blank verse, was "the finest burlesque poem in the language." But there must remain the question whether "burlesque" poems have any right to exist, and Dr. Johnson, always sententious and ingenious, was inclined to consider that they have not. He could not deny that *The Splendid Shilling* was diverting—and, indeed, if any one will have the patience to turn to it after more than two hundred years, he will find it diverting still.

But Dr. Johnson liked to be amused in his own way, and that was not the way of parody. He wrote that "to degrade the sounding words and stately construction of Milton by an application to the lowest and the most trivial things, gratifies the mind with a momentary triumph over that grandeur which hitherto held its captives in admiration." He grudgingly admitted that Philips, doing this perverse thing for the first time, had done it well, but warned the light-minded of his day that to do it again would be the contemptible repeating of a jest. Nevertheless, in every generation since then, and with more and more vivacity, parodists have flourished. Dr. Johnson, if he looks down from heaven on the poets militant below, will have to admit that what used to be called "great burlesque" has secured a place in the economy of literature.

Two qualities seem to be required to make parody

acceptable.   Let us take a famous example from Calverley :—

> " And day again declines :
> In shadow sleep the vines,
> And the last ray through the pines
> Feebly glows,
> Then sinks behind yon ridge ;
> And the usual evening midge
> Is settling on the bridge
> Of my nose."

Here the first source of pleasure is addressed to the ear
in the recovery of the measure of a heroic poem of Campbell, more universally familiar, perhaps, sixty years ago
than it is now, and therefore more widely welcome, but
still amply recognisable.   This martial strain is used, not
to lead up to a climax, but down to a bathos, and the
plunge downwards, for some obscure reason, pleases the
attention.   But the bathos itself diverts, and apart from
the resemblance to Campbell's metre, the sinking to midges
here and to fleas in the next stanza produces an agreeable
shock of surprise.

The art of the poet is to convince us that Campbell, had
he wished to sing of fleas instead of guns, would have done
it exactly in this style, since in parody the artist sinks his
own individuality as completely as possible.   He lives in
the writer whom he parodies, like a soldier-crab in a shell,
carrying his original about with him in fantastic excursions
over which that original has no control.

There is no branch of literature which is so altruistic as
parody, since it exists only in the reader's familiarity with
its model.   For example, when Mr. Squire writes :—

> " It was eight bells in the forenoon and hammocks running sleek
> (*It's a fair sea flowing from the West*),
> When the little Commodore came a-sailing up the Creek
> (*Heave ho ! I think you'll know the rest*),
> Thunder in the halyards and horses leaping high,
> Blake and Drake and Nelson are listenin' where they lie,
> Four and twenty blackbirds a-bakin' in a pie—
> And the *Pegasus* came waltzing from the West,"

he drowns his own individuality in the gallant mannerism of
Sir Henry Newbolt, and a familiarity with, and even an
enjoyment of, the naval songs of the latter is needful for
our intelligence. Here all is Newbolt, nothing is Squire,
except the humour in which the imitation floats, as in those
mirrors at country fairs, where our features are reflected
but ludicrously distorted. It is indeed very important that
the parodist should recollect that, in the words of an old
critic, he must " sit down with a resolution to make no
more musick than he found." But he may play that music
in whatever key he can.

An error into which parodists often fall is the too close
and persistent imitation of their models' most hackneyed
forms. Thus the exterior mannerism of Swinburne and
Poe in verse and of Carlyle and Meredith in prose has frequently been copied in a reproduction of what is obvious,
and of that alone. This easily becomes machine-made and
tiresome ; there was a time when every Poet's Comic
Corner groaned under feverish recollections of *Dolores*.
But parody, which is really a highly sophisticated art, calls
for a greater subtlety than that. It must enter into the
spirit of its model, and not merely echo his voice. Mr.
Squire shows remarkable skill in doing this. Listen to him,
beneath the mask of Algernon :—

" And over the high Thessalian hills, the feet of the maidens fail and
    falter ;
  Samian waters and Lemnian valleys, Ithacan rivers and Lesbian
    seas :
 And the god returning with frenzy burning foams at the foot of a
    roseless altar,
  And dumb with the kiss of Artemis and the berries of death the
    virgin flees."

Here the parodist disdains to reproduce the excessive
alliteration and the febrile extravagance of his poet's
obvious early manner and goes deeper. The subject, surprisingly, is how *Horatius held the Bridge*, and Mr. Squire

makes fun of Swinburne's tendency to plunge away from his theme, to bury it in remote allusion and to lose his head in a whirl of melodious ecstasy. The parodist laughs at all this, and exaggerates it, while loyally reproducing the delicate and characteristic choice of language and the admirable suppleness of metre. His imitation, in fact, is living and personal, not mechanical.

Even better still is Mr. Squire's *Numerous Celts*, one of the happiest pieces of mocking imitation ever published, in which the wail of Inisfail is reproduced to perfection, with the wicked sarcasm of " Uncle White Seagull and All " to punctuate and define it at the end.

Mr. Squire, I think, holds his own with the most accomplished verse-parodists of the nineteenth century, with the author of the *Heptalogia*, with Calverley, J. K. Stephen, Sir Owen Seaman, and " Evoe " of *Punch*. In prose he hardly gives me the same pleasure. Nothing here has quite the mastery of Mr. Max Beerbohm in *A Christmas Garland*, or of Marcel Proust in *L'Affaire Lemoine*. It may be, it probably is, my stupidity which forbids me to be amused by the series of *Imaginary Reviews*, which, except that they are better written, do not seem to me to differ from the ordinary gush of artless praise expended in the less prominent newspapers over real books of the moment. The ridicule, I think, should here have been more boisterous, the sarcasm more mordant. If there were an actual Mr. Pigott-Jones, the facile reviewer would doubtless welcome his *Recovery of the Picturesque* exactly as Mr. Squire does, but I fail to see anything funny in that.

On the other hand, Mr. Squire's Imaginary Speeches are very good. I cannot even smile at the Reviews, but I laugh aloud when Lord Rosebery, discussing a repeal of the licence duty on dogs, reminds the Peers that " Many a sombre and tenebrous deed has been killed before it was born by the naïve and half-divine appeal in the eyes of some devoted bloodhound." And already something of the patina of history gives gloss to the two contemporary speeches of Mr. Lloyd George, inside the House—" Just let's see if we can't agree about this business "—and outside—" The Tories ! Why, they'd sneak a marrow bone from a dog, or a penny from a blind man's tin."

Again, I think that the little essays which precede Mr. Squire's *Aspirant's Manual* are hardly in place in a volume which is intended to be preposterous and satirical. They are sarcastic, but entirely serious and sincere disquisitions on the art of writing ; they are not " parodies " of anything or anybody. They lead up to a sort of detailed imitation of a third-class society newspaper. But surely, not here, O Apollo, are haunts meet for thee !

The parodist who is also a poet accomplishes his task in a whimsical mood which is not very easy to define. He must write with appreciative gusto, or what he writes is not worth printing. He is, above all things, an admirer ; he must taste his models as though they were vintages, with a clean and sensitive palate. I fancy that Mr. Squire signs his fantastic imitations with names like Byron and Wordsworth much as Beethoven liked to write the name of the Archduke Rudolf at the top of his compositions. It is a form of infatuation, almost of idolatry. The vulgar see in parody an element of scorn, of ridicule. This is foreign to " great burlesque," which is a tribute and an analysis, not an insult.

Twenty years ago, when the dramas of Ibsen were the subjects of heated critical controversy, Mr. Anstey published his *Pocket Ibsen*, in which the plays were melted together, and their incidents presented in a ludicrous entanglement. There was Pill-Doctor Herdal, who made up beautiful rainbow-coloured powders to settle the hash of his juvenile contemporaries. All this was parody, in its fullest and most rollicking form. But what gave permanent value to Mr. Anstey's delicious volume was that it displayed a recognition of the real qualities of the Norwegian playwright, and a very fine sense of what was individual in his style. No one who had not closely studied *A Doll's House* and *Rosmersholm*, and with sympathy and admiration, could have written *The Pocket Ibsen*.

Unfortunately, the living who are parodied are often unable to rise to this finer conception, and resent what they regard as a liberty taken with their sacred speech. If they are wise, they look upon parody as a compliment, but in this finite world how few of us are wise ! I remember an instance of frailty of judgment which is, I think, still unrecorded. The excellent and then highly-popular poetess Jean Ingelow (I speak of nearly fifty years ago) received from Calverley the MS. of a parody of one of her poems, with a courteous inquiry whether she would " mind " his publishing it. She showed it to me ; I thought it extremely amusing, but, after some flutter of deliberation, Miss Ingelow decided that she did " mind," and this particular imitation—Calverley perpetrated others which gave less offence—was gallantly destroyed.

Such sensitiveness is misplaced, and recalls the distress of those who are hurt (I do not mean those who artfully pretend to be hurt) by the caricatures of Mr. Max Beerbohm. The wise man will join the laugh against himself, and be secretly gratified at being found prominent enough to be teased in public.

A FRIEND OF MOLIÈRE

A FRIEND OF MOLIÈRE

AT the time of the recent celebration of the tricentenary of the birth of Molière, it was observed that the only unpublished documents which were produced were those which owed their discovery to M. Emile Magne, whose industry in examining the treasures of the seventeenth century is inexhaustible. The mystery which shrouds the existence of the greatest dramatist of France is equalled only by the obscurity of Shakespeare, and is more surprising, because the archives of Paris are much richer than those of London. However, M. Magne contrived to throw a little fresh light upon the darkness, and in the volume called *Une Amie Inconnue de Molière* he puts together, in the narrative form familiar to him, what he has found.

The main point is certainly of great interest. He is able to show that the person to whom Molière was accustomed, as the most familiar of anecdotes has always informed us, to read his plays before they were performed was not an old serving-woman, but a lady of influence in the circle of the poet's friends. He has little detail of Molière's conversation with her to show us, and yet enough to excite a great curiosity in her adventures and character, and this curiosity he is able to gratify. The very name of Honorée de Bussy, Marchioness of Boissy, was forgotten, but M. Magne has searched the archives to such purpose that she lives in his delightful narrative.

In the sixteenth century there flourished at Poitiers a

learned lawyer whose name appears as Adam Blacvod.
The erudition of M. Magne does not extend to the English
language, and he has, accordingly, not perceived that
Blacvod is simply Blackwood. This Scotsman was an
ardent humanist and devoted servant of Mary Queen of
Scots, from whom he received his honourable post at Poitiers,
He adored his royal mistress, and in 1587 he published in
French a *Relation* of her martyrdom. This Blacvod (or
Blackwood) had three daughters, of whom the youngest,
Catherine, married the Seigneur de Bussy, while the eldest
became the wife of the famous grammarian and sceptic
François de La Mothe Le Vayer, at the mention of whose
name a Molièrist pricks up his ears.

Mme. de Bussy resided at Saumur, where her husband,
dying soon, left her with a daughter and a son. The
daughter was Honorée, the heroine of this history, born, as I
gather, in 1622 or 1623. Among her rich cousins Honorée
played the part of Cinderella, although she was far the most
beautiful of the family, and I regret to mention that we
find her mother trapesing off to balls and parties dressed in
the height of fashion, leaving Honorée to " *se habiller de
vieilles hardes qui dissimulaient sa joliesse.*" Through an
accident, however, she was seen by a finished judge of
beauty, Gaston d'Orléans, the king's brother, who insisted
that she should be clothed in brocade of gold and should
dance with him. He chose her out in a " review of the
troops of love," which must have been a sort of masque.

At this time Richelieu was exiling " in dozens " to the
provinces persons of importance whom he disliked. These
people transferred their establishments to country towns,
to which they added no little splendour. Honorée, who
refused to return to her kitchen, had a dazzling time, and
several near escapes. They married her, however, while she
was not yet eighteen, to a penniless Marquis de Boissy, who
ran through a great part of her money, but soon died. Her

conduct as a widow left something to be desired ; she went to Angers, where she was the subject of gossip in "*cet Anjou persifleur.*" I regret to say, but dare not conceal, that for some little time she was the mistress of François de Villemontée, governor of the province. This incident, however, was not dwelt upon in Poitiers, whither Honorée soon retired with her mother. In 1642 M. Magne finds the ladies in Paris, guests of Honorée's uncle, La Mothe Le Vayer, and they returned no more to their province. Le Vayer was a man of great learning, who had just been chosen to be the tutor of Louis XIV., whose studies had, as is well known, been neglected. Already the youthful Mme. de Boissy (now known as Mlle. de Bussy) was much engaged with literature and philosophy ; she was almost a blue-stocking, and quite a *précieuse*. In her uncle's house there was everything to encourage her tastes. He lived in the midst of the intellect of the age, as an active member of the new French Academy, and was the friend of Boileau and Guy Patin, of Voiture and of Gassendi.

The years that followed her arrival in Paris were peaceful and uneventful. The beauty and wit of Honorée de Bussy made her an attraction and an ornament in the house of her philosophic uncle. The Court became favourably aware of her merits ; she was patronised by Mademoiselle. When the troubles of the Fronde broke out she seems to have lost her head a little, not politically but amorously, since the disturbances of that time affected everybody in their weak spot. Honorée was surrounded by attentions ; nevertheless, on the whole, she was discreet.

Among her fine friends was the Great Condé, in whose honour she prepared a sort of album, where many of the best-known poets of the day wrote out, at her request, their poems in autograph. This anthology she had bound in citron-yellow morocco, and sent it as a present to Chantilly, where I understand it still exists in the Bibliothèque

Condé. She did this, M. Magne seems to think, to secure
Condé's favour, for she had fallen violently in love with the
beautiful young Marquis de La Moussaye, who lived with
the general. This was in 1647, when Honorée was about
four-and-twenty. La Moussaye assented, and they were
to have been married, but he died of fever. All the men
with whom Honorée now fell in love died one after the
other, leaving her more and more disconsolate ; she called
herself " *une femme fatale.*" She had to devote herself to
talking philosophy with Gassendi and turning *rondeaux* with
Voiture, to visiting Scarron in his famous arm-chair, and
to sympathising with her uncle about his great grammatical
contest with the fierce Vaugelas. Sad to relate, she had a
terrible carriage accident in 1656, which left her permanently disfigured, and this was followed by a serious
illness brought on by eating too heartily of roast sucking-
pig. Honorée seems to be losing the elements of romance,
but she was still a honey-pot, and the men came buzzing
round her.

Among them came the greatest of French dramatists, as
M. Magne has discovered. What took Molière to the house
of La Mothe Le Vayer ? Here the investigations of M.
Magne, hitherto so successful, have failed, but every one
fails who tries to pursue the phantom of Molière. M. Magne
thinks that it was the dramatist's admiration of Gassendi,
who was an intimate friend of the grammarian. At any
rate, Molière is found, about the time of the appearance of
Les Prècieuses Ridicules, a member of La Mothe Le Vayer's
circle. His life at this time was a painful one, disturbed by
jealousies and intrigues, from which nothing but the pro-
tection of the King preserved him. He found rest in the
friendly household in the Rue Traversante. A relic of the
intimacy exists in two folio volumes of the complete works
of La Mothe Le Vayer, presented in 1656 to Molière by the
author's son, the Abbé, on the occasion of whose death he

wrote one of the most famous of French sonnets. At the
house of Le Vayer Molière met Boileau, but above all he
learned to prize the intelligence and sympathy of Honorée
de Bussy.

That this was the case is proved by the precious entry
which M. Magne has found among the memoirs of Tallemant des Réaux. It runs thus :—" Molière read all his
plays to [Mme. de Bussy], and when *L'Avare* seemed to
have failed, ' It surprises me,' he said, ' for a lady of excellent good taste, who never makes a mistake, assured me it
would be successful.' And, as a matter of fact, when the
piece was revived, five months later, the public was pleased
with it." This comedy was originally acted at the Palais
Royal, on September 9, 1668, but it is evident that as
Molière had read " all his plays " to Honorée de Bussy,
even if we take this statement broadly, the friendship
was of long standing. M. Magne is inclined to think that it
began about 1658.

The great sonnet—*Aux larmes, Le Vayer, laisse tes yeux
ouverts*—was written four years earlier than the prose
comedy. After the death of his brilliant son, whom Molière
had loved and celebrated, the cynical old grammarian, at
the age of eighty-one, had determined to marry again.
He had found a learned spinster, possessed of a considerable
fortune, willing to knit her destiny to his, and the first
result of these unexpected nuptials was that Honorée de
Bussy ceased to keep house for her uncle. She took a
dwelling in the Rue de Richelieu, where Molière continued
to visit her, not neglecting the old philosopher now settled
in the Rue du Mail. Without rivalling the contagious
enthusiasm of a Mrs. Blimber, it may yet be pardonable
to wish that the conversations of the friends might have
been preserved. Molière read " all his plays " to Honorée,
and her remarks must have been the beginning of criticism.
All the Grimarests and Souliés and Monvals of the future

L 2

merely trod painfully in the footmarks of the vanished Mme. de Bussy.

A thought almost too whimsical for publication occurs to me. We have seen that the charming lady was known to have been the victim of an excessive partiality for roast sucking-pig. When Molière came to read to her the fifth act of *L'Avare*, where Maître Jacques says ambiguously to Harpagon, " *Je parle d'un cochon de lait* "—did the cheek of Mme. de Bussy blanch and the eye of Molière glitter? Of course not, and I cannot think how an idea so foolish can have occurred to me ; " *il n'est pas question de cela !* "

After 1668 there is no further trace of the friendship, but M. Magne, whom nothing escapes, has noted a point of proximity. He has found that at the time when *L'Avare* was produced, the great painter, Mignard, to whom we owe the wonderful portrait of Molière now at Chantilly, was living close to Mme. de Bussy, in the same Rue de Richelieu. He was just finishing his interior decoration of the Val de Grâce, the church which Anne of Austria had founded. To gratify the artist, Molière wrote a poem *La Gloire du Val de Grâce*, which appeared early in 1669. M. Magne has discovered that Honorée de Bussy gave a reception at which Molière's poem was recited before a fashionable audience. The gazetteer Robinet, who was present, says that the reading was a treat, a *régale*, and no doubt the reciter was the poet himself.

We should dearly like to know what attitude Honorée took up with regard to *Tartufe*, when her friend was attacked by a storm of orthodox insult. Probably she kept aloof from the discussion, for, with the passage of years, her earlier " libertine " notions of religion were becoming modified. No chronicler records the presence of Molière at any of Mme. de Bussy's further receptions, and in 1673 he died. Indeed, her thoughts had passed into a new channel, for her life, just as it seemed about to close, began to open again. When

she was approaching the age of fifty, she became the object
of a sentimental passion on the part of a wealthy officer of
her own years, Jules de Loynes, seigneur of Villefavreux.
They were married, and they were completely happy in a
long mutual infatuation. Each lived to the age of eighty,
and when Honorée died at length, Jules made no effort to
survive her. The end of her stormy career was long and
cloudless sunset.

To his biography of Honorée de Bussy, M. Magne has
appended the detail of his other discovery, which is less
picturesque but perhaps more important. Much effort
has been spent in trying to define the real philosophical
doctrine of Molière. It has been supposed that he was
definitely the pupil of Gassendi, and followed implicitly
the teaching of that philosopher. To prove how delicate
the ground is, equal effort has been made to prove that
Molière, by virtue of his friendship for Boileau, belonged
to the opposite camp, and was a Cartesian. Others, again,
have held that he merely held aloof, in the scepticism of
La Mothe Le Vayer. Boileau published an *Arrêt Burlesque*,
which has hitherto been dated 1674, after the dramatist's
death, but M. Magne has discovered that this was issued
as early as 1671, and that Molière was concerned in it.

This *Arrêt* was a farcical squib in which Boileau ridiculed
an Act of the Parliament of that year by which it was forbidden to teach in the University of Paris any other philosophy than that of Aristotle. M. Magne has unearthed a
pamphlet by François Bernier, in which he says that
Monsieur Molière " is watching the action of the gentry of
the Sorbonne, and intends [in 1671] to expose their intrigues
in a comedy which he is preparing for the diversion of the
Court." Molière did not carry out this crusade, and the
evidence of Bernier may be taken with a grain of salt, yet
the suggestion is interesting. It is not essentially improb-
able that the satiric genius which exposed to the laughter

of posterity so many contemporary foibles, and whose
sympathy with liberty of thought was patent, might wish
to ridicule the attempt of certain blind or stupid pedants
to limit the domain of philosophic speculation.   He says
himself in the immortal preface to *Tartufe*: "I have
expended all the art and all the care I could command in
distinguishing the hypocrite from the truly pious man."
In like manner, he might have shown the difference between
the mechanical, barren Aristotelian and the explorer of
true experimental intelligence.   He lacked the time, or
perhaps the determination, to do this, but we are grateful
to M. Magne for discovering that he was credited with a
wish to "expose the intrigues" of the University.

BON GAULTIER AND FIRMILIAN

BON GAULTIER AND FIRMILIAN

A PREFATORY note to the recent and first collected edition of Aytoun's Poems ever issued, states that " in the *Oxford Poets* it is the rule not to give any critical " (or apparently biographical) " appraisement of the poet." This is a rule which, in the present instance, it would have been wise to waive, since it is idle to pretend that Aytoun, who has been dead for nearly sixty years, is still a familiar figure to the public. More than most writers, he needs an introduction to render his verses, which are excessively allusive, intelligible to the public, and I fear that the majority of readers will glance at this volume without realising that it is the central illustration of an amusing episode in English literature well worthy of moderate revival. Mr. Page has performed his purely bibliographical duties so excellently that I can but wish the absurd " rule " he speaks of had allowed him to tell us who Aytoun was, and, at the very least, when he was born and died. A few words about this poet's relation to his contemporaries would have been still more welcome, and are, indeed, indispensable.

Aytoun was a product of the Edinburgh of the beginning of last century. He was a Scot of Scots, nurtured on the pious doctrine of White Rose Jacobitism, and of Scottish romance in general, by a stalwart mother who armed him in spear and belted brand, and sent him forth to fight the armies of Whiggery as a leal stout cavalier of the olden times. Aytoun grew up to be an ornament to Edinburgh society, a Writer to the Signet, a professor, and a charming, courtly companion, but to the end of his days he was flaunting his bonnet blue that wore the white cockade. He would have no truck with a degenerate England and an infidel London ; he was Tory Scotch to the core. All his triumphs were North British, and he adorned the picturesque office of Sheriff to Orkney and Zetland.

For such a man, in his youth, Edinburgh manifestly offered an asylum in the office of *Blackwood's Magazine*, and he was the faithful champion of *Maga* from 1838 (or earlier) until his death in 1865 ; he had been born in 1813. *Maga* had grown milder in the thirties than she had been twenty years before, when she persecuted Keats and Leigh Hunt so cruelly, but she was still very fierce, still blowing defiance to modern ideas through her aristocratic nostrils. She preserved her reputation for a wild species of coarse wit, for a fanatical adherence to the standard of King James, and for an encouragement of everything which was typically and truculently Scottish. It was in this environment that the remarkable talent of Edmondstoune Aytoun flourished, and a recognition of it is necessary for our appreciation of what he wrote.

Edinburgh indulged a strong curiosity about the new literature of Germany, and Aytoun spent nearly a year at Aschaffenburg when he was just of age. This was almost the sole absence from Scotland which he ever made, and he returned to Scotland with a profound admiration for Goethe ; the Germans were the only modern foreigners whose writings he admired. He translated a great deal of Teutonic poetry, and in particular *Faust*, in 1833. I think that his version of that drama has never been printed. He gradually gained, by dint of persistence, a considerable facility in prose and verse, and in 1844 he began to publish in *Blackwood's* a series of *Lays of the Scottish Cavaliers*, which he collected in 1849. These historical ballads were in the manner of Scott ; but, although Aytoun and his admirers stoutly denied the fact, their style was also plainly affected by Macaulay's *Lays of Ancient Rome* :—

> " The elders of the city
>   Have met within their hall—
> The men whom good King James had charged
>   To watch the tower and wall."

It is absurd to pretend that the writer of that had never read Macaulay. Aytoun's *Lays* however, enjoyed a substantial success, and ran through thirty large editions. *Flodden* is spirited and pathetic ; *Montrose* full of Tory fervour ; but the misfortune is that Aytoun's verse is no improvement on the sturdy Scots prose of the old chroniclers whom he copiously quotes as his authorities. It is not unkind to say that Aytoun's *Lays* resemble the historical compositions that popular Royal Academicians used to exhibit half a century ago. Then, in 1858, Aytoun published a romantic epic, in the manner of *Marmion*, which consisted of a soliloquy by Bothwell as he lay dying in the Swedish castle of Malmö. This poem, suggested by Bulwer Lytton during a visit to Holyrood, suffers from the absurd supposition that the expiring bandit could induce even the most venal of nurses to listen to an unbroken babble of nearly six hundred rhyming lines about his own past adventures.

All this, though welcomed at the time, was not really promising, but Aytoun found his gift. He was born for burlesque, and it is by his parodies and satires that he lives. He formed the acquaintance, and the lifelong friendship, of another young Edinburgh lawyer, Theodore Martin, and they roused in one another a spirit of high facetiousness. *Blackwood's Magazine* being open to them, they made it the vehicle for boisterous and anonymous *jeux d'esprit*, in which they laughed at the events and the personages of the time. To sign these japes in prose and verse, but particularly in verse, they chose the pseudonym of " Bon Gaultier " (it may be noted that they pronounced it *Gaulteer*).

It was long impossible, and it is still difficult, to distinguish the portion of the respective friends in what Martin called, long afterwards, "the Beaumont and Fletcher partnership of Bon Gaultier." But Martin had the lion's share. In 1845 they published, anonymously, *The Book of Ballads*, an extraordinary-looking little 16mo, now extremely rare, plentifully adorned with gold and colour within and without, and illustrated by Alfred Crowquill. This venture passed almost unnoticed at the time, but the ballads were reprinted, in an enlarged form, four years later, and then achieved for Bon Gaultier a lasting popularity.

In the tiny first edition, by the help of Mr. Page's notes, I find only eight pieces certainly by Aytoun, but he added others later, and Martin has recorded that many of the ballads were composed by both writers in unison. "Bon Gaultier" forms the natural link between *Ingoldsby* and Calverley, the art of Praed being something apart, and more delicate. Aytoun occasionally imitated his own serious *Lays*, and the romantic ballad manner proved very funny in parody. *The Broken Pitcher* and the absurd account in Scots vernacular of Queen Victoria's State visit to France are as amusing as ever they were.

But we come, by a process of exhaustion, to Aytoun's permanent masterpiece. About 1850 there began to be made a great fuss about "the coming poet." Everybody was looking out for him, and a forgotten, but very active and benevolent critic, the Rev. George Gilfillan, was finding him under every bush. Most of his discoveries were at once pronounced to be mares' nests, but a group of clever writers responded bravely to his call. These were known as the "Spasmodists," and for a while they occupied a very prominent position in the eye of the intellectual public. *Faust* was their grandfather, Bailey's shapeless *Festus* was their father, and the leading members of the family were Alexander Smith in his *Life Drama* of 1852 ;

Sydney Dobell, in his *Balder* of 1853 ; and Stanyan Bigg, with *Night and the Soul* in 1854.

These poets wrote much else that is beside my present purpose. Mr. Oliver Elton, who is the only leading critic who has given attention to this curious by-path of English literary history, neatly sums up the qualities of the " Spasmodists " as " a staggering, exhaustless grandiloquence of image, the oddest rhetoric, cracked and strained and iterative, and sustained rant." They had more than this ; all the leaders—even poor Stanyan Bigg, who lacks so much as a tombstone in the vast cemetery of the *Dictionary of National Biography*, and who is not mentioned by Mr. Elton—had flashes of noble imagination. But all their talent ran to waste. Their practice, however, shook the world of poetry. They were not without their influence on Tennyson, on Browning, and even on the young George Meredith.

Into this wild world of the " Spasmodists " Aytoun plunged his needle, and the bubble burst. He published, under the pseudonym of T. Percy Jones, *A Spasmodic Tragedy*, called *Firmilian*, which is one of the three finest specimens of dramatic travesty in our language, by the side of *The Rehearsal* and *The Critic*. It differs from these by its sustained solemnity, the fun consisting not in farcical language, but in the monstrosity of the sentiments and the extravagance of the plot.

At their best, Bailey had been magnificent, Smith sweet and Dobell romantic ; and *Firmilian* is each of these in turn. Indeed, often the Marlowe-like soliloquies of the latter totter into genuine poetry, and this makes the parody more emphatic and more fatal. Whatever the " Spasmodists " were, they were not vulgar ; it was the shapelessness of their dramas, their incoherence, and their bombast which were deplorable. *Firmilian* simply exaggerates these faults of taste, and sums them up with a preposterous energy which takes the reader's breath away. The poor

" Spasmodists " had not a spasm left in their quivering bodies, and they sank to silence.

The hero of *Firmilian* is a student of the University of Badajoz, who holds the fashionable theory that poetry is the loftiest of all sacred callings and the poet above all moral responsibilities. He has long been engaged on a tragedy of *Cain*, but fails to make progress with it, because he has never experienced the agonies of remorse. He comes to the conclusion that he must steep his soul in crime if he is ever to excel. He determines to " ope the lattice of some mortal cage and let the soul go free " ; in other words, to murder some one that he may know what " mysterious guilt " really feels like. But who shall be the victim ? That calls for some reflection, but finally he poisons an amiable fellow-student, whose sister, Mariana, is sole heir to his vast wealth. She happens to be affianced to Firmilian. The murderer is not suspected, and he puts another friend out of the way. Most annoyingly, he still fails to feel any remorse, and determines to act on a wider scale. He blows up the cathedral when it is crowded with worshippers. Still no remorse ; what is he to do ? He ascends the Pillar of St. Simeon Stylites, where he is joined by his dearest friend, the most successful poet of the hour, Haverillo (Alexander Smith), to whom he owes a thousand kindnesses. He hurls him over the pillar into the square below, where the critic, Apollodorus (Gilfinnan) is in the act of shouting :—

> " Pythian Apollo !
> Hear me—O hear ! Towards the firmament
> I gaze with longing eyes ; and in the name
> Of millions thirsting for poetic draughts,
> I do beseech thee, send a poet down !
> Let him descend, e'en as a meteor falls,
> Rushing at noonday— "

[*He is crushed by the fall of the body of Haverillo.*]

Aytoun's tragedy is the very type of high intellectual burlesque, and Mr. Page is to be thanked for placing it, after long obscurity, within the range of the ordinary reader.

BEOWULF

BEOWULF

Mr. CHARLES SCOTT MONCRIEFF, who has published a striking version of our earliest classic, speaks in his preface of the "many slighting references" to *Beowulf* that have been made of late. Slighting references, indeed! Beowulf has been the spoilt child of English scholarship, and Mr. Scott Moncrieff might as well say that Mr. Lloyd George has been "slighted." I have counted the numbers in Mr. R. W. Chambers' bibliography, and I find that since the beginning of the present century no fewer than 281 publications, not merely British and American, but German, French, Danish, Norwegian, Dutch, and Swedish as well, have been dedicated to the illumination of *Beowulf*. Slighted, quotha! Mr. Chambers, who is a scholar of the rarest erudition, knows them all, and he has summed up in a work of extraordinary research the activity of this swarm of commentators.

I almost wish he had not been so bewilderingly complete. There is not a silly theory buried in some *beiblatt* in Greifswald or Marburg but he digs it up, worries it, and lays it triumphantly at our feet, while he darts off to hunt up another little corpse. There is too much of it all; my poor head whirls round; and, without the least disrespect to Mr. Chambers' unparalleled learning, I wish that he had left dead foreigners to bury their dead, and had given us the conclusions of his own research without quite so much painful apparatus. He should remember that he speaks with authority.

Amid this seething mass of illustration, *Beowulf* remains

even now difficult to handle. I should like to see the Anglo-Saxon text which Professor Sedgefield published for the University of Manchester in 1910, Mr. Scott Moncrieff's new version, and as much of Mr. Chambers' commentary as deals directly with the substance of the poem, printed together in a single volume. That would put the reader in possession of all that he can possibly need to enable him to understand and enjoy one of the strongest and most stimulating products of the mediæval mind. Somebody has spoken of the ill effect of our modern craze for drowning the sacred poets in themselves, but it is worse to drown them in Teutonic conjecture. When it comes to discussing gravely the question whether the ocean-creek into which the Mother of Grendel descended with her prey, was not really a cesspool, the limit of scholastic extravagance seems to have been reached. Still—if you yearn for everything—Mr. Chambers gives it to you.

The poem of *Beowulf*, though so incessantly talked about, has hitherto been little read except by scholars, whose account of it the intelligent public has had to take on faith. Anglo-Saxon is a difficult language, and William Morris's version (with all respect be it said) was hardly more intelligible than the original. I know not what possessed the delightful author of *The Earthly Paradise* to adopt the horrible jargon in which he versified Mr. Wyatt's literal prose. But prose, however careful, gives little idea of this poem, the meaning of which seems to disappear when it is rendered in the language of a twentieth-century report.

Hence I, for one, am exceedingly grateful to Mr. Scott Moncrieff, who has, for the first time, permitted an ordinary reader like me to appreciate what *Beowulf* really is. He has cut a path along which I can walk with pleasure through what Morris left an impenetrable jungle. I will not say, that all is now perfectly lucid, or that there are no snags which catch the travelling foot. There are, I can see, hopeless obscurities here and there in the text itself, and the need of preserving the Old English tricks of alliteration and emphasis by repetition has occasionally strained the translator's skill ; the metal is sometimes too hard to yield to his tools.

But, on the whole, here is *Beowulf*, with its immense importance in the evolution of English poetry, for the first time presented to us as a mediæval poem which we can read currently and appreciate without effort. To have done this a second time—for Mr. Scott Moncrieff did it once before in his *Roland*—is a great feat, and one the performance of which deserves cordial recognition.

How, then, does this outermost planet, this mysterious Neptune of our poetic system, strike an unbiased reader who examines it through the new translator's telescope ? In the first place, I am struck with its luminous darkness. It is a picture, not like Chaucer's or Spenser's, in the camera lucida, but in the camera obscura. It is almost submarine in its effect ; we seem to be looking down into a translucent pool of ocean, fringed and shaded by seaweeds, in whose depths monstrous fishes are slowly swimming, and fierce crustaceans are energising, and noiselessly engaging in combat. The Icelandic poems, of the *Elder Edda* and what not, are mysterious, too, but they are suffused with the upper sunlight. The atmosphere of *Beowulf* is almost lunar, or rather it is permeated by an inexplicable radiance of which we cannot trace the source. To pass to particulars, it is steeped in aristocratic romance, of a kind which seems new, that is to say, which leaps over the civilisation of Latin and Greek fancy, and returns to a primeval, even to a savage ancestry. It is partly historical, and to this it owes its peculiar fascination, because here is something definite, based on the long progress of the race. Here are persons, who, remote as they are, share in some measure our own passions and capacities, but it is embroidered, as it were, with ornament of sheer fabulous invention, which transcends our experience, and is indeed incredible and preposterous. Here are real kings and fighting men, actual ships and familiar landscape, and here are also giants and genii, impossible monsters and feats of physical endurance to which the wildest credulity, it would seem, could never give credence. This mingled stuff, melted in a sombre colouring of romance, is the central feature of *Beowulf*.

It seems to me that the commentators have in some respects misread the poem. In the first place, I am quite unable to see that it deserves the sentimental prominence which has been awarded to it as the earliest expression of the English attitude to life and action. People have talked as though the author of *Beowulf* was a far-away precursor of Mr. Rudyard Kipling.

This is surely a patriotic illusion. There is nothing English about *Beowulf*, so far as I can see, except the curious and agreeable fact that it comes to us composed in the language employed in Mercia, that is to say, Leicestershire, about the year 700. Not an English place or person is mentioned in it, except one king who may or may not be English, for I have my doubts about Offa. Whether it is likely that a poem mainly describing the seacoast and maritime adventure should have been conceived in the neighbourhood of Ashby-de-la-Zouch I leave to more learned pens than mine. But all the scenes and all the personages are clearly Scandinavian. The good King Hrothgar obviously built his hall of Heorst or Hart on the eastern shore of Denmark—Mr. Chambers thinks it was at Leire, in Zealand ; the Geats who avenged his wrong must have come over the Cattegat from Sweden.

The landscape is consistently Danish ; Beowulf and Broca had their swimming match under what closely resembles the Klint of Moen ; the Whale's Headland where Beowulf's barrow stood, and where the dead dragon was

flung over into the sea, is evidently a ness in the Baltic.
There is nothing English in all this, and I ask myself in vain
how the bard in Mercia, who, unless he had travelled, can
never have smelt salt water, imagined such scenes. I feel
that we have not the material for even a conjecture as to
how, by an accident most fortunate for us, a purely Scandinavian poem came to be composed in an English dialect.

Another amiable fallacy seems to be that *Beowulf* is
suffused with the spirit of Christian piety. I fail to find a
trace of Christianity in it. The writer was so far not a
heathen that he believed in one God and rejected, or
neglected, the mythology of a still earlier race. He was
apparently acquainted with some parts of the Old Testament. Grendel and his mother are described as of the seed
of Cain, and the poet seems to have heard of Noah's Flood.
There is not unfrequent reference to a " Wielder of Victories," a power that gives wisdom to earls and kings, and
" wieldeth times and.climes." Especially is a tribute paid
to this " Wisest Lord, the Justice of Heaven," when the
hero overcomes the powers of evil.

But the allusions are all deistical ; there is not a trace
of acquaintance with Christ or the Christian plan of salvation. The poet is removed from the Icelanders, who worshipped Odin and Thor, solely by his belief in one God
instead of many. It has been said that the author of
Beowulf was " a pious Christian." I am sure he was " pious,"
for his reflections are inspired by a lofty morality, but the
signs of his Christianity escape me. The methods of the
poet are so contradictory that it is dangerous to take his
intention for granted, but it seems to me that it was not the
adventures of Beowulf so much as his character which
attracted the poet, and if this is true it sharply distinguishes
him from the Scandinavians, for whom the story was everything and the psychology accidental.

Judged by any modern standard, the method of *Beowulf*

is bewildering in the extreme. The poet seems to have
drawn no distinction between the real and the unreal.
Sometimes he is delightfully exact in his descriptions, and
we move amongst actual persons. It strikes me that he
must have been a sailor by profession, perhaps a pirate,
because the moment he begins to write about ships and their
movements a veil seems to fall, and a vivid scene unrolls
itself. The critics have generally praised, as the most bril
liant passage in the poem, the swimming match between
Beowulf and Broca, which is elaborately told and extremely
engaging. But when Unforth, who relates this particular
episode, assures us that the heroes swam for seven days and
nights without resting, holding drawn swords in their hands
to protect them against *nicors*, or sharks (Mr. Scott Moncrieff says " whale-fishes," but whales do not bite), that " a
mighty mer-deer " dragged Beowulf to the bottom of the
sea, where he fought and rose again, and continued his
swim, we feel we are in the realm of fable. Whereas the
description of how the ships started to the help of Hrothgar
is truth itself :—

> " The boys all ready
> Stepped on the stem ; the stream was washing
> The Sound on the sand ; those seamen bore
> In the breast of the bark bright adornments,
> Wondrous war-armour. Well out they shoved her
> (Wights willing to journey) with wooden beams bounden.
> Went then over the waves, as the wind drave her,
> The foamy-necked floater, to a fowl best likened."

This is experience ; and so is the still more vivid account of
the return of " the crowd of haughty bachelor-men," laden
with honour and treasure, to their Geatish haven.

The same inconsistency marks the conduct of the story
itself. Hrothgar, the melancholy chieftain, throned with
his gentle queen in the gold-decked wine hall he had built,
sitting in serenity encircled by his thanes, is an actual
human figure. But Grendel, the giant who comes marching
down on them over the misty moors, and slits open the

sleeping warriors and sucks their blood, is a mere shadow thrown by ghastly fear. There is a grandeur in the solemn horror of his approach, but he is not an individual, he is a theory of destructive wickedness. As for his mother, who follows him, with like cannibal intent, and steals a thane and eats him, and dives to the bottom of a pool where she has a cave,—unless we suppose her story to be an echo of a raid actually made upon a human coast colony by some hungry sea-beast, she is insufferably absurd.

But the reader must turn to the mysterious little epic, now so beautifully rendered by Mr. Scott Moncrieff, and judge for himself. Professor W. P. Ker has said that " nothing equally heroic " appeared in English literature until *Samson Agonistes*, and this is true. There is something uplifted, something morally magnificent, about this sombre story which gives it a unique significance.

MARK AKENSIDE

MARK AKENSIDE

SOMETHING very subtle links the practice of literature to the profession of medicine. What it is I cannot tell, but the fact subsists that if you see a surgeon or a physician meditating alone, there are ten chances that he is busy composing a sonnet to one chance that an engineer or a bank manager or a brewer is doing the same. It is no new thing ; from early times the doctors have been apt to be men of letters. Their profession has two faces, as was said of Rabelais, one turned to time, one to eternity, and the author of *Pantagruel* was the type of the literary physician. He abounds in all countries, but with us in England he has been particularly frequent, from Lodge, whose *Rosalynde* inspired the *As You Like It* of Shakespeare, down to the present Poet Laureate, whom I remember on the staff of St. Bartholomew's. Keats is the most illustrious example, but there are many others.

It was, however, in the eighteenth century that the literary doctors flourished most freely. They began with Sir Samuel Garth and his famous poem of *The Dispensary*, and with Blackmore, who rhymed to the rumbling of his chariot-wheels. They included Mandeville, who wrote *The Fable of the Bees*, and Arbuthnot, everybody's physician and author of *Law is a Bottomless Pit*, and Armstrong, whose verses were excellent, but are said to have " marred his practice as a physician." The poet's frenzy is thought by patients to be inconsistent with a good bedside manner. But of all the literary doctors who adorn the history of our country, the one in whom the gifts of literature and science

were most nicely balanced was Mark Akenside, whose two
hundredth birthday has lately been celebrated, not, I am
afraid, with much enthusiasm.

His real name is Akinside, and so it is printed on some of
his earlier publications. But when he came up to London
to practise he changed it to Akenside. The original form I
suppose he felt to be a little embarrassing for a family practitioner. He was the son of a respectable butcher of the
Presbyterian persuasion. When the poet was seven years
old his father's cleaver, with which, I am afraid, he was
playing, fell on his foot, and cut it so severely that he was
lame during the rest of his life. It is said that this misfortune constantly brought before his mind the lowness of his
birth, about which he was always too sensitive.

Mark Akenside was born at Newcastle-on-Tyne on
November 9, 1721. The principal forces of what we call the
Age of Queen Anne were in full movement, though Addison
was already dead, and Prior dying. A new school was just
beginning to be heard of in the hands of Young and Thomson. The butcher's son at Newcastle was exceedingly precocious, and before he was sixteen years of age gave signs
of an originality which deserves attention, and should have
developed along more favourable lines than it actually did.
If the original edition of *The Virtuoso* did not exist with the
date, April, 1737, printed upon it, it would be difficult to
believe in its genuineness, since it is the earliest of all the
pseudo-Spenserian imitations which were presently to
become so common and to influence poetic taste so vividly.
The astonishing butcher's boy employs the difficult stanza
of *The Faerie Queene* with complete success, and this is a
sign of that resistance to the all-absorbing heroic couplet
which was to mark almost the whole career of Akenside.

It is a sad fact that *The Virtuoso* promises a better poet
than Akenside, with all his ambition, ever contrived to
become. The subject of it is a satire, or skit, directed, with

juvenile impertinence, against the growing interest in physical science, and this by itself is odd in the first work of a boy who was to become a distinguished man of science. He jeers at a savant who

> " could tellen if a mite were lean or fat,
> And read a lecture o'er the entrails of a rat."

How many lectures was not Akenside himself doomed to deliver over entrails ! What can have inspired him—since Pope's sneering description of the pedants who approached the Goddess of Dulness, each with " a nest, a toad, a fungus, or a flower," was not published until four years later ? He was now, we gather, preparing, somewhat against his will, to become a surgeon, for another poem, printed in 1737, a blank-verse rhapsody called *The Poet*, describes himself as surrounded with " chests, stools, old razors, and fractured jars," in a high state of juvenile indignation. He must have been looked upon as a prodigy, for the Dissenters of New-castle-on-Tyne presently clubbed together and sent him to Edinburgh to study for their ministry. He had, however, no spiritual vocation, and about 1739 we find him entered as a medical student. Next year, being nineteen years of age, he was elected a member of the Edinburgh Medical Society, and proudly signed himself " Surgeon." He was now well started on his double career.

It was as a poet that he first earned distinction. The curious may examine, with stupefaction at the precocity they reveal, his successive publications. In October, 1739, his *Odes* began to appear in the pages of *The Gentleman's Magazine*, and we have to notice that this was at a date many years before either Gray or Collins reintroduced that form of lyrical expression. This, I think, is a feature of Akenside's work which has never been acknowledged ; he was an innovator, an inaugurator, at this moment of crisis in the evolution of English poetry. He completed his medical studies in Edinburgh at the age of twenty, for such studies were early concluded in those days, and he returned to Newcastle to practise as a surgeon.

We may suppose that he found little professional occupation at first, for he seems to us absorbed in poetical writing. But already a kind of icy formality of speech, which was soon to paralyse his genius, was beginning to take hold of him. His *Ode For the Winter Solstice*, which was separately published in 1740, is an elegant production, but so flowery and artificial in diction that the mind slips over it and gets no grip of the thought, which, moreover, on close examination, is found to be too slight for such exuberance of language.

But the young surgeon persisted, and in 1744, when he was in his twenty-third year, he published anonymously a quarto which created a great sensation, and placed its author immediately among the recognised poets of our language. This was *The Pleasures of the Imagination*, which is still spoken of with respect, though read with increasing difficulty. The purpose of this elaborate didactic poem, which had occupied Akenside, it is said, for several years was to lay down principles in the constitution of the human mind to account for every species of pleasureable emotion caused by natural scenery or by any of " the elegant arts." Philosophically, Akenside is a faint forerunner of Hegel, and his poem an attempt to define æsthetic beauty. He acknowledges what he owes to Aristotle, Virgil, and Horace, but is silent as to his far heavier debt to Shaftesbury, whose *Characteristics* he had evidently studied.

Dr. Johnson was very unkind to *The Pleasures of the Imagination*, where, he said—and not quite unjustly—" the words are multiplied till the sense is hardly perceived." That is, I have admitted, Akenside's weakness. But when Johnson talks of the young Newcastle doctor as " laying his ill-fated hand upon his harp," he is too picturesque, and

we remember that Akenside became an extreme opponent
of the critic's political convictions. Johnson hated a Whig,
and shut the gates of mercy on a political apostate. Most
readers in the eighteenth century did not share his view,
and *The Pleasures of the Imagination,* which Akenside completely rewrote without improving, enjoyed an unbroken
popularity for at least half a century.

In the same year, 1744, Akenside published his *Epistle to
Curio,* a vigorous political satire on the theme of " just for
a handful of silver he left us " ; and in the next a collection
of *Odes on Several Subjects,* which were highly successful.
In 1746 he wrote his *Hymn to the Naiads,* which has been
compared to frozen Keats. It has considerable beauty and
elevation, and is accomplished to the last degree. The
peculiar dignity of eighteenth-century rhetoric never rose
to a chillier altitude, and the vogue of this hymn had a great
influence in stereotyping a certain species of " poetic diction," as it was called, a language violently and successfully
attacked by the leaders of the Romantic Movement half a
century later. In spite of those attacks, however, the
prestige of Akenside survived the prefaces of Wordsworth,
and is visible in no less a poem than the *Alastor* of Shelley.
This is a sample of the *Hymn to the Naiads :*—

> " The immortal Muse
> To your calm habitations, to the cave
> Corcyian, or the Delphic mount, will guide
> His footsteps ; and with your unsullied streams
> His lips will bathe ; whether the eternal lore
> Of Themis, or the majesty of Jove,
> To mortals he reveal, or teach his lyre
> The unenvied guerdon of the patriot's toil."

Akenside was now only five-and-twenty, and he had
already composed almost the whole of his existing poetry.
His inspiration flagged, and after writing some further odes,
which were quite unworthy of him, he was silent as a poet
until close upon the end of his life, when, as I shall presently

point out, a new fervour possessed him. But a curious event occurred, the exact history of which is lost. The poet left the north and came up to Hampstead, where he started a medical practice. He had already become acquainted with the Chief Clerk of the House of Commons, whose name was Dyson.

The practice at Hampstead was a failure, and Dyson, whose admiration for Akenside was unbounded, brought him to Bloomsbury, gave him an allowance of several hundred pounds a year, with a chariot, on the understanding, it would appear, that he should, for the future, give his unbroken attention to science. He did not quite abandon the Muses until they, with their habitual freakishness, had abandoned him, but he became a serious and industrious man of science. His Gulstonian Lectures on the " Origin and Use of the Lymphatic Vessels " were read in the Theatre of the College of Physicians in 1755, and they advanced " a new theory," which few will have the leisure to investigate to-day.

He was appointed Croonian Lecturer, and held the office for several years, but gave up the task " in disgust " because some of the students complained that there was too much about the history of the revival of learning in his lectures, and not, as I conjecture, enough about the lymphatic vessels.

He continued, however, to advance in medical reputation. The man who was appointed principal physician to St. Thomas's Hospital, and, a little later, physician to the Queen, must have secured the suffrages of his profession. I regret that the account of the poet's behaviour in the former of these capacities is not all that could be wished. He was accused of being " supercilious and unfeeling," and of having evinced a particular " disgust to females," surely an unhappy trait in a hospital practitioner. It is alleged that on his visiting days he would be preceded by ushers with brooms, whose duty it was to sweep the more evil-smelling of the patients out of Dr. Akenside's path. These stories are doubtless much exaggerated, and the poet was a man capable of fine and generous actions. That his failings were haughtiness and irritability cannot, I fear, be disputed; he was apt to be either " peevish " or " oracular " with strangers. There is a story of a prodigious quarrel between him and another very pompous medical big-wig, Dr. Hardinge, on the subject of a bilious colic, which would make a cat laugh. These high priests of the medical profession took themselves very seriously indeed in the eighteenth century.

The year before his death Akenside woke to poetry once more. It is probable that few of those who nowadays turn over his pages reach the fragment of a fourth book of *The Pleasures of the Imagination* which he started in 1770. If they did, they would find such passages as this :—

> " Would I again were with you, O ye dales
> Of Tyne, and ye most ancient woodlands, where
> Oft as the giant flood obliquely strides
> And his banks open, and his lawns extend,
> Stops short the pleasèd traveller to view,
> Presiding o'er the scene, some rustic tower
> Founded by Norman or by Saxon hands :
> O ye Northumbrian shades, which overlook
> The rocky pavement and the mossy falls
> Of solitary Wensbeck's limpid stream,
> How gladly I recall your well-known seats
> Beloved of old, and that delightful time
> When all alone, for many a summer's day,
> I wandered through your calm recesses, led
> In silence by some powerful hand unseen."

These lines were written in the year when Wordsworth was born.

PEARL

PEARL

THE canon of English literature is now so closely established by the researches of scholarship that the man who
can boast of having added a considerable poet to its history
may consider himself a very fine fellow. Sir Israel Gollancz
is in that proud position, and must feel like—

> " Some watcher of the skies
> When a new planet swims into his ken."

More than thirty years ago he successfully demonstrated
that to the three great figures which illustrate the revival
of literature in the fourteenth century we must add a fourth
in no respect unworthy to be named with Chaucer, Langland, and Gower. This is the bard, unluckily still anonymous, whose writings have come down to us in a single
manuscript in the British Museum, traditionally known as
"Cotton Nero A.x." This small quarto volume contains four
poems of very diverse character, but all apparently composed by the same unidentified hand. All four are marked
by a fine originality of style quite independent of influence
from preceding or contemporary native literature. It is
very provoking to be unable to give this writer a name, and
Sir Israel Gollancz was justified in making one of those
happy conjectures which infuriate pedants, but amuse the
reasonable reader.

There was a certain poet of that age who enjoyed a high
reputation, but whose works have completely vanished.
Chaucer dedicated his *Troilus and Creseide* to " moral
Gower " and to " philosophical Strode." But who was

" philosophical Strode " ?   Nobody knows anything about him, save that there was a Radulphus Strode, " a noble poet," according to a catalogue in Merton College, who wrote an elegy called the *Phantasma Radulphi*.   It is all pure guesswork, but Sir Israel Gollancz's conjecture that the author of the four Cottonian MSS. was Ralph Strode is so pleasing that we may indulge in it until fuller light breaks in upon our darkness.   In that case *Phantasma* would be the vision called *Pearl*, since it does not fit the other three poems.   Of these, one is a romance of *Sir Gawain and the Green Knight*, while the other two are didactic pieces, entitled *Cleanness* and *Patience*.

But much the most attractive is the extraordinary tribute by a father to the memory of his little dead daughter, which was deciphered and given to the world, with a translation, by Sir Israel Gollancz in 1891.   This is *Pearl*, which takes its place as one of the minor classics of the English language, and which can but be more and more highly valued the more it is studied.   The original edition of thirty years ago attracted wide attention.   Tennyson, not easily moved to enthusiasm in matters of this sort, welcomed it in an excellent quatrain :—

> " We lost you, for how long a time,
> True Pearl of our poetic prime !
> We found you, and you gleam reset
> In Britain's lyric coronet."

But the edition of 1891 has long been out of print, and the new issue, carefully revised and expanded, is particularly welcome.

A great source of weariness to readers of early English literature is the incessant obsession of allegory.   It is so natural to suppose that a fourteenth-century poem must mean something quite other than what it pretends to mean, that scholars have not hesitated to search in *Pearl* for recondite senses of all sorts. An American critic sees in it a fundamental interpretation of the Eucharist ! Fortunately, there is no evidence of any such theological intention on the part of the author, and it is a charm in all his poems, but particularly in *Pearl*, that we may take them exactly as they are, without attempting to force into them any deadening religious allegory. The poet has been supposed to be hostile to Wycliffe, but perhaps the only evidence of this is his conservative attitude towards religion. He was no reformer ; he accepted the dogmas of his day as he found them ; and he poured out his beautiful verse in response to emotions which were wholly natural and normal.

It is the human emotion in *Pearl* that makes it precious. We find no wire-drawn sacerdotal metaphysic here, no remote pedantry of the schools, but we are brought face to face with a passion of simple grief which is intelligble to every one of us. We listen to a father from whom his little darling daughter has been snatched by a mysterious decree of Providence, and who seeks for consolation in a vision of her eternal happiness.

The author's greatest treasure has been an oriental pearl, doubtless a Margaret, his only child, a little girl who died before she was two years of age. It is curious that in all his reverie and his plaintive reminiscences the poet never once refers to the child's mother. There are hints that he is entirely solitary, that, perhaps, his wife had deserted him, leaving with him for sole company his Pearl, " so round, so royal, so sweetly small, so wondrous smooth." After the child's death, wandering utterly disconsolate in the garden where her little body was buried, he throws himself down and lays his head among the spiced flowers, white, blue, and red, which bloom there against the sun. Burying his face among the peonies and gilliflowers, he falls asleep, worn out with the weariness of his hopeless and intolerable sorrow. Then, in a trance, he finds himself walking between

cliffs towards a forest, in a landscape of almost intolerable
splendour of light and colour :—

> " Wondrously the hill-sides shone
> With crystal cliffs that were so clear ;
> And all about were holt-woods bright,
> With boles as blue as hue of Ind :
> And close-set leaves on every branch
> As burnish'd silver sway'd and swung . . .
> And the gravel I ground upon that strand
> Were precious pearls of Orient ;
> The sunbeams were but dim and dark
> If set beside that wondrous glow."

He pushes on through the lush vegetation of this magical
scene till the path descends to a wonderful river, whose
whispering waters are like the transparency of a beryl.
Across this river lies a country bathed in radiant splendour,
which he perceives to be Paradise itself. But the water is
deep and swift, and much as he longs to cross it he sees no
possibility of doing so. He walks along the bank until, on
the other side, under a cliff of crystal, he sees a child seated,
" so debonair, a maid of grace," and recognises in her his
own lost Margaret. She left him before she was two, yet
the girl he sees is of mature growth, but he recognises her
at once, ripened into intelligence by the subtle airs of
Paradise. Still, he is stricken with silent amazement, and
can hardly believe her to be his daughter until she rises,
" bedight with pearls," and comes down to the opposite
shore. She is wearing a rich crown, which she doffs, and
hails her father with blithe obeisance, removing his last
scruple whether he may regard this radiant being as his
daughter. He speaks to her, pouring out the record of his
lonely days and aching nights, and tells her how " pensive,
broken, forpined " (" for-payned," tormented) he is, " a
joyless jeweller " bereft of his one pearl of price.

The remainder of the poem is mainly occupied by conversation between father and child. Pearle greatly blames
him for his intemperate grief. What he lost was but a white

rose ; what he finds on the shore of heaven is a jewel of permanent value. He yearns to cross the river and join her, but that he may not do till his earthly pilgrimage is over. He must, however, restrain his sorrow, which has taken a form of impious excess. In order to restore him to some peace of mind, Pearl has prevailed to grant him this vision of her immortal joy. She is now the bride of heaven, a lady in the court of Mary immaculate, Empress of Courtesy, and she offers her father the privilege of seeing the castle in which she lives with all her starry peers. They proceed on either bank of the river, when suddenly the father sees the jasper city of the Apocalypse set high up on the gleaming cliff. A procession of maidens ascends to it, and threads its streets of golden glass.

Among these moons of purity and sweetness he suddenly perceives his own daughter walking in rank, and his separation from her becomes absolutely intolerable. Although he has been forbidden to attempt to cross the river, he can resist no longer. He rushes down the bank and flings himself into the water. The shock awakens him, and he becomes conscious that all has been a dream. But he has learned the lesson of resignation, and he will no longer defy the Divine Will by the violence of his grief, since he has seen his Pearl in her radiant happiness, and must grieve no longer as those who have no hope.

The date at which this beautiful poem was composed is uncertain. But Sir Israel Gollancz brings forward internal evidence which makes it probable that 1370 was the approximate year. *Gawain and the Green Knight* seems to have preceded, and *Patience* and *Cleanness* to have followed *Pearl* in each case by two or three years. There are strange pictures in the MS., presenting a sort of portrait of the father, who seems, in these, to be a man under thirty years of age. He would, in this case, be a little younger than Langland and Gower, and almost exactly as old as Chaucer ;

he was obviously the direct contemporary of all three.   It
is therefore curious to observe how little likeness he has to
any of them or to any English poet of his time, in spite of
a certain kinship with Chaucer through their common
devotion to the *Roman de la Rose*, which was, as Sir Israel
Gollancz says, the " secular Bible of the mediæval poets."

The editor and translator believes that the author of
Pearl had read, and had been influenced by, a Latin poem
of Boccaccio, the *Olympia*, written soon after 1358, an
elegy on the death of that poet's youthful daughter Violante.
The parallel does not seem to be very close, but it gives Sir
Israel Gollancz an opportunity of presenting to us this
interesting and little known eclogue in a skilful blank-
verse translation.   The Middle English of the author of
Pearl is much more difficult for the unpractised reader than
that of Chaucer or Gower, or even of *Piers Plowman*.   The
learned editor has issued the texts of *Patience* and of
Cleanness, but without adding such a translation as makes
his *Pearl* easy and agreeable reading.   I wish that he
would give us all four poems in a modern form, and if he
issues them as the *Poetical Works of Ralph Strode* I shall be
the last to show ingratitude by throwing a stone at him.

EARLHAM

EARLHAM

MR. PERCY LUBBOCK has published a book all about a
house in Norfolk. Not many of his readers, and certainly
not that ingenious author himself, can have seen the fair
courts of Earlham so long ago as I did. The methods of
Mr. Lubbock irresistibly invite the autobiographical mood,
and nothing can prevent me from admitting that I was
there more than sixty years ago. The memories of a little
child are capricious, and mine in this regard have no value,
yet I drop my grain of mustard seed into Mr. Percy Lubbock's full granary without a blush. My charming and
amiable stepmother, to whom I long ago introduced an
indulgent circle of my readers,* was faintly connected,
like so many Norfolk people, with the populous and famous
house of Gurney. In the autumn of 1861 she made a pro-
tracted visit, from her new Devonshire home, to her old
haunts in Norfolk, and in the course of it she stayed at
Thorpe with her redoubtable bachelor uncle, Mr. John
Brightwen, in his fine house close to Norwich. In that swift
advance, my kind stepmother swept me along in the swirl
of her flounces, and I found myself in such clover as I had
never dreamed of. Thorpe itself—now I am told razed
to the rock and swallowed up in Norwich—was then a
noble mansion lifted almost precipitously above the waters
of the Yare, as may still be seen in the lithographs of
Cotman. It was suggested one day that " Eliza " would
do well to " pay her respects to the Gurneys," and, accord-

* In *Father and Son.*

189

ingly, accompanied (as it seems to me) by bluff old eighteenth-century " Uncle Brightwen " himself, we adventured a sort of state visit to Earlham in the large Brightwen barouche. It was, as I now find, but a distance of a few miles from Thorpe to Earlham, yet, half-sunken among the crinolines of the ladies, and drawn with dignity through the breadth of Norwich and out into the country, the expedition seemed endless in its delight.

John Gurney, who was a notable Norfolk Quaker, was, his descendant tells us, " a worthy though not an interesting man," but he rebuilt in 1786 the famous house at Earlham, which dated from 1642. He married, moreover, a certain Miss Catherine Bell, whose beauty is preserved in an admirable portrait by Gainsborough. This excellent couple had no history, except that they begot a marvellous family of sons and daughters, who illuminated the local history of their time, and of whom some passed out of it into permanent fame. These children were active as philanthropists in the forefront of their age. There was Samuel Gurney, " the banker's banker," whose foibles were Liberia and the sorrows of our coloured brethren ; there was Elizabeth, who became Mrs. Fry and the most active of prison reformers ; there was Daniel, another banker, notable as a county antiquary ; above all there was Joseph John, sturdy opponent of capital punishment and active in every species of good works.

This great generation, with the seven sisters in their scarlet cloaks and purple boots, had become the merest ghosts in Mr. Lubbock's childhood. In mine, also, they were mainly memories, but very fresh ones, especially through Amelia Opie, under whose wing (I think) my stepmother had originally penetrated the halls of Earlham. I must not divagate, but yield only for the moment to the temptation of recalling, in shadowy retrospect, that golden day in 1861, when we rolled up, " palpitating with excitement," to the semicircle of steps which gave entrance to the beautiful old spreading mansion.

These gracious and lively inmates who animated the scene in Mr. Percy Lubbock's childhood were a quarter of a century younger on the day I speak of than they were in the years of which he speaks. I cannot, ransacking my infant memory, recall any of them distinctly, but I remember the house, inside and outside, sufficiently to infer that the passage of years made little change in it. I recall a certain dim crowd of children, grown to the estate of men and women before Mr. Lubbock knew them, and a variety of elders, yet only vaguely, as trees walking. But I remember much more clearly the aspect of the house, and I think that this fact, so far as it goes, confirms and excuses Mr. Lubbock's contention that it was the house itself, primarily, which impressed itself on a visitor. The passage which I am about to quote warns me off from any attempt to describe what I remember, because it presents with focus and authority, in strong lines, exactly what I could but falteringly attempt to revive. All this " comes back to me," as people say, filling up, with colour and definition, a phantom outline still alive in my mind :—

" The house was various, endless, inexhaustible. Mounting the stairs again (after how many years ?), the shallow stairs that rose from the hall, I hardly know which way to turn—here, perhaps, on the first landing, at a door which takes me into the ' ante-room,' I suppose originally the chief parlour. It was high, clean, formal, with the air of a room little used ; there was not an object on a table, not a blue china cup on a cabinet, that had shifted its place in fifty years. But at the end of the long room was a small extension, a projection in a bow-window, that was in familiar use. A cool, green light fell through the windows, which looked northward into an avenue of great limes, murmurous and odorous in summer noondays. . . . The space in the bow-window was raised like a daïs above the level of the room ; there was a green velvet window-seat, and a huge old Chinese jar, standing on the floor, holding relics of ancestral lavender and rose-leaves. There on the window-seat our grandmother drew us round her, and read to us, sweetly and playfully, ancient moral anecdotes, stories out of tiny little volumes that she cherished—or Bible stories, if it were Sunday."

This grandmother is the heroine of Mr. Lubbock's book, as the mansion of flint and brick is its hero. She had been the wife of John Gurney, who died young, and, a very short time before my visit, she had married the Reverend William Nottidge Ripley, rector of St. Giles's, Norwich. All this family history, complicated by the great number of children and connections, is patiently and amusingly unravelled by Mr. Percy Lubbock, but deserves our attention mainly in so far as it gravitates round the exquisite figure of Laura Pearse, originally Mrs. John Gurney, then Mrs. Ripley, for fifty years the centre about which the serene and opulent life of Earlham revolved. Persons desirous of refreshing their memories as to the facts and dates in the chronicle of the Gurneys of Earlham must turn back to the well-known manual of Augustus Hare. They will find nothing that is statistical and little that is anecdotal in Mr. Percy Lubbock's reveries.

This book, which is oddly, and, I think, rather daringly, conceived, has but a single subject, namely, the solid mass of Earlham with the author's grandmother as the soul of it, described exclusively as they impressed a sensitive and observant child. The child wanders, in a restless ecstasy, up and down the staircases and through the congeries of rooms, haunted by the warm, fitful presence of the delicious wayward chatelaine. But the house, in these memories, predominates even over the grandmother; she appears occasionally, but the house is present, like a dumb, huge guardian or immense lidless eye of red brick, on every page. Mr. Lubbock has written a book which reminds me of no other, a book in which a beautiful old house is treated as though it were a benevolent personage, full of human life and movement, but in itself more interesting, because more consistently beautiful, than any of its inhabitants.

The conception of this book I have called " daring," because it rests for its attraction on nothing which is usually

summoned by the author of such a monograph to diversify
the monotony of his theme.   It is Earlham that we get, and
nothing but Earlham, and the pictorial and sentimental
aspects of Earlham exclusively in their relation to a child's
eye and heart.   From Mr. Lubbock's early childhood the
great Norfolk mansion, with its broad and populous hos-
pitality, was the scene of autumn holidays in each recurring
year.   Whether the author saw or even visited Earlham at
a maturer age, why and when he ceased to repeat his
ravished impression of it, we are not told.   What is presented to us is solely that which a man may remember of
what a little child saw and felt, sensuously and sentimentally, in the wholly restricted circle of one house and garden.
We are kept within the bounds of Earlham as inside a
magician's ring ; there is no escape from it, as there is no
desire for escape.   Even to Norwich, in those days still so
picturesque (though far more picturesque in mine), we are
only allowed an excursion at the very close of the book.
Absorbing adventures by one's self, through the hall of the
house, "in the depth of the soundless afternoon," are
described as though they were expeditions to Thibet,
while the flight of the stairs is ascended with as much pomp
as if it were Aconcagua.   The "light flap of the awning
which hangs in the doorway " stirs our nerves as though it
were the trump of doom.   The intricate maze of the shrub-
bery has all the terror and the charm of an uncharted
wilderness.

It is plain that a book carried out unshrinkingly on
these lines runs a very great danger of becoming tedious
and being thrown aside.   The charm depends entirely on
the skill with which the writer sustains the beauty of his
delicate tissue.   Let him once relax, or, taking fright at
his own audacity, let him once call to his aid some adventi-
tious form of entertainment, and all is lost.   He has to
penetrate to the very secret haunt of memory and stay

there until the substance of his mind is illuminated and
charged by all the lost impressions of childhood :—

> " The magic music in his heart
> Beats quick and quicker, till he find
> The quiet chamber far apart,"

and, having found it, he must be suspended there until those
impressions flood his mind to the exclusion of all others.
This Mr. Percy Lubbock has done, and, therefore, unless
we resign ourselves in sensitive response to the mood of a
child, it is possible that we may find the absence of anything like narrative bewildering and even dull.   Unless
we are in passive harmony with the object of Mr. Lubbock,
and let the author lead the reader, like another child,
through the rooms and round the garden, the perusal of
Earlham may be difficult.   It will not be everybody's book,
but there will be many to whom it will appear as nothing
less than a little masterpiece.

A very modest and even unenterprising author, Mr.
Percy Lubbock does not seem to have yet attracted the
public notice which his skill demands.   In an age when the
art of poetry receives far more attention than the art of
prose, he is in the front rank of living prose artists.   If this
has not been said before, I take the liberty to say it now,
and to invite an examination of my claim, which I am willing
to rest upon a passage from any chapter of *Earlham*.   We
command a hundred authors who write with vigour, with
lucidity, and with the ease which comes from experience,
but we have very few who combine rich but subdued
colour, and grace which is never effeminate, with cadences
so natural and so delicate that their technical beauty is felt
rather than revealed.   Mr. Percy Lubbock is a mannered
writer, and it is plain that he has been influenced by two
eminent masters of artificial prose, Henry James and Marcel
Proust, but particularly by the latter.   The effect of
Proust's fascinating progress from one atom of experience

to another has, in one respect, I think, been deleterious to
Mr. Lubbock.   The impression of childish days in *Du
Côté de chez Swann* is only saved from monotony by constant
thrills of language, little electric shocks, which, indeed, do
not always or entirely save it.   But these shocks and thrills
—which Henry James introduced, sparingly enough, by
occasional lapses into colloquial speech—are absent in
Mr. Lubbock, whose style has the rich uniformity of a
seventeenth-century prose writer—he often recalls Jeremy
Taylor and his compeers—and something of the impenetra-
bility which made the reform of prose under Addison and
Swift compulsory.   It may suggest my meaning if I put it
that the style of Mr. Percy Lubbock is less a painted picture
than a woven oriental carpet in which the lovely pattern
recurs with uniformity.   Anxious to find fault with *Earlham*
and so to justify my critical office, I can discover nothing
else to carp at.

THE LAUREATE OF WEDDED LOVE

THE LAUREATE OF WEDDED
LOVE

WHILE I turned the pages of Mr. Osbert Burdett's *The Idea of Coventry Patmore*, there rose up vividly before me the image of that marvellous man as I used to see him at Hastings forty years ago, stretched in his study chair before the fire, smoking innumerable cigarettes, smiling and blinking at his guest, as he rolled out paradox after paradox, with a crackling laugh and a sort of bark at the close of each sentence. His conversation was what that of the Sphinx might have been, if we conceive the Sphinx to have been an angel, too. In it a dogged sort of cynicism was mingled with celestial hues of ideality; mystery was dyed with a startling tinge of common sense. At the time I speak of, when it was my privilege to be a thrilled pilgrim at the shrine, there were hardly any other worshippers; that was the dark hour of the public neglect of Patmore.

Born in 1823, he had published *The Angel in the House* before he was thirty, had enjoyed a marvellous popular success with it for some ten or fifteen years, and had then sunken into a disfavour with the public, whether expert or inexpert, which was quite as surprising. He had adopted, after long silence, a sterner and more abstruse method of writing in *The Unknown Eros*, and had met with no recurrence of popularity. It was not until Patmore's fiftieth year that the tide began to turn again, and that a new generation awoke to the lofty music of his odes. But even then few perceived that a common thread ran through these and connected them with the despised and rejected

Angel in the House ; that, in fact, only the man who wrote the one could have written the other.

That even his most enthusiastic admirers failed to recognise his life-long purpose to the full was often a subject of regret to Patmore, who, like many rigid and dictatorial persons, was secretly longing to receive the appreciation which he seemed to disdain. I therefore wish with all my heart that he could have lived to read Mr. Osbert Burdett's volume, for it would have given him sustained satisfaction. When I say that no previous critic has approached Mr. Burdett in his successful interpretation of Patmore's "idea" I do not mean that critical opinion will acquiesce in all Mr. Burdett's conclusions. I think there will be many things to be said on the other side, but, at all events, among those who express dissent the spirit of Patmore himself will not put in an appearance.

It is already much to have set forward an exposition of a poet which exactly agrees with the poet's own "idea," and that Mr. Burdett has done, for the first time. He has developed—perhaps he goes too far in claiming to have "discovered"—a continuity of aim throughout the whole of Patmore's writings, whether in prose or verse, and he defines and illustrates this "idea" in terms which have indeed, as it seems to me, been suggested by others, but never carried out so fully and coherently as by Mr. Burdett.

The position is this. Up to the year 1875 Coventry Patmore was almost exclusively known as the author of what the general public accepted as a sentimental novel, exactly as it accepted the *Barchester Towers* of Trollope and the *Chronicles of Carlingford* of Mrs. Oliphant, except that, while these were written in prose, that was in easy octosyllabic verse. For a time the book sold in vast numbers (ultimately amounting to a quarter of a million), but it was bought by readers who formed no conception of its real aim, and therefore when the first amusement in

the story and the treatment of contemporary manners had
subsided, *The Angel in the House*, and its increasingly less
successful three continuations, were laid on the shelf and
forgotten.   The public thought of it as D. G. Rossetti did
when he wrote : " Of course, it is very good indeed, yet
will one ever want to read it again ? "

Those people who treat it, as the egregious Chorley did,
as a mere " tale, not very wise, about a Person and a
Spouse," never will wish to read *The Angel in the House*
again, but, if they are intelligent, will turn, as authoritative
criticism has continued to turn, to the great mystical odes
of Patmore's later period.   These no reader of judgment
fails to perceive are magnificent, but the usual expression
is one of surprise that the majesty of *Psyche's Discontent*
should have proceeded from the trivial mind which had
told how, when Jane bought

> " A gay new bonnet, gown, and shawl,
> Frederick was not pleased at all."

The mission of Mr. Burdett is to show that there is no
discrepancy whatever, and that the " realism " of the
earlier style and the sublime mysticism of the later are part
and parcel of one perfectly consistent genius.   This is why
I say that whoever likes Mr. Burdett's book, Patmore
would have liked it most of all, for this was what he continued to assert in season and out of season.

Let the " idea " be bluntly stated.   Mr. Burdett holds
that in the history of the spirit three attempts have been
made, and only three, to make love the basis of a com-
prehensive philosophy.   The first was made by Plato, the
second by Dante, the third by Coventry Patmore.   The
Platonic theory of love was " a pyramid standing on its
apex," and was confined to the celebration of friendship.
The second theory was an idealisation of woman, as the
romantic object of an unselfish passion, which either became

etherealised into a pursuit of Divine Wisdom, or materialised with the Troubadours and the mediæval Courts of Love into a sort of sublimated adultery. In neither marriage was an element, and as the experiments of later poets have all been based either on the Platonic or the romantic theory, a great section of the life of love has been wholly excluded from poetry.

This bachelor attitude, as Mr. Burdett calls it, left the ground free for Coventry Patmore to propound a new poetic philosophy based exclusively on marriage. He therefore made it his life's work to write a breviary for wedded lovers, finally carrying the theme, originally of a tender and homely character, up into the heights of mysticism, and using it to interpret the relation of the Divine Husband to his spouse, the Soul. On this Mr. Burdett expatiates, and it is impossible to deny that Patmore himself took this view of his mission.

But when we turn from promise to performance we may part company a little, and for a little while, with the enraptured commentator. I hate to seem to belittle the writing of Coventry Patmore, for which I have nurtured a sincere and ardent admiration all my life. But there is such a thing as moderation, and when I am asked to give *The Angel in the House* equal rank with the *Symposium* and the *Vita Nuova* I hesitate.

For this hesitation there are two obvious reasons. The one is of substance, the other of form. Mr. Burdett (assenting to Patmore's reiterated appeal) declares that wedded love is as proper a subject for epical treatment as Platonic or romantic love. But is it ? We cannot conceive of an epic in which there is neither danger, nor sacrifice, nor sorrow. The progress of our interest depends on the tragic element, on vicissitude and distress. But in the Patmorean epic of happy married lovers these elements are inevitably missing. The more perfect the felicity, the less chance is there for evolution ; the ideal comfort depends on being stationary :—

> " Ten years to-day she has been his.
>   He but begins to understand—
>   He says—the dignity and bliss
>   She gave him when she gave her hand."

The consequence is that, while *The Angel in the House*, and to a less degree *The Espousals*, are starred with passages of the loveliest lyrical psychology, *Faithful for Ever* contains very few, and *The Victories of Love* practically none at all. The subject, when confined to modern happy marriage, peters out, and the " epic," as Mr. Burdett calls it, sinks into the sands.

But there is a second consideration, that of form. Mr. Burdett has no patience with those of us who value *The Unknown Eros* far more highly than all but excerpts from the earlier books. He does not seem to have given sufficient thought to the matter of execution. If we admit that in his theory Patmore was the equal of Dante and Plato, can we seriously grant the same rank to his practice ? To intend to do a thing is not the same as to do it. Sir Richard Blackmore intended to be sublime, but that does not make his epics as fine as *Paradise Lost*. It would be ugly and unfair to quote over again the trivial passages in the " Vaughan " series of volumes, since they give an unjust impression of the distinguished powers of their author ; but I do not see how any one can deny that they are often flat and sometimes ridiculous.

Patmore had a sublime " idea," and he attained splendid effects in lyrical psychology, but he was ill-advised to descend to the details of a middle-class contemporary household, where his art failed him, not because he was not a substantial poet, but because genius itself was powerless to develop into " epic " variety the successful monotony of such a happy, prosperous pair as Felix and Honoria. The treatment of a domestic theme probably demands more technical skill, more passion of the craftsman, than any other ; and there is this further danger about such a theme, that it is inevitably soon exhausted, however much it may be hung about with lyrical ornament. We may quote Patmore against himself ; the almost perfect success of *Amelia*, in its splendid brevity, has only to be compared with the long-drawn dreariness of *Faithful for Ever* to show that this species of love is suited to an episode, not to an epic.

At the same time that Mr. Burdett publishes his monograph, an interesting light on the same subject is thrown by Mr. Everard Meynell, who issues a *Catalogue of the Library of Coventry Patmore*, with various notes, personal and bibliographical. The poet seems to have been one of those retentive people who keep everything that they write or that is written to them. His copies of St. Augustine, St. Bernard, and St. Catherine of Siena, are marked by annotations which show his study ; and he had a devotion for St. Catherine of Genoa, who is less well known. That the *Exercises* of St. Ignatius had been accepted by the Church as " almost canonical " Patmore took as a final answer to his doubts as to the ultimate fate of his own poems.

Of curious importance to him were the various works of Swedenborg, deeply scored by his pen. Patmore studied Swedenborg just before he himself began *The Unknown Eros*. He wrote that he never tired of reading Swedenborg ; " he is unfathomably profound, and yet simple." It is odd that neither St. Teresa nor St. John of the Cross occurs among the poet's books, and he showed little regard for the English mystics. I remember discovering that he had never met with Crashaw, and I presented him with a copy of that poet's works, particularly drawing his attention to *Love's Horoscope* and the *Hymn to St. Teresa*. Yet in acknowledging the gift he made no reference to these, but only to *Music's Duel*, a wholly secular poem, which he told me he considered " perhaps the most wonderful piece of word-craft ever done." All investigation of one of the most original minds of the nineteenth century is welcome, and I rejoice that Patmore continues to attract so many readers.

EDWIN ABBEY

EDWIN ABBEY

TWIN leviathans sprawl over my table, stretched like a couple of promontories. Nothing so large has been seen in literature since the Theologians, two hundred years ago, gave up presenting their sermons in folio to an intimidated public. It is impossible not to ask oneself who are the enthusiasts that are prepared to put down six guineas for this huge picture-book? The answer, doubtless, is that it is not designed for general consumption, but is of the nature of a monument. Not in Parian marble nor in bronze of Syracuse, but in two vast tomes of biography, illustrated by two hundred reproductions, does piety in this case seek to undo the ravages of time.

There is much to be said in favour of this species of sarcophagus, but it is difficult to know what to do, in everyday life, with a portable memorial of such bulk. There ought to be a gallery exclusively devoted to Edwin Abbey's work, as in certain other cases has been done, and in the centre of that gallery there ought to be placed two lecterns, and a copy of a volume of Mr. Lucas's biography be chained to each. So the visitor might contemplate *Departure of the Knights on the Quest of the Holy Grail* or *With Jockey to the Fair*, and then withdraw to the lectern and read all about it. This would be doing proper justice to a surprising work, which for the purposes of common life strikes the cynic as unwieldy.

Let me not be presumed to think slightingly of this biography. Mr. Lucas, I gather, did not know, and perhaps had never seen, the popular American artist. But he is a practised craftsman, if ever there was one, and he has manipulated the material placed in his hands with the utmost skill. He was faced with the necessity of mentioning scores of names, many of which never meant much to the reading public and now mean nothing at all. He has by dint of research and inquiry found out what it was essential to our comfort that we should know about most of these names, and has unobtrusively moulded this information into his narrative. The reader not experienced in the carpentry of books may very well fail to perceive this feature of the *Life*, but it is an important element in the pleasure as well as the profit which he obtains from the reading of it.

Sometimes, we may smile to observe that the torrent of American names has carried even Mr. Lucas off his feet, but as a rule he clings to every plank and gets safe to shore where an adventurer less active than he would be swept down the rapids. The book is a manifest and a very spirited effort to stem the dreadful torrent of oblivion ; and from that point of view alone, to the future student of contemporary artistic history it will prove invaluable. The particularly distressing question of how much final impression the majority of these industrious and competent efforts of artistic energy will make on future minds is beside Mr. Lucas's question. He has had to construct the monument, and he has done it in masterly fashion. How many hurrying wayfarers will stop to look at it, and take off their hats in reverence, is no business of his. Here is the great twin memorial, and it could hardly have been better executed.

Edwin Abbey was one of the most sociable of human beings. This characteristic is the point from which any outline of his full career is bound to start. He was not an isolated talent, developed in retirement, but was always working at the centre of an active and voluble group. He was far from voluble himself, but his cheery and comfortable presence formed a kind of rallying point, and he worked best at the heart of a society of other artists. This must be borne in mind in consideration of that torrent of names of which I have spoken ; there could not be a biography of Abbey that was not humming with companions. When he moved, it was in a swarm, as though he had been a sort of queen-bee, and everything about him was serviceable and cosy.

He was born in a city whose name is extremely appropriate to his nature, namely, in Philadelphia, on April 1, 1852. His parentage was simple ; he was the grandchild of a typefounder of English and French extraction, and the son of an impecunious agent in yellow pine timber and tobacco. His mother was a woman of refinement and sense beyond the common. There is an amusing daguerreotype of the artist at the age of two years, seated in a high chair and flourishing a pencil, his eyes fixed before him with an expression of stern æsthetic elevation.

His vocation as an artist was patent almost in the cradle. He had, of course, to earn his living as early as possible, and at sixteen he was doing it by illustrating school books, geographies, and " readers." His earliest masters were the imported English illustrated journals such as they flourished in 1868. It appears that Abbey never had what in Europe would be counted an artistic education ; in 1889, when he was already famous, he naïvely notes in a letter, " I have never painted from the nude at all, *think of that !* " We do think of it ; and it leads to reflection.

The early advances of Edwin Abbey in America are recounted with great fullness by Mr. Lucas, but they are of comparatively little interest to the European reader. Americans, on the contrary, will be delighted with them. He competed, in charming good humour and boisterous high spirits, with a host of other young art journalists, particularly for the firm of Harper's. We find him unable to admire what was not " pretty," and constantly anxious to draw " in a sympathetic way." He worked with extreme assiduity, but made at first only a poor income ; nevertheless, he was steadily advancing in skill and in position. To produce " a charming water-colour of a young girl leaning against a stile " was the limit of his ambition at the age of twenty-five, and we may very reasonably doubt whether he would have achieved any conspicuous success if an event had not called him out into that wider field of experience which he practically never left again. It was suggested that he should pay a visit to England that he might " gather enough English atmosphere " to qualify him to illustrate some of the English poets with authority. But if he came as " a retrospective Columbus," as Mr. Lucas puts it, to discover the Old World, the Old World discovered Abbey and made an artist of him, and retained him.

At this point the narrative becomes extremely interesting. Towards the close of 1878 the young draughtsman landed in Liverpool, and for a little while, marvellous to relate, was almost alone in England. He went straight to Stratford-on-Avon, and was infatuated with Warwickshire at first sight. He had, however, to leave it and go up to London, to an attic in Bloomsbury. His early English adventures and impressions are recorded in his letters to his mother, which are of a charming freshness and piquancy. Most of these letters, it appears, have been destroyed, which is a great pity, as Abbey had a pen hardly less picturesque than his pencil.

Extraordinary was the instinct by which this gregarious young man, without apparent effort, fell smoothly into the circle which suited his talent best. " What a lucky fellow I am," he writes, " to drop right into the society I most enjoy and from which I can learn so much." He was thrown into the company of Boughton, Alfred Parsons,

Alma Tadema, Whistler, and a dozen others who were flourishing in the appreciative art-world of London forty years ago, all unconscious of Mr. Roger Fry and the other iconoclasts looming drearily in the future. Later, Abbey went to Paris, and widened his horizon still further. He had that joyous faculty for admiration which was a pleasing feature of the generation to which he belonged. Perhaps it was a credulous generation, but it was very happy. Bastien Lepage was the idol of 1880, and to Abbey " everything looked cheap and commonplace and feeble beside that wonderful masterpiece, the " Joan of Arc." Fashions change in literature, but they change with much more disconcerting violence in plastic art.

No doubt the blossoming time of Abbey's remarkable genius came between 1880 and 1886. He made endless drawings, chiefly for American periodicals, and these designs became more and more exquisite in fancy and competent in performance. He published in 1882 a folio edition of the *Hesperides* of Herrick, to which Austin Dobson contributed a critical preface. This is one of the most delightful " illustrated " books in existence, and it gave Abbey a position at once in the front rank of draughtsmen. The engravings were very numerous—Abbey was always liberal in his work—and they possessed a surprising consistency. He had wandered among the villages of central England, and he had seized the bloom and tone of ancient rustic life in its most tender and unspoiled effects. His *Herrick* made him famous, and as soon as it was issued he set himself to a new task, an edition of *She Stoops to Conquer*. He worked slowly at this ; and he writes : " I'm doing a little poem of Pope's to keep my hand in while the big thing simmers." This was the *Ode on Solitude*—" Happy the man whose wish and care "—a choice delightfully appropriate.

Hitherto Abbey had worked almost wholly in black-and-white drawing for reproduction. Now he began to paint seriously in water-colour. His *Widower* of 1883, and his *Stony Ground* of 1884 were much admired for their sober delicacy and suppressed Puritan humour. They were specimens of his sentimental draughtsmanship translated, with elaboration, into colour. The success of these works seduced Abbey more and more completely away from black-and-white, and he became a painter, presently a painter in oils, finally a mural painter of vast compositions and a decorator of public buildings. He enjoyed every species of success; his fame steadily increased, and culminated in his receiving the commission to paint the Coronation of King Edward VII. Mr. Lucas's second volume is " roses, roses all the way," till near the end in 1911.

But to me the charm of the record resides in the first volume, with its record of poverty cheerfully borne, difficulties robustly overcome and steady progress made in the centre of a laughing group of devoted friends. It is Abbey at Broadway, the wonderful colony in Worcestershire, that the mind chiefly rests upon in contemplation of the radiant group, who painted, wrote and dreamed there among the old gardens and the russet cottages nearly forty years ago; and it is difficult for a survivor not to be convinced that it was there and then, and not in Westminster Abbey, surrounded by a crowd of assistants, that the real genius of Edwin Abbey was exhibited.

The purchaser of these large volumes may almost be left to come to his own conclusion on this matter. In later life Abbey indulged in extraordinarily brilliant colour, set off by equally intense blackness. In this mannerism he had quite a school of imitators. A great many of his gorgeous paintings are here reproduced, but, of course, they lack their colour. I have to remind myself that this book is a monument not to resent the excessive multitude of these illustrations, which, to be perfectly candid, becomes not a little

fatiguing in the second volume. I wish the artist back in
the big bald barn at Broadway, where he had such pensive
visions of *Corinna going a Maying* and *Sally in our Alley*. I
am obstinate in thinking that those beautifully simple and
antiquely sentimental recoveries of old English society, and
not huge allegories for the dome of the Pennsylvania State
Capitol, are what Abbey will be remembered by longest.

THE OXFORD SAUSAGE

THE OXFORD SAUSAGE

PICKED up on a suburban bookstall, a little volume, annoying me at first by what seemed its impenetrable reserve, ended by exciting my curiosity to the last degree. *The Oxford Sausage* bears no editor's name, its anonymous preface is designed to mislead, and its contents show no evidence of design. It is a collection of facetious copies of verse, illustrating university life, and its title-page claims that all of them are witty, *tota, merum sal. Tota* is going too far, but many of the poems are funny, and all are unfamiliar. But they cannot have been highly familiar even to readers of this reprint of 1815, since the Oxford they illustrate was the Oxford of more than half a century earlier than that.

The Oxford Sausage, as I will presently explain, emanated from Trinity ; in the following year, 1816, a graceful youth named John Henry Newman matriculated at that college. The contrast between old and new could not be made more emphatic. The first discovery about the *Sausage* is that it was, in 1815, a reprint ; the original having appeared, with a like furtiveness, in 1764. Half a century had made a great difference in social manners, yet there is no change, or very little, in the verses. In order that I might reduce and recognise the allusions, I called to my aid a powerful ally in my learned friend, Dr. William Hunt, who responded with zealous generosity. It is due to Dr. Hunt's help that I am able to give some account of an amusing and, as it seems, entirely forgotten volume. Anthologies are in the fashion to-day. Here is one which was popular in the

Universities (for Cambridge had her share) in the days of
Dr. Johnson.

The carefully concealed editor of *The Oxford Sausage* was
a man famous in his day and by no means forgotten now,
Dr. Thomas Warton. He was the author of the earliest and
long the best *History of English Poetry*, he was a poet himself and in his day a metrical innovator, but he was above
all an Oxford man. His whole life was spent in the odour
which breathes around *The Oxford Sausage*, an atmosphere
of strong tobacco and foaming ale, Latin quotations, and
endless conversation. By 1764 Warton was already a Fellow
of Trinity College and Professor of Poetry, as well as the
author of many serious works ; so that he might well not
be anxious to appear as the compiler of a book of local
songs, all frivolous, and some not decent. So he wrote a
preface, warning readers not to try to discover who the
editor was, and especially not to suppose him to be the
author of the anonymous *Companion to the Guide to Oxford*
and of *Terræ Filius*, because " most unluckily the author of
those pieces will never be known."

This was very sly, because these were not the same
person, *Terræ Filius* being the work of a rapscallion called
Nicholas Amhurst, long dead by 1764 ; and the *Companion*
—oh ! what a deceitful professor—being written by Warton
himself ! He slipped into the *Sausage* several poems of his
own, of course without his name. Dr. Hunt has identified
some of them for me, but there is one, the satire called *New-
market*, which there could be no mystery about, since
Warton had openly published it thirteen years earlier. I
wish that Dr. Hunt could find it in his heart to turn for an
hour from sterner investigations and publish an annotated
edition of *The Oxford Sausage*. No book is in more need of
editing, and no one more capable of fulfilling such a task
than the late President of the Royal Historical Society.

The exposure of university life which Gibbon makes in

his *Autobiography* has often been quoted, and has been
charged with exaggeration. " The Fellows or monks of my
time were decent, easy men who supinely enjoyed the
gifts of the founder. . . . From the toil of reading, writing,
or thinking they had absolved their consciences." The
verses in *The Oxford Sausage*, whether satirical, Bacchanalian, or merely frivolous, confirm the judgment of Gibbon.
Here is part of a picture of " the peaceful Fellows," probably
from the pen of Warton himself :—

> " No chattering females crowd their social fire,
>   No dread have they of discord and of strife,
> Unknown the names of Husband and of Sire,
>   Unfelt the plagues of matrimonial life.

> " Oft have they basked along the sunny walls ;
>   Oft have the benches bowed beneath their weight ;
> How jocund are their looks when dinner calls !
>   How smoke their cutlets on the crowded plate !

> " O, let not Temperance too disdainful hear
>   How long our Feasts, how long our Dinners last ;
> Nor let the Fair with a contemptuous sneer
>   On these unmarried men reflections cast ! "

Historians, such as Mr. Christopher Wordsworth, confirm
the impression which these verses give. In the generation
previous to *The Oxford Sausage*, the University, strongly
Jacobite and disloyal to the House of Hanover, had been
kept from stagnation by its political anxieties. But after
1745 slumber fell on Oxford. Professors were silent, college
tutors grew inefficient, discipline was relaxed. The first
Lord Malmesbury, writing of the very year when the
Sausage appeared, describes the utter looseness of rule.
Undergraduates could absent themselves when they pleased,
and go off to town. His own tutor, " a worthy man," did
not " concern himself with his pupils." This is the tone
revealed throughout the verses of *The Oxford Sausage*.

But Thomas Warton himself was far removed from the
lazy type of the college don, who

> " to thoughtless ignorance a prey,
> Neglects to hold short dalliance with a book."

He was full of intellectual curiosity and creative energy. Nevertheless, the stamp of the Oxford of 1750 was upon him. In the common-room of Trinity College, where through so many evenings he drank beer and smoked a churchwarden, flung his grizzle wig over the back of his chair, and discoursed on black-letter folios and the versification of Chaucer, there hangs to this day his admirable portrait painted by Sir Joshua Reynolds.

When Warton was brought to Streatham to be presented to Fanny Burney, that stringent judge of men pronounced him " unformed in his manners and awkward in his gestures. He joined not one word in the general talk." No doubt, the elegant author of *Evelina* was not of the world of Tom Warton, who was unaccustomed to the society of females ; yet when he got back to Trinity, he would once more become the life and soul of the common-room. There he talked with wit and copiousness, though unfortunately in a voice which was said to be like the gobble of a turkey-cock. He was a privileged enthusiast, who was known to have once, at least, ventured on wearing a crown of laurel. His heavy body was not prone to violent exercise, but he was fond of walking along the river, with a pipe in his mouth, while he chatted with the watermen. We may think of him so, or trying to rouse enthusiasm by lecturing in Latin to a languid class of students. Either way, he was the antithesis of the typical college don of the period, and the idle, guzzling University which he mocked and loved is mirrored in his *Oxford Sausage*.

Good-natured in the extreme, Warton shows his easy temper by printing in *The Oxford Sausage* a skit upon himself ; or, perhaps, was that a blind—who knows ? Michael Wodhull, of Brasenose, was the author of the *Ode to Criticism*, which ridicules *The Triumph of Isis*, a serious poem which Warton had published in 1749. But Wodhull was a famous book-collector, whose library contained black-letter treasures which Warton may have been anxious to consult. He is not so kind to all contemporary antiquaries, since a parody of the ballad of *Chevy Chase* pokes fun at Browne Willis, whose books about the English cathedrals are still of value. Faded shadows, most of the famous figures in this book, but I should like to know more about Herbert Beaver, who is not in the *Dictionary of National Biography*. He is the author here of *The Cushion Plot*, a very vivacious ballad, recounting the adventures of Dr. Shaw, head of " Teddy " Hall, who was called " Gaby " :—

" When Gaby possession had got of the Hall,
  He took a survey of the Chapel and all,
  Since that, like the rest, was just ready to fall,
            Which nobody can deny.
" And first he began to examine the chest,
  Where he found an old cushion which gave him distaste,
  The first of the kind that e'er troubled his rest,
            Which nobody can deny,"

this cushion having embroidered on it, in letters of gold, a device which might be either Jacobite or Georgian. Dr. Hunt has found out that Beaver, who was Superior Beadle at Law to the University, had a public scuffle with one Yeats, which occupied the idle attention of Oxford. Here was a subject for a ballad of which *The Oxford Sausage* failed to take advantage. It is difficult to account for a footnote which speaks of St. Edmund's Hall as a " College," and its Principal as the " President." A foreigner making this double blunder would be withered by Oxonian sarcasm.

Light is thrown by various poems in the *Sausage* on the relaxations of University life. The gentlemen commoners, being men of fashion, affected riding, horse-racing, and driving. On Sundays they rode

" With hat new-cock'd, and newly laced,
  O'er mutton-chops and scanty wine
  At humble Dorchester to dine."

Cock-fighting in the pit in Holywell had been forbidden by the Vice-Chancellor, but was winked at elsewhere.

There was some tennis for the richer and some billiards for the poorer men, but very little. Undergraduates, scarcely more than boys in those days, amused themselves with walks, skittles, and quoits. There is here a mention of rowing for pleasure :—

> " No more the wherry feels my stroke so true ;
>   At skittles in a grizzle can I play ?
> Woodstock, farewell ! and Wallingford adieu !
>   Where many a scheme relieved the lingering day,"

sighs the scholar promoted to the immobility of a Fellowship. The exercise of the skittle-yard was looked upon with favour by the college authorities as encouraging a game " founded on arithmetical and geometrical principles." The absence of any mention of cricket or football will be noted. I think that neither of these games was played at all prominently in Oxford during the eighteenth century ; to Cambridge I fancy that lads coming up from Eton may have brought a certain amount of school tradition with them, but not to Oxford. Every year, from 1754 at least, there was circulated through the University by the bellman a copy of rhymes called *The Oxford Newsman's Verses.* These were occupied with every description of local tittle-tattle, but there occurs in them not a word about those amusements which now absorb undergraduate attention.

The editor of *The Oxford Sausage* was but thirty-six years of age, but his ways were already settled, and it is notable that he consistently looks backward and not forward. He would not have sympathised with Lord Haldane's call to the heights, nor is there the slightest hint that he saw around him any revival of enthusiasm or earnestness. Warton had plenty of humanism, but it was not in the least idealistic, and in this respect he was abreast of his time and not a step in front of it. But he looked back with veneration on the isolated scholars who had preserved Oxford from reproach in the previous generation, and particularly on the wonderful and isolated figure of

Thomas Hearne, the *architypographus* to the University, whom Warton can scarcely have known in person, since Hearne died, in his rooms in college, in 1735, when Warton was a child. The *Epistle* from Hearne is doubtless a mystification ; in it the spirit of the great persecuted antiquary sarcastically congratulates Warton on the disfavour now shown by the Oxford fellows to every kind of research. I fail to grasp the allusion in the lines :—

> " Cruel as the mandate
> Of mitred priests, who Baskett late enjoined
> To throw aside the reverend letters black,
> And print Fast Prayers in modern type."

But it is part of a lamentation appropriately put in the mouth of Hearne, who, though no house in Oxford " had so rich a furniture " in his eyes as the Bodleian, was not merely dismissed from his post there as a punishment for his non-juring convictions, but was positively forbidden, in the midst of his unrivalled investigations, to enter the Library. This was a shameful piece of tyranny. I find little reference in *The Oxford Sausage* to discord between Whigs and Jacobites, doubtless because after 1760 the Jacobite question ceased to be a burning one, though it is neatly summed up in Beaver's ballad of *The Cushion Plot*, to which I have already referred.

From a *Panegyric on Oxford Ale*, which I am disposed to attribute to the pen of Thomas Warton himself, I take a passage characteristic of English versification in 1764, modified as it had become by the influence of Thomson and Young, and equally descriptive of the duller side of college life :—

> " All powerful ALE ! Thy sorrow-soothing sweets
> Oft I repeat in vacant afternoon,
> When tatter'd stockings crave my mending hand
> Not unexperienced ; while the tedious toil
> Slides unregarded. Let the tender swain
> Each morn regale on nerve-relaxing Tea,
> Companion meet of languor-loving nymph :

> Be mine each morn, with eager appetite
> And hunger undissembled, to repair
> To friendly Buttery ; there on smoking crust
> And foaming Ale to banquet unrestrained,
> Material breakfast ! "

Tea, at about a shilling an ounce, was still a luxury, not to be wasted on a serious meal like breakfast, but to be reserved for some special occasion when, as *Terræ Filius* tells us, the scholar had the privilege of sipping it, " after Prayers, with some celebrated toast."

GEORGIAN POETRY

GEORGIAN POETRY

ELEVEN years ago appeared the first volume of a work destined, I believe, to occupy a prominent place in the history of contemporary literature. The accomplished connoisseur, who faintly conceals his name under the initials " E. M.," had been struck by the fact that English poetry was blossoming anew in a parterre which was but rarely and negligently visited. A number of young writers, actuated by similar aims, were putting forth little volumes which contained beautiful passages, but were seldom observed by reviewers or by the public. Guided solely by his own taste, he gathered an anthology out of the best of these and published it as *Georgian Poetry*.

The success of the venture was immediate and prolonged. Poets whose isolated productions had been unnoticed woke up to find themselves famous beneath the ægis of " E. M." Rupert Brooke and James Elroy Flecker were the main ornaments of the first collection, and when a second instalment came (in 1916) it was inscribed to their memory. What I hold before me to-day is the fifth volume of *Georgian Poets*, 1920–22, and while the general order and character of the work remain unchanged, time has not been negligent in modification. Several writers who, in 1912, were threatening to become middle-aged, have been placed on the retired list ; and death has made further inroads.

The principle on which the selection was originally conceived is maintained. Seven new writers have this time been introduced, with varying advantage to the scheme.

On the other hand, there are seven of the older members who " do not exhibit this year," as the formula runs in the case of older Academies. This is unfortunate, since among the absentees are the three most energetic of the Georgian set—Mr. Masefield, Mr. Ralph Hodgson, and Mr. Siegfried Sassoon. It cannot be denied that this particular volume labours under a disadvantage from their temporary abeyance.

No previous instalment of *Georgian Poets* has had any but the briefest preface from the editor's pen. But in this case " E. M." has signed a more or less facetious introduction. He takes up several objections which wandering reviewers have ventured to make and he replies to them. His answers give me a text for a further reply, although I am certainly not one of the reviewers to whom he refers. He says, with amusing exaggeration, that he has been treated as a sort of President of an Academy, fitted to " bestow and withhold crowns and sceptres, and decide that this or that poet was or was not to count." Well, in quieter language, that is exactly what he has shown himself fitted to do, and, what is much more remarkable, his competence in doing it has been almost universally admitted.

" E. M." should bear his honours patiently, for it is undeniable that his scheme has responded to the need for gregarious selection which affects groups of persons, engaged, with unequal skill, on the same task. Force is obtained by eliminating the weak elements and welding the strong together, and to do this is to found a successful Academy. Certainly, " E. M." had no such aim when he originally insisted on the recognition of certain gifted poets who had achieved no notoriety. But this is what his venture has come to be. The choice of names included in the list is not an arbitrary one. It advances a young writer to the honour of *hors concours*, and the successive biennial volumes of the publication are really no more nor less than the transactions of the Academy of Georgian Poets. The diffidence of " E. M." is misplaced.

Another objection which, as I learn from this preface, has been brought against the poets is that their works display " an insipid sameness," and that they are " merely a small clique of mutually indistinguishable poetasters." " E. M." seems to be a master of the art of making an opponent ridiculous by exaggerating his strictures. To say that the admirable poets who owe much to " E. M.'s " discrimination, but still more to their own genius, are " indistinguishable " one from another is absurd. But the emphasis of the benevolent editor ought not to blind us to what is a real and a very curious peculiarity. The poets who have become prominent in the present century are, with all deference to " E. M.'s " sarcastic explosion, remarkable for their general identity. They form a school in a degree which has rarely been seen in this country, but has frequently marked the poetry of Italy and France, and was present, with us, among the Elizabethan lyrists. The close resemblance of the style of Coleridge to that of Wordsworth at an early date is a parallel instance. I will name no names, because I am anxious to avoid all offence, but in the volume before me I have marked five or six passages from different poets which might certainly appear as the work of a single writer without exciting the slightest suspicion.

Among the great Victorians it was otherwise. No one could possibly be persuaded that a page of Browning was written by Rossetti, or be doubtful whether a stanza was the work of Swinburne or of Patmore. But a strong personal note of character is lacking among many of the Georgians, and " E. M." should remember that although the shepherd knows his individual sheep by their faces, a whole flock is apt to look very much the same to a candid public. When the standard of artistic merit is so high as it is in the present case, similarity is hardly in itself a defect.

Criticism of contemporaries must always be limited and superficial, since growing organisms cannot be definitely measured. But, in comparing the output of 1922 with that of 1911, I have to confess that I see little evidence of evolution, of progress. Perhaps it is an error to expect from poetry, which is eminently a perfection of early youth, any sign of growth. Most of our lyric poets have written their best pieces, and have exhibited the fullness of their powers, before they were thirty. But it was my hope that the new writers, now admitted to the sacred ranks from which expulsion is impossible and where fame becomes mechanical, would go a little further than their forbears, and strike out in new directions.

Of this I see but one example, Mr. Edmund Blunden, whose future will be watched with the most eager anticipation. He displays all the characteristics of a mind inspired by the close and independent contemplation of nature exercised in imagination. That he is under the spell of John Clare is evident ; and is curious, since Clare never boasted a disciple before. Mr. Blunden will grow out of this, when he perceives that why Clare was not a poet of the first rank was that his attention was hampered by incessant beauties, and that he lacked the gift of selective apprehension. Already, in the very remarkable piece in which " The Giant Puffball " speaks, Mr. Blunden has got beyond Clare, and I have no doubt that he will rise much further yet. No more interesting star has appeared of late in our poetical heavens.

The determination to be anything rather than rhetorical is a snare to the Georgians. They are pertinacious in avoiding any appeal to the movement of experience and thought. They reject general ideas in favour of a pictorial representation of the physical phenomena of life, and they approach more closely than any previous school of English poetry has done to the method of the cinematograph.

They will have everything concrete, nothing abstract.
An example is the clever and accurate piece of rhymed
observation called *Miss Thompson Goes Shopping*, where
every artifice of style is expended on a long description,
excessively minute, of a spinster's excursion down the street
of a country town in the evening to buy articles for her
house. It could not be more vivid in its congregation of
details, but at the end of it the reader asks what is the use
of such a catalogue of trivialities.   The poet stands entirely
outside Miss Thompson, whose footsteps he dogs, while his
photographic apparatus melodiously clicks out its couplets.
But the result is a " film picture," and nothing more. The
same almost crazy fear of being " rhetorical " plunges the
poets in occasional bathos. They are so determined to be
simple that they succeed in being silly. When one of the
new Academicians remarks,

> " I know a farmer in Camden Town
> Killed a brock by Pentonville,"

and when another says,

> " I lingered at a gate and talked
> A little with a lonely lamb,"

they fail to ask themselves whether the confessions are of
general interest to anybody.   Coleridge, who wrote an ode
to a Young Ass, whom he hailed as " brother "—

> " I love the languid patience of thy face— "

nevertheless rebuked Wordsworth " for attaching himself
to the low in his desire to avoid the genteel."   So difficult
is it to see ourselves as others see us ! But the Georgians
would do well to quit addressing poetry to lambs and
donkeys and badgers, in spite of the precedent of W. W.
and S. T. C.
  If we take the contents of this volume as typical of what
is best in the poetry of the present day we may regard the
Georgians as jewellers, while the Victorians were sculptors.

The broad outline, the radiating vistas of intellectual and moral life do not interest these young poets in the least. Their eyes are not lifted to the mountains, but are occupied in minute inspection of the ground. They listen to the whisper of their own inner feelings, and the daisy at their feet doth the same tale repeat. The result is that they lack in some degree the sense of proportion. They know not what to withhold, and they sow with the whole sack. No generation of writers, I suppose, was ever more obsessed with the charm of nervous sensibility, cultivated for its own sake, and not shrinking even from an apparently prosaic diction in order to emphasise its penetration. As a French contemporary has put it for them :—

" L'ombre mouvante est dans les choses minuscules."

All this is very interesting and very sympathetic, yet there may be a danger in this eclectic refinement of the Georgians. They are exquisite, but poetry should not always be " breathing through silver." In their critical performances we see the Georgians shrinking, as if in physical pain, from the robustness of Mr. Kipling, from the trumpet-note of Sir Henry Newbolt, from the breadth of Mr. Noyes, from the sonority of Sir William Watson. They hardly attempt to conceal that they think these manifestations of energy vulgar.

If, however, I have been drawn to express my consciousness of some lack of variety and some narrowness of purpose in certain of these sectarian singers, I am not insensible to their accomplishment. They are admirable artificers of verse, and I rejoice to find them less and less drawn away from wholesome tradition by the lure of metrical experiment. Apollo be praised, there is not in this fifth volume a single piece of prose cut up into lengths and called *vers libre !* To pass to particulars, the passionate and wayward fancy of Mr. Walter de la Mare is still dominant, as it has been from the beginning. He has always struck the peculiar chord to which all the others have gone dancing, each in his own way. Landscape, poignantly felt and searchingly described, continues to be a leading feature of the Georgians, and Mr. Lascelles Abercrombie, in *Ryton Firs*, brings the very colour and form and smell of Gloucestershire across our senses. Where the subjective tone prevails, the objective of *Full Moon* is welcome. I am constrained to quote this amusing little piece, by V. Sackville-West (Mrs. Harold Nicolson), the only woman, I think, yet admitted to the Georgian Academy :—

> " She was wearing the coral taffeta trousers
>   Some one had brought her from Ispahan,
>   And the little gold coat with pomegranate blossoms,
>   And the coral-hafted feather fan ;
>   But she ran down a Kentish lane in the moonlight,
>   And skipped in the pool of the moon as she ran.
>
> " She cared not a rap for all the big planets,
>   For Betelgeuse or Aldebaran,
>   And all the big planets cared nothing for her,
>   That small, impertinent charlatan ;
>   But she climbed on a Kentish stile in the moonlight,
>   And laughed at the sky through the sticks of her fan."

Mr. Francis Brett Young is delightful in the plaintive futility and shadowy pathos of *The Quails ;* Mr. Squire very moving in his *Elegy ;* Mr. Robert Nichols—but if I proceed I shall have to mention all the poets, or almost all. " E. M." is to be warmly congratulated on his fifth Transactions, but before 1925 I hope he will have recaptured Mr. Masefield and Mr. Hodgson and Mr. Sassoon.

THE WOLSELEYS

THE WOLSELEYS

THE classic instance of the publication of letters
exchanged between husband and wife is the correspondence
of Robert and Elizabeth Browning, authorised by their son
a quarter of a century ago. The letters of Lord and Lady
Wolseley, now given to the public, resemble those of the
Brownings in their mutual confidence and warm unbroken
cordiality, but the circumstances which they represent are
very different. The letters of Robert and Elizabeth were
all written within a comparatively short time and in a
consistent mood. They are almost to be described as the
continuation of talk, binding one confidential interview
to another. They have great intensity, but suffer from a
certain monotony of theme and manner.

The letters of the Wolseleys have not this uniformity of
time or mood. They are a series of groups or fragments,
called forth by the professional absences of the husband or
the rare excursions of the wife. In consequence, they offer
no outline of the careers of the couple, and are in part only
made intelligible by the brief introductions of Sir George
Arthur. It is plain that the editor has been anxious not
to put himself prominently forward, and it may be held
that in some respects he has carried modesty too far. He
starts the book with a strange abruptness. Neither the
year of the birth nor of the death of either protagonist,
nor the date of their marriage is given, and I think the
volume may be searched from cover to cover without any
revelation of Lady Wolseley's christian name or maiden
surname. A prefatory page (or a paragraph) of skeleton

biography would have been a great aid to the reader, who cannot be expected to carry in his head the data which he needs for appreciation of the sequence of events.

Garnet Wolseley and Louisa Erskine were married in 1867, three years before the earliest letter in this book was written. He was thirty-four, and had already modestly distinguished himself in various overseas directions, as may be read in his *Story of a Soldier's Life*. After returning from China he had been sent to Canada, where his record was respectable but not brilliant, when the outbreak of the Red River Rebellion suddenly gave him an opportunity of showing what he could do. He conducted the expedition with extraordinary rapidity and economy, and he added the province of Manitoba to the Commonwealth of Canada. He was not made Governor, as he hoped to be, but he returned home a popular hero.

The next batch of letters deals with the Ashantee War, Wolseley's second and still more brilliant campaign. He was by this time known as a reformer at the War Office, and his energy and perseverance had gained him strong friends as well as inveterate enemies. He describes to his wife adventures that culminated in the capture of Coomassie, and he comes back to be feted by Royalty at Osborne, where " a splendid man, six feet high, in red coat and powdered hair, has just come in for letters ; so good-night, pleasant dreams." The next group of letters deals with Zululand and the Kaffir Rising of 1875, and the next with Cyprus. The quality of Lord Wolseley's correspondence steadily improves. He learns what to say in his private communications, and what to omit. The impact of his wife's active and cultivated mind is seen on his, and after a while the two write in a manner so identical that it is only by the subject or the situation that we can tell one from the other. Lady Wolseley never allowed her affection to blind her to a motherly function which she exercised over the lighter and least professional side of her husband's mind. She taught him to observe and to describe what he observed. She even was untiring in trying to correct his incorrigible spelling.

The official biography of Lord Wolseley, which Sir George Arthur and Sir Frederick Maurice are understood to be preparing in concert, will be so largely taken up by the splendid actions and the exacerbated disputes of his brilliant public career that the details of his domestic happiness cannot expect to be prominent. Hence the merit and the value of these delightful letters addressed to and by the one faithful and clear-sighted companion, who, in Sir George Arthur's felicitous phrase, after having " stimulated and strengthened him in his feverishly busy noon, cheered and made easy his quiet evening." In the midst of his marvellous success, Wolseley had moments of disappointment and discouragement. Typical of these is the very remarkable letter from Dongola, of November 24, 1884, when a wave of premonition of the fate of Gordon, and the practical failure of the expedition, seemed to have swept over him. Here is a Wolseley of whom the world knew nothing, writing to his unfailing comforter in London :—

" It is troubles of this sort that make men old before their time, and I have been so hounded down by enemies at home, that the thought of failure is to me more dreadful than it would be to one who would merely be regarded as having failed to accomplish a very difficult or impossible task. My only real trouble is time. My task would be simple if I had a couple more months of cool weather before me than I can calculate upon. I know you don't take the same views I do upon the interposition of God in all our doings. I wish you did. How often I have escaped death by a hair's-breadth, always with the feeling that God watched over me. This was when no responsibility rested on my shoulders ; but I have realised it far more since chief command lies on me."

We learn with what tenderness, with what playfulness and with how bright a wit Lady Wolseley dispersed, at all events for the moment, the clouds of her great husband's legitimate anxiety.

The character of Lady Wolseley cannot be comprehended

without recognition of the fact that she, like her husband, was of the romantic order. I use the word in no slighting or dishonourable sense when I say they they were " adventurers." Neither had been born in a great hereditary position ; they rose side by side into a social prominence which they enjoyed, but the basis of which they always knew to be uncertain. Neither was ever quite at ease in Zion ; there were always Philistines to be looked out for, hiding behind the bushes. Through the difficulties of a life the very energy of which was for ever hurting somebody's susceptibility, Lord and Lady Wolseley proceeded, borne along, like the nautilus on a summer ocean, on the tide of their own high spirits. They met with adverse waves, which vexed them both, but over which they rode with purple wings unfurled. In 1882 Wolseley finds the Court influence " all steadily against me. I have done all I could lately to mollify the Queen's dislike to me and to gain her favour." Lady Wolseley is snubbed by great ladies, but these always get the worst of it, while the irresistible Field-Marshal finally conquers even the coldness of Victoria.

All this will come out, of course, more plainly and consecutively in the memoir, yet already in these letters we read between the lines. No doubt Sir George Arthur has omitted much, for the pair were reckless in invective, but, on the whole, there is nothing here that seems to me scandalous. I only hope that the various ladies described as " fascinating hippopotamuses " and " fat old humble-bees " have by this time passed into a better world, along with " that crocodile, Gladstone." But their initials (with a dash) may not conceal them from outraged relatives, whose feelings, perhaps, will be best kept to themselves.

Louisa Erskine had qualities which clearly fitted her to be the wife of the Field-Marshal. Her mind and will grew with his, and as time progressed their practical identity

of purpose became complete. Both, being human, had
faults, but these did not affect their personal relation.
She was natural and sincere to a remarkable degree, and she
spared on no proper occasion her " mild reproof," even to
her adored companion. Lady Wolseley had a directness of
speech which was sometimes disconcerting, and the slight
difficulty in her social relations made her curiously vigilant.
Her repartees were acid and direct, and she uttered them
with remarkable gusto. But it was not until she was
attacked, or conceived that attack was coming, that she
made use of these weapons. In the company of people whom
she liked she was extremely agreeable, and even coquettish.

Every mood in her manner is reflected in the Field-
Marshal's letters ; she pipes and he dances ; they dance
together, with peals of laughter, at the grassy edge of the
abysm. She had a great influence in keeping him, in the
midst of his complications, actions, and advances, the
light-hearted boy which he remained until he was over
sixty-five. Lady Wolseley's letters have no air of composition, but they were delightful to receive. There was
always some turn of absurdity in them, some touch of
heightened colour. She wrote so well that it may seem
surprising that she resisted what must have been the
temptation to write for the public. But she was a mixture
of indolence and energy, and it was quite enough for her
to amuse her General. Their occasional separations were
distinctly beneficial to their mutual attitude. It was said
of two more famous relatives and letter-writers that if
they were too much together " *elles se tuaient l'une l'autre.*"
Occasional separation was the best way to prevent a watch-
ful affection from becoming too exorbitant.

The noble pair possessed, or cultivated, several tastes
which their correspondence amply illustrates. The
primæval tendency of the soldier to reward his own labours
by the acquisition of loot took, in a warrior so highly

civilised as Lord Wolseley, the subdued form of a passion
for bric-à-brac. This amounted in his wife's case to an
infatuation ; she so actively purchased beautiful objects,
and got tired of them, and then sold them to buy others,
that she almost deserved the title of *brocanteuse*. I remember how, a great many years ago, expecting to be with her
in Venice, Sir Redvers Buller warned me : " Don't let her
drag you into the curiosity-shops, or your life will be a
burden to you ! " The letters, on both sides, are full of
information about " a little old box about the size of an
orange, in real old Russian enamel, very quaint," which
Lord Wolseley annexes in Moscow, and Napoleon's wash-
hand-basin from Elba, which Lady Wolseley longs for at
Marienbad. When the Sultan sends the wife a large green
velvet box containing a handsome star made up of " good "
diamonds, rubies, and emeralds, the husband becomes
quite lyrical. The love of delicate sparkling things which
they shared was very innocent and amusing. Their taste
in books, in pictures, in the theatre (which they both loved),
was identical. They liked eighteenth-century memoirs,
old-fashioned novels, and Victorian paintings that were
not *too* Victorian. They called Tennyson " old Pass-the-
Salt."

Sir George Arthur promises, as I have said, a full and
military memoir of the Field-Marshal. I hope he will not
too long delay the production of it, since the general effect
of these letters on readers whose memories are short, or
whose imaginations are defective, may be unfortunate.
Here is a great man displayed absolutely as his valet would
be shocked to see him, in his dressing-gown, without his
jack-boots, and careless of his dignity. Amusing to think
how very different the private correspondence of an eminent
Continental general would be from these frank and unpre-
meditated letters ! No Frenchman, for instance, could
write even to his wife without a certain *panache*, without

waving ever so little the banner of *la gloire*. Lord Wolseley, just before the battle of Tel-el-Kebir, reflects " how much pleasanter is death from clean bullet wounds than from loathsome diseases, to be killed in the open air with the conviction that you are dying for your country." That is as near as he ever gets to the heroic, and the moderation, simplicity and joviality of those letters may, for the moment, do his great memory some harm with idle readers. Sir George Arthur's future volumes will correct any such silly censure. They will show that Wolseley was great enough to be perfectly natural, to be on easy terms with life. Let no vivacity of private speech lead us to forget what England owes to the courage, the sagacity, the organising genius of one of the greatest of all her historic soldiers.

As Lady Wolseley will pass into the background in the official biography, I must give here an example of her sprightly pen. This is the sort of thing with which she enlivened the mail-bag of her exiled General :—

" Well, yesterday we had our luncheon with our neighbours. I said, going, ' We shall have roast pheasant (*un plat fin*),' and roast pheasant we had ! Madame *mère* is a very mysterious person, huge, with a nice face. Head, with a sort of Cenci, mummy, Madonna (I can't say *what* it is) wrapping up of white thin silk ; draped black garment strangely pinned about with little brooches. A gigantic spar or marble heart pendant on her bosom (very ample that, too). If it was all meant for simplicity, it was marvellously laboured. The parlour-maids, too, were most extraordinary. They might have been odalisques, or nautch girls, or *vivandières*, or anything except parlour-maids."

This has something of the Sévigné touch, and Lady Wolseley reminds the friends who knew her, as well as those who now for the first time meet her, of some great lady in the times of Louis XIV. and XV. The parallel might be carried far. Socially, like so many of the old French nobility, she was not quite sure of the stability of the fabric on which she had arrived, but what matters to us is that she was always perfectly sure of her Field-Marshal. He never failed her, and in a maelstrom of society they would have been found clinging to one another. That gives this otherwise trivial collection of domestic letters its permanent value as a document.

But, will it be credited—as schoolmasters say—this bulky volume is rendered useless for all historic purposes by possessing *no Index ?* Not a name nor a passage in it can ever in future times be referred to ! Something very serious will have to be done to publishers if they go on behaving in this way. I am weary of expostulating with them.*

---

* I allow the text to remain as I wrote it, since it gives me an opportunity to applaud the action of the publishers, who, in consequence of my appeal, have not merely added an index to the second edition of the *Wolseley Letters*, but have determined to offer copies of that index to the possessors of the original book. Would that the power of this poor pen of mine could lead more often to such virtuous resolutions !

M. BOURGET'S NOVELS

M. BOURGET'S NOVELS

THE book-world of Paris is waking up once more to a great animation, but it cannot escape the notice of an observer that the War has had an extraordinary effect in altering its general character. The imaginative literature of France has suffered a sea-change, and coral has been made of the bones of those who danced so gaily along its shore a decade ago. The War defined and accelerated a movement which was already beginning, while circumstances not obviously connected with the great struggle have combined to hurry it on. Briefly, we look around in vain to-day for the principal novelists who adorned the beginning of the century. They have disappeared; some are dead, like Octave Mirbeau; some, like M. Maurice Barrès, are occupied on other tasks; some, like M. Pierre Loti, are silent.

But there is one eminent novelist, on whom the passage of time and taste seems to have no effect, one servant of the public who caters with unabated industry for the pleasure of his old-fashioned readers. This is M. Paul Bourget, who has been writing for more than forty years, and who wrote novels all through the War, and who has gone on writing novels ever since. The simultaneous publication of two solid and elaborate romances, quite independent of one another, should recall to our minds the persistency of an old and faithful favourite.

In these days we read little about the work of M. Bourget in current Parisian criticism. And this gives me occasion to repeat what I have several times ventured to point out, that English writers on French literature make a serious mistake when they simply echo the latest opinion of the boulevards. If M. Bourget is not at this moment widely discussed in France, it is because he has been so much discussed in past years that there is nothing fresh to say about him. His work is extremely copious, and it is remarkably uniform. Its merits and deficiencies have been so abundantly reviewed that there is, for the moment, nothing fresh for a Frenchman to say about them.

But in England we can hardly permit ourselves to take so completely for granted a very prominent and gifted veteran of letters, nor need we accept without demur the hasty judgments of the young critics who are tired of M. Bourget and predisposed to express their satiety with petulance. For us, who read less and must make a selection, it is proper to take a somewhat different view of the veteran author of more than fifty volumes of fiction, verse, philosophy, and description. Very few of us, I imagine, can pretend to have read all these books, or half of them ; but our imaginative education is incomplete if we do not take the mass of them into more sympathetic consideration than they receive at this particular moment in Paris.

To realise what M. Bourget stands for, it is necessary for us to recollect what the state of French fiction was when he began to write, which was, I think, about 1874. He was a pupil of Taine, and, of all the young men who sat under the shadow of that spreading tree, he was the most earnest and the most active. It was the age of the Triumph of Naturalism and of Zola, when that consummate propagandist, by precept as well as by practice, and supported by a horde of young followers, had succeeded, as it seemed, in driving out of French fiction everything that was not documentary and external. The novelist was to be a Naturalist—that is to say, he was to be exclusively occupied with the substance of the human machine ; his sole business was to reduce the spiritual elements to physical—in other words, to attend to the outer envelope of life. It was the central dogma of Zola that the novel must not be aware of any standard of morality, but must review conduct as it exists, from a material and experimental point of view.

When this was quite accepted, and when it was recognised that no future romances were ever to deal with the phenomena of the soul, young M. Bourget produced *Cruelle Enigme* and *Un Crime d'Amour*, in which an analysis of the soul was the only theme, and the excuse for the story. Zola went on from bad to worse, with *La Terre* and other such human secretions, but the axe was laid at the foot of the naturalistic tree, and young M. Bourget was the woodman.

Then, in 1889, occurred an incident which will always secure a place in the history of literature. The three or four novels which M. Bourget had hitherto published were studies of fashionable society, a little too musky and precious for everybody's taste, and dealing mainly with the spiritual agonies of frail ladies of title. No doubt this was done on purpose ; the scenes of the Naturalists being laid in squalid conditions, the new novelist emphasised the refinements of " high life." This M. Bourget has always been blamed for exaggerating, and, indeed, there are more countesses and marchionesses in his novels than in the pages of the *Almanach de Gotha*.

But his next book, *Le Disciple*, was wholly serious. It presented a sort of Spinoza, a M. Adrian Sixte, an elderly philosopher of spotless life whose scientific theories, accepted by a libertine pupil, provoke the latter to commit an odious crime. Great moral questions were started by this book, which led to a famous public discussion between Brunetière, who was all for discipline, and M. Anatole France, who was all for liberty, as to whether ideas react on morals ; whether, in fact, those who start emancipating theories are responsible if their teaching leads in crude hands to criminal conduct. It was a very nice point, and was argued with great heat and vehemence, very much to the advantage, of course, of M. Bourget and his publisher. But the novelist's line was now clearly marked. He was in future to be the champion of philosophy as the handmaid of religion, and that is what he has been ever since.

Most successful novelists write because they possess an irresistible faculty for story-telling. M. Bourget, on the contrary, is a practised psychological analyst, who took to novel writing as an illustration of his theories. The world does not very kindly embrace the analytical novel, while few novelists have undergone the mental training which would fit them to produce it. In English literature, I can think of no writer of fiction who is to be compared with M. Bourget except George Eliot, in her later forms. The author of *Daniel Deronda*, if she had been a Frenchwoman, might have written *L'Etape ;* the parallel is, indeed, somewhat close. The objections which are brought against M. Bourget's studies in experimental psychology are exactly those which, after her great splendour began to wane, were brought against George Eliot. In each case the simplicity and vitality of narrative are injured by what has been noted as the danger lying ahead of every philosophical novelist— namely, that of being " too exposedly constructive."

In M. Bourget's fashionable novels, the loud sound of the intellectual wheel is apt to drown the murmur of the stream of narrative. He is too prophetic ; he stands aside and bids us notice what his characters are going to do, and why they will do it ; and also how inevitable, with the sort of character which he has invented for them, their particular line of action is. In short, he spoils his art by an excess of science, and defines his aim too rapidly for a genuine imitation of contemporary manners. In this connection, however, it is only fair that I should translate a passage from one of the new novels before me. After a page of moral analysis, in the course of *L'Ecuyère*, the author says :—

> " This philosophy may seem very serious, as the framework for a frivolous anecdote of Parisian life twenty years ago. But the most trifling facts of nature, closely examined, may serve to enable a biological observer to demonstrate great laws ; and why should the historian of nature be refused the privilege of applying the same method to the incidents which he relates, giving them their full value by indicating the causes which led to them ? "

We might answer that the great masters of analysis, like Richardson or Marivaux, are content with the facts, and avoid indicating the causes. It is a weakness in George Eliot that she persists in subordinating observation to philosophical doctrine, and this is M. Bourget's weakness also. Henry James, in a fine letter recently published, dared to bring this home to his French colleague ; he warned the author of *La Duchesse Bleue* that the persons of his novels " act too immediately in character." The truth of this charge might be exemplified from almost any one of M. Bourget's powerful and strenuous but too mechanical inventions. It is with him too constantly the psychology that wags the story, not the story that carries the psychology.

These considerations need not unduly debar us from enjoying the two new stories, *L'Ecuyère* and *Un Drame dans le Monde*, but they ought to be present with us when we read them. The former is simplicity itself when stripped of its philosophical trappings. It is the very pathetic story of a young English circus rider—settled with her father, a worthy horse-dealer, in a corner of Paris—who attracts the notice of an idle young nobleman. She is pure and simple, and he jilts her with savage selfishness, but under a pressure of circumstances most ingeniously invented. All M. Bourget's bitter morality, his *sæva indignatio*, is concentrated on the analysis of the false suitor's character.

The end of *L'Ecuyère* is complete tragedy. *Un Drame dans le Monde* is more sensational, and more directly addressed to edification. It deals with the result of a double crime, poisoning and the destruction of a will, committed by a young woman of brilliant but uncertain position for the purpose of continuing a life of pleasure and passion. Easy to conceive how M. Bourget treats such a subject, what an " *examen de conscience* " he makes of it all, with what a judicial severity he scourges the laxity and the luxury. But I fear lest I seem to present him to my readers, who, however, must by this time know him well, as tiresome or dreary. He is never either the one or the other. Long practice, infinite pains, and a native gift of narrative have made M. Bourget one of the most skilful craftsmen of our day. His firm and elastic, if somewhat monotonous style shows no sign of fatigue. He is as adroit as ever he was in preparing for a crisis and in recording an event. Any one who desires to read an excellent story of contemporary Parisian manners cannot do better than defy the young lions of the *Bou Mich*, and invest either in *Un Drame dans le Monde* or, better still, in *L'Ecuyère*.

THE LIVES OF THE SOPHISTS

THE LIVES OF THE SOPHISTS

THE wonderful Loeb Library continues indefatigably its task of lighting up the dark places of antiquity. The torch is this time thrust into a couple of caverns where nothing seems to have disturbed the bats and owls for hundreds of years. I believe that somebody translated Eunapius into English in the reign of James II. ; I should suppose that that version is not easily accessible. Of Philostratus' *Lives* I find no translation earlier than this of Professor Wilmer Wright, for which the general reader, no less than the scholar, will be grateful. Even to people who are moderately well-read this work of Philostratus and the whole of Eunapius are new, and I may go so far as to say that Philostratus is welcome.

Personally, I would willingly leave Eunapius in his interlunar cave. Philostratus is familiar to readers of out-of-the-way books as being the author of the *Life of Apollonius of Tyana,* an odd and interesting experiment in biographical eulogy. From an age of which so many important monuments have entirely disappeared, a substantial mass of the writings of Philostratus of Lemnos has been preserved. He was born about 170, and left his island at a tender age to attend the lectures of Proclus of Naucratis in Athens.

Owing to this fact we gather some interesting particulars about the great Greek schools. Youths who wished to listen to Proclus, who was the prime attraction of the Athenian world of letters, had to pay down a sum of 100 drachmas. Then they were free of the lecture room

for the rest of their time. As there had been unseemly
squabbling as to precedence in the schools of some of the
other sophists, Proclus made an arrangement by which
young boys sat in front, with the row of their " pedagogues "
—the servants who had brought the boys to school—just
behind them, and adult students in the rest of the hall.
It is difficult to understand how he adapted his wisdom to
so mixed an audience. Proclus, in his hours of ease, traded
in books and papyrus, and he possessed a large library,
which he threw open to his students.

It is thought that Philostratus came to England (or
Ireland) with Septimus Severus, and he was certainly the
favourite of that monarch's philosophic Empress Julia
Domna. She was a Syrian and a determined blue-stocking,
in whose company Philostratus lived successively at Per-
gamon and at Antioch. Perhaps it was for her that he
began his *Lives of the Sophists*, but more probably it was
the amusement of his old age, when Julia Domna was dead,
and he had retired to Athens.

Professor Wright gives reasons for thinking that this book
was written after 230 and before 238, when Gordian, to
whom it was dedicated, committed suicide. Philostratus
had no desire to be classed with grammarians ; " he wrote
like a well-bred Sophist who wished to preserve for all
time a picture of the triumphs of his tribe, when Sophists
were at the height of their glory." In opening his com-
pendium of gossip, he reminds Gordian of the conversations
about the Sophists which they engaged in long ago, in the
Temple of Daphnean Apollo.

Gordian seems to have warned Philostratus that he did
not want to know all about the ancestry of the learned men,
but anecdotes of their tricks of speech and specimens of
their oratory ; and this is what Philostratus gives. He
makes a forgotten world of intellectual activity rise out of
oblivion for an instant and move before us. His book has

the same relation to a serious biography that a " film " has to a novel. There is a procession of figures, and each one is in the flash-light for a few moments.

The earlier part of the volume may be passed over rather lightly. It deals with the eminent Sophists of the great period from the fourth century before Christ. Philostratus repeats what he has been told, or has read, about such illustrious persons as Isocrates and Æschines, but if we wish to study what is known regarding these celebrated men we have much fuller sources of information than Philostratus can give. We must remember that he was writing at a time when he himself was as distant from Isocrates as Dante is from us. We are apt to forget the immense prolongation of the classic ages, and the fact that successive generations revered, and forgot, and recalled to reverence persons who seem to us to belong to a single movement. The essay on Isocrates by Jebb contains twenty times as much accurate information about him as do the gossiping paragraphs of Philostratus. But it is pleasant to learn that, six hundred years after the death of Isocrates, the carved siren on the tomb of that orator still testified to his " persuasive charm."

Plato, the pungent enemy of the Sophists, has permanently darkened their light for us, in spite of Grote and Henry Sedgwick, and, above all, of Henry Jackson. The world will never forgive the Sophists their irrelevancy, nor forget that they were charged with " indifference to truth." But the testimony of Philostratus shows that six centuries after the Sophists began to flourish their works continued to be read and admired ; and who can desire more immortality than that ? They taught what courage is, and what justice, and how the universe was fashioned, in rhetoric of studied splendour, which was admired so long as men enjoyed such rhetoric, and found in it their chief intellectual stimulus. The white marble pillars of the Temple of Apollo,

through which the Ægean is seen far below in the colour
of a hyacinth, Isocrates walking up and down among his
disciples, and whispering—for he had a very weak voice—
in that charming rhythm of balanced sentences which made
immortal the name of the " old man eloquent," as Milton
calls him—all ⁺his forms a vision which may still fascinate
and tantalise the inward eye.

After a fashion, it fascinated the eye of Philostratus, but
what really makes his gossip valuable is what he is able to
relate out of his personal memory.   But something must
have happened to his book, from the centre of which a huge
fragment seems to have fallen away.   Imagine a Lives of
the English Poets, which should regale us with anecdotes of
Chaucer and Lydgate, and should then, without apology
or transition, be found to be talking about Browning and
Swinburne.   That gives an idea of Philostratus, who leaves
unexplained a gap of four centuries, beginning again with
Nicetes of Smyrna, who seems to have started a sort of
oratorical renaissance on Asiatic lines.   Nothing of Nicetes
has survived, but the younger Pliny heard him lecture.
Nicetes might, therefore, have been personally known to
Damianus, from whom Philostratus gathered orally a great
deal of what he relates.   At all events, the biographer
suddenly passes out of the dimness of antiquity into contemporary light, and we can only wish that his own genius
had been more ardently illuminated.   However, let us be
thankful for what we get.   I am thankful for Herodes
Atticus, of whom I knew nothing but that Gibbon mentions
him.   Herodes is the hero of Philostratus' book, and though
the great Sophist died when the biographer seems to have
been a child, the latter grew up in the splendour and perfume of the magnificent man who overshadowed the garden
of Greek culture in his own day like a magnolia.

We may wonder how a reputation like that of Herodes
could ever disappear, but before the invention of printing

no genius was safe from oblivion. I suspect that Herodes
was too glittering to last, that his talent had in it a tropical
element, and that its own redundancy was fatal to its
permanence. Although he was the most celebrated
sophistical writer of the second century, of the numerous
compositions of Herodes only one oration remains, and
that, Professor Wright considers, is manifestly spurious ;
it has none of the qualities for which Herodes was
celebrated.

During the late war, an admirable anthology of English
literature was prepared by a French professor, who had the
misfortune to be taken prisoner by the Germans. His
book appeared in Paris without his revision, and, through
an error of the printers, Pater's celebrated rhapsody about
the smile of Mona Lisa appeared attached to a short
biography of Mr. H. G. Wells. Suppose that the entire
corpus of the writings of Wells and Pater should perish,
and the first edition of this French anthology alone survive,
we have a parallel to the fate of the unhappy Herodes.
His famous works are all lost, except one piece of declama-
tion, which is obviously not his. I can imagine nothing
more tragical than to meet his magnificent ghost roaming
along the slopes of his native Marathon and trying to explain
to foreign professors, unaware of his presence, that he never
wrote a word of what they edit in his name.

Philostratus gives us as good an account as he can of the
style of Herodes, which he considered to reach the very
summit of oratory. His type of eloquence, he says, " is
like gold-dust shining beneath the waters of a silvery,
eddying river." This suggests something like the manner
of Renan, delicate and ironic, the matter even more delightful than the manner. " The structure of his work was
suitably restrained, and its strength lay in subtlety rather
than in vigour of attack." His model among the ancients
was Critias, whose style is said to have been " agreeable

and smooth like the breath of the west wind." How tantalising it all is! Evidently Herodes was an ardent reformer in literature, or rather resuscitator. He thought much of good taste, the taste of his own age being barbarous, and of conciseness, the principal error of his own age being a tumid prolixity. He taught the value of purity, grace, and temperance in speech; he recalled his hearers to the majesty of the Athenian classics. His epitaph in the Panathenaic Stadium set forth the words: "Here lies all that remains of Herodes, son of Atticus, of Marathon, but his glory is world-wide." It was world-wide still when Philostratus wrote in the succeeding generation. Great men had meanwhile arisen and had passed away, but Herodes continued to outshine them all. I know few things more pathetic than the complete disappearance of this example of " the glory that was Greece."

Perhaps fate thought that Herodes had so many of the good things of life during his long and serene career that he claimed no posthumous good fortune. No man of letters has ever been more handsomely conspicuous. He was born to vast wealth, which was so augmented by family bequests that he became the richest private citizen in the Empire. His grandfather, Hipparchus, much admiring the story of Miltiades, had aspired to be tyrant of Athens. The Emperor Nerva had discovered the plot, and deprived Hipparchus of his fortune, but, later on, millions of drachmas flowed in on Herodes from all sides. He did not imitate his grandfather's error, but devoted himself exclusively to literature—that is to say, when he was not endowing nations with theatres and colossal statues. When the Athenians forced him to accept the highest honour of their city, he accepted it only on condition that he should be allowed to present to Athens the most splendid stadium of pure white marble which the world contained, and he kept an army of workmen busy on this monument for four years, when he escorted to it the robe of Athene in a ship manned by a thousand rowers, and so presented his gift.

All this munificence was accidental ; it was forced upon him by his generosity and by the reputation of his boundless wealth. His heart all the time was in the pursuit of literary excellence. But what kind of literature was it that he cultivated in his unclouded career of nearly eighty years ? Even from Professor Wright, lucid and careful as she is, I cannot gather. Herodes is like a cloud on the horizon of a sunset to me ; even as I try to observe him, he changes and vanishes. Probably he wrote too ambiguously, and perhaps what he composed was too much an imitation of the Attic masters of four hundred years before him. In Philostratus' day, Herodes was principally read in a small volume containing the cream of his discourses, essays, and letters, in which " the flowers of antique erudition " were collected. Why has not that small volume survived, instead of the single dissertation which is not his at all ?

Another illustrious philosopher was Dio Chrysostom of Prusa, of whom eighty speeches or moral essays have been preserved. In good time, I suppose, we shall receive him from the Loeb Library. Mrs. Wilmer Wright says that next to Lucian, Dio " is the most successful and the most agreeable to read of all the Atticizing writers with sophistic tendencies." I hope Dio will console me, when I come to read him, for my disappointment at missing Herodes. But there is an anecdote which alarms me. The Emperor Trajan set Dio by his side in his golden triumphal car and took him for a long drive, during which Dio held forth in his best strain of philosophical persuasion. Trajan turned at last to him and said, " I don't understand a word that you've been saying, but I love you as I love myself ! " That is how I feel about the Sophists.

LORD ROSEBERY AS A CRITIC

LORD ROSEBERY AS A CRITIC

THE literary activities of Lord Rosebery are little known to the latest generation of readers. If my memory does not betray me, he has not published a book since his *Chatham ;* that was in 1910, and nerve-shattering events have bewildered the memories of the race since then. Moreover, even before that date, with the exception of his little monograph on Pitt, in 1891, he had scarcely chosen to take any public place as a writer of books. Hence his lifelong connection with certain phases of literature remains unknown to those who have not had the advantage of listening to his addresses on Burns, or Chalmers, or Johnson and the rest of his favourites, or of reading them in some ephemeral form, at the moment of their delivery.

This great statesman has always been vaguely apprehended as "interested in literature," but his close application to certain books and authors has not been perceived. For this reason, if for no other, a vivid curiosity awaits his *Miscellanies Literary and Historical*, and a cordial welcome. The contents have been put together by Mr. John Buchan, who prefixes a brief and modest note. The author, Mr. Buchan tells us, "stands aside in benevolent neutrality," but has slightly revised the text. No political speeches are included. In 1899 Mr. C. Geake in like manner obtained permission to print Lord Roseberry's *Appreciations and Addresses*. That volume is not at my hand, but I think that Mr. Buchan prints nothing included by Mr. Geake. Indeed, the chapters are almost exclusively later than 1900 in date of composition.

Lord Rosebery has nothing to say to us here about recent books or authors. His mind is more than a hundred years old, and it disdains to acknowledge the existence of modern imaginative literature. It is not merely that, by accident or design, Lord Rosebery evades the mention of contemporary writings, but that, with certain slight exceptions which I shall presently notice, he succeeds in appearing to be unaware of them. His taste is formed within the compass of the close of the eighteenth century, and his intellect bears the stamp of 1790. He precedes the French Revolution; he is conscious of, but not unduly impressed by, Rousseau and Montesquieu; he has not perceived the approach of the Romantic movement. It is not that his curiosity or his love of the picturesque take him back to the study of life a hundred years ago, but that he actually belongs to the eighteenth century.

It is essential to perceive this very interesting and remarkable fact, since, without a recognition of it, criticism of Lord Rosebery's style and attitude to literature is unintelligible. It is no question of imitation. He is unlike the great writers and orators of George III. in detail. He is less excessive than Burke, less angular than Windham, less ponderous than Gibbon, but he is of their race. He moves in their atmosphere, he weighs events by their standards, his thoughts are of the same order as their thoughts. He loves that extinct age of rhetoricians, because he understands them and because nothing but the accident of time divides him from their generation.

When once this idea is firmly implanted in our consciousness, the literary essays of Lord Rosebery present themselves to us in a fascinating light. To follow his method we must bear in mind the fact that he is always in pursuit of what another eminent coæval of his, Sir Joshua Reynolds, called " the invariable, the great and personal ideas which are fixed and inherent in universal Nature." The eccentric

and the speculative have as little attraction for Lord
Rosebery as the ultra-personal and the paradoxical have.
He has no feeling for mysticism ; what the cant of this
hour calls " spiritual truth " leaves him cold.   He exposes
no consciousness of that æsthetic sense which was pro-
digiously cultivated in the nineteenth century.   He is
older than Landor or De Quincey, although so much of the
eighteenth century clung about the robes of those authors
that they seem a little antiquated to us.

Lord Rosebery's interest in broad ideas is compatible,
indeed, with a very remarkable power of describing scenes
of human interest ; but so it was also with the Boswells
and the Gibbons.   He strikes the imagination with his
portraits, such as that of the dying Burns and the declining
Randolph Churchill ; but the gift of brilliant portraiture
was never more highly developed than at the close of the
eighteenth century.   In a curious phrase, he says that
Burns " lived in an age when the average of the poets
was sublime."   Now, who were the poets in 1785 ?   They
were Cowper, Crabbe, Erasmus Darwin—excellent writers
in their own way ; but what were they by the side of the
Wordsworth, Coleridge, Byron, Shelley, whom Lord
Rosebery was born, intellectually, too early to perceive ?
There was Blake—but I am very sure that Lord Rosebery
does not consider *him* " sublime."

The prose of Lord Rosebery invites, therefore, close
attention, as a portent in our 1923.   The address delivered
at Glasgow on the centenary of Burns in 1896 is worthy of
analysis ; it might, with the change of a word or two,
have been uttered immediately after the poet's death in
1796.   Robertson, who had known Burns, is called, with a
touch of bravado, " the late Dr. Robertson."   The speech
on Burke, delivered at Bristol in 1904, invites comparison
with Burke's famous *Letter to the Sheriffs* of that city ; it
might have been delivered to identically the same sheriffs.

Everywhere in the critical portion of these two volumes we meet with a great simplicity based upon long experience and political common sense, but embroidered with magnificent outbursts of imagination. As we read we seem to listen ; it is the ear which responds to the amplitude of these daring accents :—

"Pass, heavy hearse, with thy weary freight of shattered hopes and exhausted frame ; pass, with thy simple pomp of fatherless bairns and sad moralising friends ; pass, with the sting of death, to the victory of the grave ; pass, with the perishable, and leave us the eternal."

In a pleasing sentence Lord Rosebery praises the prose of Cowley, and quotes a noble passage, but it fits ill with his own soberer rhetoric.

It would be false, however, to say that Lord Rosebery is an imitator of Burke or Gibbon. Only, as I have said, he belongs to their generation ; he occupies the platform at their side. He is less emphatic than the one, much less uniform than the other. In some respects he even seems to go back further than they do, to be a little their precursor. He has more than they have of the undulating pomp and graceful ease of Bolingbroke, who, though he had not much to say, said it in a way which lifted English prose to a higher accomplishment than it had enjoyed before him. I observe in Lord Rosebery, with interest, an occasional use of inversion for rhetorical effect—an artifice almost abandoned since 1800.

Lord Rosebery is a little blunt in his appeal, like some of the minor prose-writers of the age of Hurd, a critic whom I imagine he vastly prefers to Pater or Ruskin. He is not seduced by any of the falbalas of criticism ; indeed, he appears to be unaware of their existence. For instance, of Samuel Johnson, he writes with candour, vigour, and wit, but his views on Johnson's style are unaffected either by revised opinion or by modern investigation. He speaks of Johnson's works as the best judges spoke of them a

hundred years ago. " His twelve volumes sleep, I fear, on
our shelves; at least, they do on mine," he says. Even
the thought of the Lichfield celebration, in 1909, at which
Lord Rosebery presided, " could not overcome my repug-
nance to read *Rasselas*." This is characteristic of the
writer who thinks M. Albert Vandal " the first of living
historians." It is consistent, and I would not have it
otherwise.

The general impression which Lord Rosebery's style gives
the reader is of conversational charm. It never fails to be
various and vivid. Not like Macaulay, who deafens the
ear at last by the persistent clatter of his tongue, holding
the table bored and bound by the monotonous emphasis
of his method, Lord Rosebery understands every art of
retaining attention by variety. If he is earnest for a few
sentences, he relieves the tension by a certain playfulness;
he is careful not to be sonorous too soon, but saves up his
most brilliant effects for the end, and closes the diapason
of his address on a loud brief note of human pathos. Occasionally, where the appeal has been too grave, he touches
a light key in daring contrast, as where, in the midst of a
political disquisition, he suddenly refers to Addington's
sonnet on Burns, as a production " which in the Academy
of Lagado would surely have been held a signal triumph
of the art of extracting sunshine from cucumbers."

The man who can write in this way must be a great
talker; he must be " a moon among the lesser stars " of
conversation, as Johnson said that Windham was. He
must have no inclination to dazzle or deafen his auditors,
but to hold them thrilled and charmed, to send them away
with the conviction that they have been listening to a magic
flute.

The rare occasions on which the literature of the nineteenth century occupies Lord Rosebery's attention only
prove the eighteenth-century character of his mind. He

appears to be out of his element. A speech delivered at an exhibition of Thackeray relics at the Charterhouse in 1911 has a languor which none of the other addresses exhibit. He does not seem interested in his subject, nor to have taken much trouble to comprehend it. The reader wishes that the orator's mind could be diverted to Fielding, or even to that remarkable Scottish thistle, Tobias Smollett. On either of these themes he would be sure to be delightful. The only recent author mentioned in these volumes is Robert Louis Stevenson, of whom Lord Rosebery spoke when there was a question in 1906 of a Scottish memorial. This essay is composed with genuine warmth, and is inspired by a true enthusiasm, but we feel that it is the Scotchman in Stevenson that interests the author. And the eighteenth-century obsession is here fully developed. Stevenson's diction reminds the speaker of Addison's *Spectator*, and when Lord Rosebery seeks for a parallel with the modern novelist's style he finds it where a critic of 1790 would have found it :—

" Mr. Fox said of Mr. Pitt that he himself (Mr. Fox) had always a command of words, but that Mr. Pitt had always a command of the right words, and that is the quality which strikes us in the style of Stevenson."

I would not have Lord Rosebery reminded of any one more recent than Mr. Pitt and Mr. Fox, and the application is excellent ; but how characteristic !

The remarks I have hitherto made do not cover the essays and speeches which are directly the outcome of Lord Rosebery's action as a strenuous politician who rose to be Prime Minister. Of these by far the longest and fullest is the study of *Lord Randolph Churchill*, which is doubtless the most familiar of Lord Rosebery's writings to the general public, since when it was published fifteen years ago it was universally read and discussed. The sketch of Lord Salisbury is much shorter, and is not drawn from close contact ; that of Mr. Gladstone is, but it is too brief for completeness. All these studies, however, and there are several others, show a penetrating eye and a retentive intelligence.

Very interesting are what may be called the purely patriotic addresses, delivered before students of the Scottish Universities. A conviction of the dignity of Parliaments, of the vast unity of the Empire, of the need of a living sense of the community of commonwealths, breathes through and through these eloquent addresses, in reading which we seem once more to hear the golden voice in which they were delivered. And most directly, perhaps, inspired by the heart of the speaker are the essays which deal with the history and character of the Scottish people, and with the means by which, through a recollection of past achievements, Scotch patriotism may be kept alive.

Many of these addresses were published, at the time of their delivery, in several public forms. But I take a personal interest in one, *The Scots Greys*, which, for some inscrutable reason, was not reported in any of the English newspapers. Mr. Evan Charteris and I, greatly struck with its beauty, obtained Lord Rosebery's permission to print it privately in 1907, at our own expense, as a pamphlet; this is now a very scarce bibliographical curiosity. From this address, which will be a new thing even to most of Lord Rosebery's most attentive admirers, I copy a passage which seems to me to exemplify its author's style at its highest oratorical perfection :—

" Honour to the unreturning brave, the brave who will return no more. We shall not see their faces again. In the service of their Sovereign and their country they have undergone the sharpness of death, and sleep their eternal sleep thousands of miles away in the green solitudes of South Africa. Their places, their comrades, their saddles will know them no more, for they will never return to us as we knew them. But in a nobler and higher sense, have they not returned to us to-day ? They return to us with a message of duty, of courage, of patriotism. They return to us with a memory of high duty faithfully performed. They return to us with the inspiration of their example. Peace, then, to their dust. Honour to their memory. Scotland for ever ! "

TWO BLIND HISTORIANS

TWO BLIND HISTORIANS

FEW aspects of the intellectual life are so invigorating as the contemplation of lives in which marvels of scholarship have been performed in spite of the most grievous drawbacks of ill-health and general physical disability. The classic example is Casaubon, whose career perhaps inspired Robert Browning to write his famous *Grammarian's Funeral*, where the attitude of the man who, "with the throttling hands of death at strife," decides " not to live but know," is drawn in lines of unfading beauty. But I am not sure whether it has been observed that the two most astonishing records of masterly composition achieved in the worst possible circumstances, ran exactly parallel with one another in the lives of two great historians of France and America.

I have recently finished, with an emotion which I would willingly pass on to other readers, the biography of Augustin Thierry, which has just been published by his grand-nephew. The French are, by custom, less copious and less prompt than we are in supplying the public with memoirs of eminent persons. Thierry has been dead for sixty-six years, and it is only at this late date that we receive minute particulars of his life. The biography reveals, with praise-worthy discretion and wholesome lack of emphasis, a pertinacity of intellectual courage equalled only by one who was Thierry's immediate contemporary, William Hickling Prescott, the author of *The Conquest of Mexico by the Spaniards*. The parallel is the closer, because Thierry's best, or best-known, work is similar in title and even in attitude to *The Conquest of Mexico*, but I do not think that there is any evidence that Thierry was aware of Prescott's existence.

Augustin Thierry was the son of parents in moderate circumstances, who lived at Blois. He was born in one of those dove-grey houses which hang between the Loire below them and the noble castle above them in that little town of romantic beauty. In the midst of the Terror, on May 10, 1795, a new-born baby was smuggled out to be secretly baptised at dead of night by an old priest who would not bow the knee to the violent anti-religious laws of Prairial. The attitude of Thierry's family was that of Russian " intellectuals " to-day, who groan under the impious tyranny of the Bolsheviks, and Augustin grew up intensely French, monarchical, and anti-Republican. He early showed a prodigious memory, and this has to be borne in mind in contemplating the miracle of his resistance to disability. His memory carried him through the years of darkness. No doubt, he was overworked, like the infant John Stuart Mill. His tutor at the College of Blois recorded that " his abilities were transcendant, his success astonishing " ; obviously he undermined his health by his feverish precocity.

He entered the Ecole Normale in Paris at the age of sixteen ; in his nineteenth year he was appointed to a professor's chair at Compiègne, whence he fled two years later before the Austrian invasion. As early as 1814 he published a book on the reorganisation of European society, a subject no less alarming then than it is to-day. He fell under the influence of the wild social reformer, Saint-Simon, and became his secretary. He was greatly impressed by the gesture and the imagination of Chateaubriand, but all this time he showed no turn for historical investigation. He seemed likely to give his energy to politics.

Many years later Augustin Thierry wrote that the " poésie patriotique du docteur O'Connor " first awakened

in him the sentiments which made him an historian. Who
was this? Probably Arthur O'Connor, who bought an
estate at Bignon, near Paris, and who married Condorcet's
only daughter. *The Conquest of England by the Normans*
occurred to Thierry as the subject for a great book after
the disasters of the French nation in 1815, when he was
twenty years of age, but he was not then ripe for carrying
forward such a performance. Nevertheless, he prepared
for the task by learning the English language and by beginning to examine the charters and chronicles. France lacked
historians of the modern order. England had produced
Hume, Robertson and Gibbon; Italy, Vico and Muratori;
France had not a single name to set by the side of these.
But a new school of great historians was just about to make
its appearance in France; Michelet, Guizot, Mignet, even
Thiers were the exact contemporaries of Augustin Thierry,
but he was their pioneer. History is a branch of literature
which is being for ever undermined by the spread of exacter
knowledge, yet the name of Thierry will never cease to be
illustrious.

His biographer does not give us those particulars about
his hero's study of English which we should like to possess,
but it seems from Thierry's own account that the study of
Hume had a strong effect upon him. "Suddenly," he
says, "as I finished Hume's volumes, I was struck by an
idea which came to me like a flash of light, and I exclaimed,
'All this dates from a conquest; beneath the history of
the English people lies a conquest.'" He began to push
his inquiries further, and his earliest publications in this
kind were essays on Colonel Hutchinson and on Anne
Boleyn. Finally, "with a transport of enthusiasm," he
says, "I saluted the publication of *Ivanhoe*," which appeared
in 1819. Thierry found the spirit of Walter Scott's romance
"exactly in harmony with the plan I had by this time
sketched of *The Conquest of England by the Normans*."

The health of Augustin Thierry was already shaken, but he spared himself no excess of labour. In his exhaustive reference to English sources he was helped by an ardent Irish girl, Mary Clarke, then settled with her mother in Paris. In this name we may easily fail to recognise the intimate friend of Mme. Récamier, who married the Orientalist, Julius Mohl, in 1847, and who became the Mme. Mohl, so celebrated for her intellectual salon in the Second Empire. She was a violent Orleanist, a friend of Chateaubriand, and in love for a while with the brother of Augustin, Amadée Thierry, himself a remarkable writer. Meanwhile, Augustin, " soul-hydroptic " for knowledge, as Browning puts it, was doing his best to ignore a variety of discomforts. By the age of twenty-seven his walk had become painful and irregular, he had lost the sensation of touch, he could scarcely button his clothes. He suffered from the beginnings of what would nowadays be called locomotor ataxia, and the doctors ordered a complete cessation from all reading and writing. But Augustin Thierry would not relax the tension ; he plunged deeper and deeper into his chronicles and charters.

At last, returning for a few days to Blois, and looking up at the acacias blossoming in the garden of the bishop's palace, he found that all their creamy whiteness was turned to rose-red. His eyes were going ; and at the same time rigours and shootings of pain darted from his legs to his head. Blindness came steadily on, and day by day the acts of reading and writing became more difficult, yet the sufferer would abate no jot of his ardour. At last, in the autumn of 1824, when the first draft of *The Conquest of England* was almost completed, he could no longer decipher a text nor hold a pen in his stiff fingers. He was fortunate enough to find a rarely competent secretary in Armand Carrel, and the work went on without abatement.

The *Conquête* was published in the spring of 1825, and it enjoyed an instant and overpowering success, a popular success not paralleled by any such volumes until, thirty years later, by Macaulay's. But the situation of the now blind and paralysed historian was pitiable indeed. A Chinese proverb says that " Money makes a blind man see," but Thierry lacked even this alleviation ; he was miserably poor. Friends offered him an asylum in a village, Carqueiranne, on the Riviera, and here he rested for a year. A ray of dim light came back to his eyes ; he was able to hobble about a little in the sun, and the old historic passion swept back upon him. In 1826 he insisted on returning to Paris, and " a vast design haunted his spirit," none less than to prepare a *Great Chronicle of France*, founded on documents hitherto not edited and not examined. A small pension now supplied his very modest wants. With incredible zeal and force of purpose he dictated his *Letters on the History of France*, which appeared in 1827, and repeated the success of the *Conquête*.

But one day, as he was beginning a fresh labour of magnitude, he was struck down at his writing-table by a fit, which left him long hovering between life and death. When he recovered consciousness he was totally blind and the lower part of his body paralysed. He was now thirty-three years of age, and was destined to live for twenty-eight more. Aided by his miraculous memory, by the clearness and vigour of his brain, which was wholly unaffected in spite of his diseases, and by the devotion of secretaries who carried out his instructions, Augustin Thierry was able to fill those last years with invaluable contributions to the historical literature of France. Two days before his death, and after a final stroke of apoplexy, he dictated a correction to be inserted in a new edition of the *Conquête*. The victim of darkness, perpetual pain, and miserable immobility, this astonishing man never wavered in cheerfulness, in the ardour of investigation, in the passion of intellectual benevolence.

Let us now turn to Thierry's American contemporary and parallel, Prescott, whose name is not mentioned by the French biographer. Thierry was one year old when Prescott, who outlived him for two years and a half, was born. These two historians, therefore, so singularly resembling one another in their fame and fate, spent sixty years of suffering, labour, and triumph scarcely, as it appears, ever hearing of one another. The hardships of Prescott have been the theme of many biographers; they were very severe, yet not so poignant as those of Thierry as we now face the latter. Prescott, at all events, never felt the pressure of poverty.

In other respects the symptoms and the characters of the two historians were remarkably similar. Prescott was at college and eighteen years of age when, during a " rag," one of his fellow-students threw a piece of crust at him, which hit his left eye and paralysed the retina. His general health was affected, and six months later the right eye began to fail, but the suffering proved to be a form of rheumatism, which shifted to other parts of his body. Prescott, however, was never well again; he became unable to walk, and the surviving eye slowly grew worse. He wrote, " I am afraid I shall never be able to draw upon my mind to any large amount," but as he grew blinder and more helpless his mental energy became more intense. At the instigation of Tickner, who afterwards wrote an excellent life of him, Prescott took up the study of Spanish. The first germ of his *History of Ferdinand and Isabella* dates from May, 1826, and a month later his eyesight almost completely failed. He suffered intense pain from light, even from firelight; he could only bear to read a few lines at a time, and that in an artificial twilight of dark blue curtains.

In these conditions, when most men would have resigned themselves to their fate, Prescott found himself lifted in a great inspiration to write Spanish history on a large scale from original sources. He strengthened his purpose by contemplation of the labours of Hume and Gibbon, without stopping to reflect how much those great men possessed which was physically denied to him. He surrounded himself with secretaries carefully trained to be his eyes. Nothing escaped him which could serve his purpose; unique manuscripts were brought over from Madrid. When the agony of his rheumatism made every other posture impossible, Prescott lay flat on the floor, and wrote by means of his noctograph. As life went on, he became more and more like Browning's grammarian :—

> " Back to his book then : deeper drooped his head :
>   Calculus racked him :
>   Leaden before, his eyes grew dross of lead :
>   Tussis attacked him."

Prescott became almost immovable with paralysis and ague, but still he worked on, clear-minded to the very last, infinitely loveable, uncomplaining in a serene dispassion, compiling, composing, publishing volume after volume; and he died in the midst of his huge *History of the Reign of Philip II.*, assiduous and unflinching to the very last.

The ardour and resignation of these two illustrious men, plagued beyond all the experience of their fellows by physical disabilities, yet persisting through the hopeless years in a system of energetic labour which would seem formidable to any healthy and comfortable body, can but be exhilarating to our tempers. For the case of Prescott, I nourish a tender personal memory. The first book of history which ever came in my way was his *Conquest of Mexico*, which I read when I was ten years old; I was absorbed, enchanted, and bewildered by it. While I was deep in it, my father laid down the newspaper one morning, and told me that Mr. Prescott was dead, and added that he had been blind when he wrote his books. The statement was, perhaps, the earliest distinct intimation of literature which I received, and it gravely impressed me. As a rule, I think, children do not connect the idea of a book they read with that of any person having written it. But I was brought up in a house where books were written, and I was accustomed to see my father at work, always, however, in the light. I asked myself with amazement how a blind man, in the dark, could write a book? I ask myself the question still, with even greater emphasis of sympathy and wonder, as I close this beautiful Life of Augustin Thierry, who wove a wonderful network of luminous literature in the interlunar cave of his weariness and blindness.

KITCHEN ESSAYS

KITCHEN ESSAYS

THACKERAY says, "Next to eating good dinners, a healthy man with a benevolent turn of mind must like, I I think, to read about them." It is strange that so obvious a truth should require to be stated, but we English have, as a nation, a strange foible for despising our food, or pretending to do so. We all know the man who loudly declares that he " does not care what he eats," and who evidently takes pride to himself for his indifference. Even those who are blessed with a good appetite are apt to be a little ashamed of confessing it, as though to see no difference between bad cookery and good were a normal quality, and to cultivate a palate were tantamount to encouraging a vice. This is, no doubt, a remnant of the old savage Puritanism, lingering in an odd byway of the mysterious Nonconformist conscience. It was rampant among the Roundheads, who were very fine fellows, but should not be permitted, after two centuries and a half, to continue their censorship of our dinner-tables.

The Anglican churchmen were never so outrageous. They preached moderation and sobriety, but they were careful not to pretend that it was wicked to enjoy one's meat and drink. Jeremy Taylor published two sermons on *The House of Feasting*, which are not merely exquisitely written, but defend the principle of enjoyment in set terms. This is what the Chrysostom of our divines says on the subject of morality in eating : " It is lawful when a man needs meat to choose the pleasanter, even merely for his pleasure. This is as lawful as to smell of a rose, or to

lie in feathers, or to hear music, or to walk in gardens."
Indeed, I am inclined to think Jeremy Taylor must have
been no little of an epicure in his grave way, since he compares
the impression of nice food on the palate to " the feeling of
silk, or the handling of a melon or a mole's skin." It
would have been delicious to see the great preacher, after
descending from his pulpit, being conducted by his noble
hosts to the dinner-table at Golden Grove, in order " that
the Body," as he so genially says, " may rejoice in fellowship with the Soul."

This keen but rational satisfaction animates *Kitchen
Essays*, the very lively and practical book which Lady
Jekyll has published on what our seventeenth-century
ancestors called " skill in banqueting stuff." Her recipes
and her reflections are unctuous enough to make a dyspeptic
clap his hands, even if he has to burst into tears immediately afterwards. Lady Jekyll writes about food with
gusto, although always with delicacy and reason, as one
who knows that temperance is the girdle of enjoyment.
Her book is a plea for brain-work in cookery, and she has
threaded her recipes, like so many golden beads, on a string
of humorous commentary.

This is not a cookery-book in the determined old fashion
of Mrs. Hannah Glasse and her rivals of the eighteenth
century, who doggedly described everything that a housewife could possibly need, from the making of a whipped
syllabub to a certain cure for the bite of a mad dog. Lady
Jekyll keeps strictly to business, and her original inspiration
has been no more than a religious wish to preserve, through
the vicissitudes of house-changing, the recipes collected
during years of provision, recipes which the genius of some
clever long-departed cook introduced, and which are now
in danger of being lost for ever. She greatly endears herself
to the reader by her solicitude for his happiness. While
the earlier purveyors of cookery-books seemed to cater

for greedy persons, flushed with health and strength, she has a true woman's pity for the weak. She has a recondite " refresher " for elderly persons " depressed by gardening," and the moisture gathers in our eyelids while we read of a raspberry vinegar expressly designed for old gentlemen " when exhausted by church." Lady Jekyll evidently has a beautiful nature.

Some of her receipts seem to err on the side of expense, although she is moderation itself in comparison with certain of her more famous precursors. Gervase Markham, for instance, writing in the last years of.Shakespeare's life, desires the housewife, when she has a dinner-party, to cover the table with wild boar, roe-pie, a lesser wild-fowl and a lesser land-fowl, a great wild-fowl and a great land-fowl, a hot baked meat and a cold ; and " for made dishes and quelquechoses, which lie on the invention of the cook, they are to be thrust into every place that is empty, and so sprinkled all over the table." What it must have cost ! A year's income would go in one banquet if we attempted this sort of thing to-day, accompanied by all the profusion of wines, " pleasant at the nose and quick in the taste," upon which Markham insists. Lady Jekyll is moderate in quantity, but she dwells, very properly, on quality. It will be thought that she borders on the fantastic when she suggests that an expensive dish may really prove an economy, because it may encourage a bachelor guest to leave his hostess a rich legacy. It ought to do so, of course, but the ecstasy of the palate is very volatile, and I cannot urge any impoverished family to calculate on such an effect from a *côtelette en robes de chambre* or even from a caramel of oranges and cream.

The simplicity of some of Lady Jekyll's recipes is agreeably concealed by the names which she gives to her dishes. Our kind old friend, rice-pudding, hardly recognises itself when re-christened Dundee, but she invests it, under that dreamy title, with a fresh charm and attractiveness. It is characteristic of something very fine about the temperament of Lady Jekyll that she seizes this particular opportunity, and no other, for warning us against a fault in manners which singularly besets the greedy. The common moralist would grasp the occasion of describing " *Rognons à la Turbigo* " or a " Good Cold Cream of Chicken " to add an intimation that delicious as these are, a single helping must suffice, and that this is no dish to lay before Oliver Twist. Inborn refinement checks Lady Jekyll on these too-obvious occasions, and it is only when she is dealing with plain rice-pudding—with, it is true, " a small valley in the centre " filled with an ineffable mixture—that she remarks, with sudden severity, that to ask for a second helping would be as inartistic as an encore at the opera. The lesson is subtle, but obvious. The person who would be pig enough to ask for a second plate of plain rice-pudding is ready to show himself a guzzler in grain upon every occasion.

The moments during which the exquisite constructions of Lady Jekyll are being carried from the kitchen to the dining-room are filled up by a variety of anecdotes, some of which are new and some are not, but all are amusing. Nobody has heard every story, and there is always some young man from Trichinopoly on whose innocent ears the most ancient tale falls like balm from heaven. Still, I should have thought that even that young man knew the legend of the minister who reserved the grace of " Bountiful Creator " for roast duck. But quite fresh is the story of the marquis, whose newly-engaged cook

" sent on its gay career round a decorous dinner-party of county neighbours a transparent and highly decorated pink ice-pudding, concealing within its inmost recesses a fairy light and a musical box playing the ' Battle of Prague.' Words were spoken, and, like the chord of self in Locksley Hall, this over-elaborated creation ' passed in music out of sight.' "

And I like the bishop who said that his cook knew no

alternative between a burnt offering and a bleeding sacrifice.

Until I came across the bibliography of Cookery Books, brought out some twenty years ago in New York by Mrs. Pennell, I had no idea of the abundance of the quarry after which sportsmen of this particular game go hunting. There was Apicius, who wrote in the third century, but I have never read his receipts. Why has not his *De Re Coquinaria* been included in the Loeb Library? There are many ancient editions of Apicius, the earliest printed at Venice about 1486. I suppose that he was the authority for the Doctor's Entertainment in the Manner of the Ancients, which is described in *Peregrine Pickle*. No fewer than five cooks in succession gave notice to leave rather than prepare this "elegant meal in the genuine old Roman taste," so shocking were its recipes to their professional honour. The sixth cook, engaged at an extraordinary premium, threw himself at Pallet's knees, and in "a piteous voice exclaimed in French, 'For the love of God, dear sir, spare me the mortification of the honey and oil'!" The meal was a terrible one, and when it extended to a pie made of dormice and syrup of poppies, a guest exclaimed, "Lord! what beastly fellows those Romans were!" Nor was there general approbation of the jelly made of vinegar, pickle, and honey, boiled with candied asafœtida, although the host carefully assured the company that this exactly repeated the delicious *laser syriacum* of the ancients.

The banquet broke up, it will be remembered, in shocking confusion. The palates of the Romans must have differed strangely from our own, and perhaps resembled more closely those of the Chinese. There was very little about the food of the ancients which deserved the charming name given by Platina, in the Renaissance, to his cookery book, *De Honesta Voluptate*, but Lady Jekyll might have borrowed that title with no scruple.

Most epicures to-day would rather drink tea with Lady
Jekyll than swill the resinous wine of Falernum with
Apicius. But I offer a faint reproach to the lady for
neglecting to dwell more at length upon the " equipage "
of the tea-table, as our grandmothers used to call it. The
rubric " Tea " occurs not in her appetising index. She
gives us no rules for the preparation of the most elegant
of beverages. Is she of opinion, with the poet Waller,
that " the Water is to remain upon the Tea no longer than
while you can say the Miserere Psalm very leisurely " ?
I should like to possess the opinion of so learned and so pious
a judge upon this nice point. She does not, however, ignore
the ceremony altogether, and she describes a Stollen Cake
suitable for friends who come in hungry from the garden,
while for the dyspeptic who never eats anything at tea,
her brown flour biscuits are seductive.

For the rector there is a Wardley Cake, and for
" syrens "—but who in his senses would take tea with a
syren ?—there is a Viennese confection called Venus Torte,
which sounds extremely voluptuous, and is beaten for one
hour, after which " it should form bubbles," but Lady
Jekyll omits to say where. A chapter on " Tray Food "
deals with the treatment of invalids, and contains a great
number of admirably practical suggestions. The author
appears to understand to the full what is meant by " enjoying bad health." Her mind runs, I confess, too much on
convalescence, and I do not admit that a patient who is
very seriously ill could, or should attempt to, do justice to
a slice of roast mutton with a nice little pile of capers and
a soubise sauce. When it comes to a soubise sauce, it is
time to dismiss the doctor and return to the family circle.

A specimen of the author's engaging philosophy must be
given. Lady Jekyll blames, very justly, the slap-dash
mode of cooking and eating, which has particularly become
a habit since the war. She is all for patient art in the

kitchen and prompt consideration in the dining-room.
She says :—

> " It is poor encouragement to the cook to let her carefully-
> prepared, well-garnished dish cool its heels, first on a dinner lift,
> then behind a screen, where it is dealt with by an intermediary
> hand, and at last presented, often in fragments of unrecognisable
> derivation and uninviting appearance, its tardy companions, the
> gravy and sauce-boats, the savoury rice or dressed vegetables, for
> which it called out long but in vain, never coming, like wisdom, till
> too late. Delay is almost invariably fatal to success, but a pair of
> carvers near the kitchen fire and a lightening flight straight to the
> dining-table lend an unimagined savour to the simplest food. The
> sudden irruption of an anxious chef through a dining-room bearing
> a soufflet light as thistledown, and crying apprehensively as he came,
> ' Vite ! vite ! messieurs, mesdames, cela tombe ! cela tombe ! ' was
> more than justified by the fleeting perfection of his *chef d'œuvre.*"

How wonderful is Food—Food and his brother, Drink,
when they are treated with this tender refinement ! Great
injustice has been done by wilful ascetics to these great
subjects, of which women should be, and fortunately often
are, the defenders and the apostles. Nothing is more ugly
than an ill-natured gibe at the dignity of eating. When
Macready arrives in Dublin, he notes in his *Journal*—not
apropos of anything, but simply as a reflection—" How
unbecoming in the female character is over-enjoyment of
the pleasures of the table ! " Possibly it is ; but what a
waspish way of looking at life this reveals ! We prefer to
think of Mr. Samuel Pepys, taking his ladies down the river
in the King's pleasure-boat, and " all the way reading in a
book of receipts of making fine meats and sweetmeats,
which make us good sport." Lady Jekyll's book would
have pleased Mr. Pepys.

LEIGH HUNT

LEIGH HUNT

YEARS pass by, and still the exact place of Leigh Hunt in our [literary history remains undetermined. Critics, anxious to sweep on to a consideration of Keats, are unwilling to do justice to the elder friend's poetical initiative. Hunt's faults as a writer and a man are almost proverbial, his merits rarely mentioned. His personal character suffers from the persistent popularity of Dickens's caricature, and, in spite of all the novelist's remorse, nine out of ten readers instinctively think of Harold Skimpole when they hear of Leigh Hunt. In vain has Mr. Squire acutely remarked that " the sort ᵒf gay and ostentatious wilfulness " of Skimpole is far more a premonition of Oscar Wilde than a portrait of Leigh Hunt—in vain, for the powerful magic of Dickens prevails in spite of his own too-tardy recantation.

As an author, Hunt suffers from a variety of misfortunes. He was careless, loose, and unacquainted with the virtues of the jelly-bag. Hitherto his verse, and still his prose, have remained uncollected and unrevised. Alone among the leading writers of his age, no definite or even collected edition of his works has been forthcoming. His prose, in its lax and broadcast suffusion, will probably long remain an almost impenetrable jungle. The poor dear man wrote so much and so languidly in his life-long pursuit of the five-pound note that the task of collecting his prose seems hopeless. But why his verse has been so long neglected it is more difficult to say. The reproach is, at all events, at last removed by Mr. Milford, who, in an admirable edition, has brought together, with a wonderful apparatus of bibliography and annotation, much of Leigh Hunt's poetry which was previously unattainable, and all, as I suppose, which even the minute student will ever want to refer to. That he has deliberately excluded much that is worthless is a proof of Mr. Milford's courage and discretion.

Associated with Byron, Shelley, Keats, and a group of minor poets absurdly called the " Cockney School," Leigh Hunt was considerably senior to them all. But this fact has to be approached with caution, because, although he was in one sense precocious—publishing a volume of verse which went into several editions when Keats was six years old—he showed no sign of original talent until he approached maturity. His *Juvenilia* of 1801 is simply a collection of late eighteenth-century rubbish. In his elegant but rather " sloppy " autobiography, he attempted, towards the end of his life, to give an outline of his early mental development, but he seems to have forgotten the facts. He does, however, admit that " it was many years before I discovered what was exquisite in poetry." He met Byron as early as 1809, but the author of *English Bards and Scotch Reviewers* was then equally ignorant of what was " exquisite."

Yet as early as 1805, when he was twenty-one, Leigh Hunt appears to have had a glimmering. He began his study of Italian poetry, and it is characteristic that his earliest adventure there seems to have been in Tassoni's *Rape of the Bucket*, that lively type of the serio-comic verse which combines pathos and picturesqueness with satire. It transpires that Hunt in this same year wrote an essay on Heroi-Comic Poetry, which is lost. His investigation of Italian literature proceeded ; he welcomed with rapture the *Morgante Maggiore* of " good-natured Pulci " ; he was greatly stimulated by Bojardo and Ariosto. His tropical blood responded to the warmth, ease, and audacity of Italian burlesque, while it shrank from the cold egotism of

Dante. He began to dream of producing in English, a mixed order of poetry, mingling sacred with profane works, in which lyrical enthusiasm should be blended with levity, and ease take the place of elevation. The romantic revival in Wordsworth's hands had aimed, beneath its simplicity of form, at a metaphysical sublimity. Hunt would not compete with this, but would cultivate a tender and graceful sweetness, a Tuscan elegance, throwing over homely themes a golden haze ; he would be lively and amiable, and exchange the cloudiness of the Lakes for a sky of blue Italian weather. This, I take it, was his aim, and I think that he formed it in 1805 or 1806, long before he met any of his future Cockney associates.

When he began to carry it out is another matter, and very difficult to ascertain. Leigh Hunt reached the rather mature age of twenty-seven before he " found himself " as a poet, and that was some years before the world " found " him. In 1811 he printed in *The Reflector*, a new Radical newspaper, *The Feast of the Poets*, which did not appear in book form until 1814 ; he began *The Story of Rimini*, which was delayed until 1816, in the same year, 1811, when he printed *Politics and Poetics*, a long piece in heroic couplet now retrieved by Mr. Milford. In these we find Leigh Hunt at last started on his career as a poet whose aim was to mingle " fancy with familiarity," but *Politics and Poetics*, obviously the earliest of the three poems, is still pure eighteenth-century in style.

The most valuable contributions made by Mr. Milford is the original (1811) version of *The Story of Rimini*, now printed for the first time from Mr. T. J. Wise's MS., with Byron's comments, which are probably much later in date. This rough draft already shows a great advance over *Politics and Poetics*, but moves with less freedom and playful ease than *The Feast of the Poets*, where, in my judgment, the authentic voice of Leigh Hunt as a poet is first heard.

He modified and enlarged *The Feast of the Poets* incessantly, but we ought to look back to the original text of 1811. Byron, Shelley, and Keats had, by that date, written nothing really memorable. This analysis may seem tiresome, but it is essential in an attempt to give Leigh Hunt his due as an innovator. *The Feast of the Poets* owes something to the form of Goldsmith's *Retaliation*, and even of Anstey's *New Bath Guide*, but much more to the spirit of those serio-comic Italian poets with whom Leigh Hunt now found himself in close kinship.

Leigh Hunt was over thirty years of age when he formed the acquaintance of the youthful Keats, who dedicated to him his precious boyish volume of 1817. *The Story of Rimini* had just been published, and had been received by official criticism with a storm of abuse. Wounded by the unmerited censure of certain reptiles of the Press, Leigh Hunt found healing in the bold support of this youth of twenty-two, under whose crude husk he immediately divined the folded wings of a divine genius. Keats expressed " a free, a leafy luxury " in sharing with Hunt a retirement in " places of nestling green for poets made." The story has been told a hundred times, and best by Sir Sidney Colvin, but the point which occupies me to-day is the permanent effect on Keats of the verse of Hunt, admiration of which he thought that he soon outgrew. In point of fact, he never quite outgrew it ; it is manifest, not merely in *Endymion*, but in *Isabella*, and it recurs, in a manner wholly puzzling and even disconcerting, in Keats' latest and least worthy long poem, *The Cap and Bells*, from which Keats' critics usually fly, with averted faces, pretending that it does not exist. There it stands, however, embedded in his *corpus*, and the only way to understand it is to take it as a recrudescence of the Italian burlesque manner introduced by Leigh Hunt from Tassoni and Pulci, and stamped upon the consciousness of Keats at the most impressionable moment of his life. It was a return, perhaps caused by the languor of declining health, to the old theory which had fascinated his boyhood, that pathos and picturesqueness could be happily combined in a stream of colloquial versification.

To this theory Leigh Hunt himself remained faithful, and when old age found him a contemporary of Tennyson and Browning, he was still " climbing trees in the Hesperides " in the manner of the sixteenth-century Italians. All he had gained was a certain seriousness ; he had exchanged Pulci for Tasso and translated the *Aminta*. In prison he had provided himself with the *Parnaso Italiano* in a library of volumes, which went well with his sky-blue ceiling and wallpaper of a trellis of roses. He transferred into verse, which is sometimes charming and always easy, a buoyant irrepressible gaiety rarely paralleled on the melancholy slopes of Helicon.

The worst feature of his poetry is its want of taste, its laxity of judgment, the poet's inability to perceive that the loosely-girded versification, the soft resonances and easy rhymes of Italian can only be imitated in English by a bard who anxiously avoids the semblance of vulgarity. Leigh Hunt failed to realise this, yet he was always on the verge of a great discovery. If he had been a little tougher in intellect, a little more tightly belted for the race, if, moreover, his temper had been a little less petulant and trivial, he might have carried his Italian manner in English verse to an equal point of derived originality with Spenser, who, two centuries earlier, had learned so much from his luxurious southern models. Leigh Hunt's verse is constantly over-bubbling with fancy; but of imagination, in the high sense, it has very little, and it is consequently most successful when fancy suffices to complete the desired impression. *Mahmoud* and *The Glove and the Lions* are excellent examples of Hunt's gentle humanity, though even here there are not absent blemishes which make the sympathetic reader wince.

A feature of Hunt's poetical activity which has hitherto been scarcely known is his political satire. The common story is that he was shut up in gaol for having said, in the *Examiner*, that the Prince Regent was " a fat Adonis." This, we are told, was " construed into a libel," and was certainly rude, but hardly seems to justify two years' close imprisonment. But Mr. Milford, ransacking the files of the newspaper, has found more serious excuses for indictment. *The St. James's Phenomenon* is really too vivacious. It was less than polite, it was scarcely loyal, to say of the future George IV. :—

> " His organs of digestion
> Make a noise like the wheels of mangles ;
> His tongue's a skin,
> And hollow within,
> And his teeth are dice at angles."

Mr. Lytton Strachey has been suspected of being no courtier, but he would scarcely like to sign the *Coronation Soliloquy*, although it is an extremely lively and ingenious lyric. Leigh Hunt continued to issue these noisy squibs for many years, and they form a section of his writing which deserves to be borne in mind when we estimate his talent and character. He hated tyranny and brutality ; the world he wished for was a fairy place the intrusion into which of cruelty, insolence, and cowardice was to be resisted in violent terms. He must forget his birds and his blossoms for a minute while he drove the intruder forth with harsh cries. His political satires, now for the first time brought together, remind us in some degree of Moore's *Twopenny Postbag* and the like, but they are rougher and more sincere.

The verse of Leigh Hunt cannot be safely considered except in the light of his prose, and both must be measured by his character. In this connection I am tempted to quote from a paper in his newspaper, *The Tatler*, which has never,

so far as I am aware, been reprinted since it appeared in
1831, and may therefore be almost called unpublished.
The young Arthur Hallam had spoken lightly of Leigh
Hunt as belonging to the school of Shelley and Keats, and
as being, as he put it, their *caposetta*. Hunt was moved to
his own defence, and on August 1 he answers thus :—

" [Mr. Hallam] says [I was] diverted from my poetical aims
' by a thousand personal predilections and political habits of thought '
. . . My sympathies with humanity were always pretty strong ;
they had had a remarkable education ; but their political directions
were an accident. . . . I am nothing if not *social*. In temperament
as well as origin I am somewhat of a foreign and Southern species,
and have perhaps been as little understood in my way as my admirable friends [Shelley and Keats] in theirs. I never claimed to set
up a school of any kind, and must beg leave to disclaim having done
so. . . . Mr. Shelley was a Platonic philosopher of the acutest and
loftiest kind, poetising. He came out of the schools (if the word
must be used) of Plato and Æschylus. Mr. Keats was a poet of the
schools of Spenser and Milton. I myself (if in self-defence I may be
allowed to characterise myself at all) came out of the lower forms of
the narrative schools of poetry, of which, perhaps, I might call
myself a runaway disciple, sentimentalised. To move a tear with
a verse is the highest poetical triumph I can boast of. Generally
speaking, I am something between poetry and prose, a compound
of the love and wit of Nature."

METAPHYSICAL POETRY

METAPHYSICAL POETRY

WITHIN the last few years more attention has been paid to the poets called " metaphysical " than they had enjoyed since the time in which they flourished. Indeed, it is not necessary to make this reservation, for in their own age they seem to have been little appreciated for the qualities we now perceive in them. What the actual valuation of poetry in the seventeenth century was it is very difficult to decide, so much text has been preserved and so little intelligible comment.

To turn to the prose remarks made by contemporaries of the poets is simply to be bewildered, all seem so wide of the mark. When Winstanley, writing in Herrick's life-time, says of the *Hesperides* that " but for the interruption of trivial passages it might have made up none of the worst Poetick Landskips," what does he mean ? When we are told of Randolph that he was " of such a pregnant Wit that the Muses seem not only to have smiled, but to have been tickled at his Nativity " we seem listening to gibberish. I do not think that there is any evidence that readers in the seventeenth century saw in *Lycidas* or in Marvell's *Garden*, or in *They are all gone into the World of Light*, or even in *The Pulley*, what we see now. The critics inquired whether the poets excelled in " the Epænitick " or " the Bucolick " style, not whether they achieved beauty of expression or spirituality of thought.

There was apparently such universal public insensibility to these finer qualities that I have sometimes asked myself what it was that encouraged the poets to go on writing so well, and in such multitudes. The only real seventeenth-century appreciation of poetry occurs in the encomiastic pieces prefixed to the little books of verse by friends.

Attention was first drawn by Dr. Johnson to the unity of style which links together a certain company of poets who begin with Donne and end with Cowley and Flatman. He classed them together in a famous passage of his *Life of Cowley*, written in 1777. He spoke of " a race of writers that may be termed the metaphysical poets," as though he was inventing the adjective, and he has gained, and still seems to retain, the credit for it. He is not very helpful in his *Dictionary*, where he defines " Metaphysickal " as " versed in metaphysicks." People speak of " what Johnson has called Metaphysical Poetry." But it is a curious fact that he borrowed the epithet, no doubt unconsciously, from a great writer who had lived with the poets he described, and in his youth had been one of them. In the very interesting preface to his *Juvenal*, in 1693, Dryden had written that Donne " affects the metaphysics, not only in his satires, but in his amorous verses." This is the hint which Johnson expanded in the remarkable pages on Wit which have been so often quoted.

What Dryden, and after him Johnson, exactly understood by " metaphysic " is doubtful, but we may assume that they opposed it to natural or simple fancy. They were affected by the ingenuity, the subtlety, and what Johnson calls the " watch for novelty " which distinguish Donne, for instance, from the straightforward sentiment and lucid imagery of the Elizabethans. Mr. Grierson very justly points out that real metaphysical poetry, such as that of Lucretius and Dante, is inspired by a philosophical conception of the universe, and he notes that in this high sense Milton himself was no philosopher. We do well to put away from us all lofty imaginings about the *rôle* assigned to the human spirit in the great drama of existence. This was no part of the business of people like the two Vaughans and the Matchless Orinda.

When we come to essay a definition of what really was the aim of the English lyric poets from Donne to Cowley we find it easy to see that they had a common purpose, but difficult to state it in adequate language. Perhaps we get nearest to it when we say that their object was an application of the psychological method to the passions. The poet, tired of pastoral superficialities, looked deeply into his own soul, and found himself in possession of certain data, which he produced with more or less skill in terms of the imagination. He illustrated these spiritual phenomena, and endeavoured to make them intelligible and tangible by calling to their illustration images drawn from common experience. There was a constant temptation to employ an excess of ingenuity in the use of this imagery, which was deliberately heightened so as to startle the reader and to rivet his attention. The innumerable songsters of the Elizabethan period had been satisfied with the commonplaces of sentiment tricked out in beautiful language :—

> " The withered primrose by the mourning river,
>   The faded summer's sun from weeping fountains,
> The light-blown bubble, vanishèd for ever,
>   The molten snow upon the naked mountains
> Are emblems that the treasures we uplay
> Soon wither, vanish, fade, and melt away."

This might in a sense be called philosophical, but it was just the kind of thing that irritated Donne and drove him into discords. He must delve deeper than this, or not at all ; and so strong was his influence that from the moment when his " metaphysical " experiments began to be read the poets ceased to tune their oaten pipe with fluency and sweetness. They were ready to sacrifice everything, even beauty, in order to obtain a closer insight into the movements of passion.

Where did this impulse come from ? Dr. Johnson
suggests that it was borrowed from the Italian writer
whom he calls " Marina." But Giovanni Battista Marino,
although in the latter part of the seventeenth century he
exercised an extraordinary fascination over the continent
of Europe, does not seem to have been much known in
England, although Drummond knew him. Moreover, the
famous epic of *Adone,* which was the vehicle of that fascination, did not see the light in Italy until 1623, when Donne
was fifty years of age and had written all his most remarkable poems. It is not possible to explain George Herbert
or Cowley by a reference to Marino, for there is no real
similarity. The great poem of the fantastic Italian is a
wilderness of description, a sort of labyrinth of perfumed
and incongruous conceits, like the garden Mistress Mary
planted with silver bells and cockle shells and pretty maids
all in a row. Marino makes no sort of effort to discover
uncharted provinces in the soul of man, whereas it was the
real originality of the English metaphysical poets that
this is exactly what they did endeavour to do, often very
awkwardly, but always conscientiously and seriously.

We may perhaps allow that their style was affected by
the general dryness which fell upon all European literature
after the Renaissance, and that their fondness for extravagant conceits ran parallel with the excesses of Marinism,
but that is all we can admit. The influence of Marino was
never felt in England as that of Petrarch, for instance, had
been felt at the end of Elizabeth's reign.

The more we reflect upon this problem, the more importance shall we give to the individual genius of Donne.
We are only beginning, after three hundred years, to realise
what a giant he was. Mr. Grierson, to whom we owe the
best existing text of Donne's poetry, has always been an
enthusiastic exponent of the potency of the mighty Dean.
He does not fail to notice, in the essay which opens his

anthology of *Metaphysical Lyrics and Poems*, the freshness of Donne's imaginative point of view. With great reluctance we have been forced, by the investigations of Sir Sidney Lee and other scholars, to recognise that what we had been accustomed to admire as the harmony and sweetness of the early lyrists is but in a relative degree their own. The voice is the voice of the Italian Jacob, although the hands may have an English roughness.

Mr. Grierson puts it with an outspokenness which is almost shocking, but can hardly be refuted. " Over all the Elizabethan sonnets," he says, " hangs the suggestion of translation or imitation." Often the lack of individuality is double or treble ; we have English imitations of French translations, Drummond's version of Desportes' copy of Tansillo's paraphrase of some classic poet. These English imitations were charming, but we cannot assign to them the value which is more and more obviously due to Donne's profound originality.

It is instructive to turn from the sugary and flowery fancies of the Elizabethans to the subtle hyperboles of which Mr. Grierson has collected a precious handful. Compare Greene's *O were she pitiful as she is fair*, so delicate, pensive, and melodious, with Donne's *Prohibition*. Each piece is an appeal to a woman, for her own sake, not to reward the poet's devotion with neglect or dislike. But see into what profundities Donne drops his plummet :—

" Take heed of hating me,
Or too much triumph in the victory !
Not that I shall be mine own officer
And hate with hate again retaliate ;
But thou wilt lose the style of conqueror,
If I, thy conquest, perish by thy hate.
Then, lest my being nothing lessen thee,
If thou hate me, take heed of hating me."

The great gift which Donne passed down to his disciples was an intellectual intensity of expression. He taught the poets to regard mellifluousness with suspicion, if it con-

cealed poverty of thought, and to be more anxious to find
words, even stumbling and harsh words, for their personal
emotions, than to slip over the surface of language in a
conventional sweetness. This intensity is what marks
every one of the Metaphysicals down to Flatman and
Traherne, in whom, under pressure from French rhetoric,
the school finally expired. But even Flatman, who is so
imperfect, preserves on occasion that brave splendour of
expression which they all learned from Donne :—

> " We are misguided in the dark, and thus
>   Each star becomes an *ignis fatuus ;*
>   Yet pardon me, ye glorious lamps of light,
>   'Twas one of you that led the way,
>   Dispelled the gloomy night,
>   Became a Phosphor to the Eternal Day,
>   And showed the Magi where the Almighty Infant lay."

This is from Flatman's *Review*, a poem which Mr.
Grierson does not quote, and which, indeed, in its entirety
would be unworthy of a place in his anthology, but in which
the flash of the great metaphysical manner is thus suddenly
revealed.

Donne had turned in middle life from a contemplation
of the tortures of earthly love to a scholastic analysis of the
mysteries of religion, and though the Metaphysicals continued to celebrate the conduct of their amours, it was in
their spiritual rapture that they rose to the highest
sublimity.

Mr. Grierson has some excellent remarks on this subject,
and it has been left for him first to observe how suitable
the metaphysical method was to interpret the passion of
Christian worship. It is not a little to the credit of the
Metaphysicals that almost all the English religious verse
which is also poetry is of their composition. In George
Herbert we have the orthodox Anglican, who has been
Public Orator and a courtier to kings, addressing with
intimate tenderness One who is the King of Kings. In

Crashaw the transcendental Catholic flings his soul like so much nard and cassia on the altar-flame. In Henry Vaughan, the mystic, almost the Rosicrucian, loses himself in a dream of that " shady city of palm-trees," under which the staggering spirit might sink down in an ecstasy and lose all sense of mortal disability.

So with other types of the passionate worshipper in a reverie or trance. So with the saintly Mildmay Fane, so with Traherne—both of whom Mr. Grierson (I know not why) ignores ; so even with poets like Marvell and Cowley, in whom the religious element confines itself to respectful piety, and never skirts even the borderland of ecstasy, there is that same intense observation of the movement of the passions applied in serious meditation which seems to me to be the peculiar attribute of the Metaphysicals. We meet with it in all our serious verse, of course, since even the theological aspirations of Herbert and Crashaw may be paralleled in Wither on the one hand and in Charles Wesley and Christina Rossetti on the other. But it is in the poets from Donne to Traherne, covering a space of nearly one hundred years, that we find it expressed with an intensity and a unity of style that we look for in vain elsewhere, a style that undulates in a marvellous way from the passion of love to the passion of piety, so that when the poet exclaims—

> " Love, thou art absolute sole Lord
> Of Life and Death."

we hardly know, and perhaps do not need to know, whether the address is made to the sensuous human instinct or to the Divine abstraction which dwells in

> " That endless height which is
> Zenith to us, and our Antipodes."

LAMARTINE AND THE ENGLISH POETS

LAMARTINE AND THE ENGLISH POETS

SOME months ago, in writing of the early works of Sainte-Beuve, I commented on the desirability of close examination being made if it still were possible, of the influence of English authors on the juvenile taste of the Frenchmen of that age. Since then I have been gratified to learn, from my friend M. Jusserand, that a student in Paris has undertaken this particular task. But very much remains to be done. Between the abdication of Napoleon in 1815 and the determination of Canning to cut England off from the Concert of the Powers, there was a brief period during which the intellectual influence of Great Britain was strong in Paris. From that time it declined, and the intellectual division of the two countries became more marked than the political.

By the time that Dickens and Balzac, Tennyson and Hugo became dominant, all sympathy between English and French literature had ceased. But there was an earlier period in which it was very considerable, and the history of the interchange has never been written. It would probably, at this distance of time, be difficult to revive it, but something more searching than has yet been attempted might be done. At all events, in the case of Lamartine, the splendid edition of the *Meditations*, on which M. Lanson has expended years of labour and learning, is a mine from which a good deal may be extracted and expanded. I propose to try to-day to find out what some of the relations of Lamartine to English poetry were.

Alphonse de Lamartine de Prat was born at Macon in
1790 ; he was, therefore, considerably older than the
other French poets of the Romantic revival, but he was
exactly of the generation of Byron and Shelley.   His
youth was buried in a remote Burgundian home ; such
foreign influences as he met with were likely to come from
the still dominant eighteenth century.   The pastoral childhood he spent in the farmstead of Milly is celebrated in
many familiar passages ; " no man," he says, " was ever
bred closer to Nature nor sucked at an earlier age the milk
of rustic things."   The French poets anterior to him had
been creatures of town and college ; he alone was exposed
to no artificial conditions.   Like Wordsworth—

> " Fair seed-time had his soul, and he grew up
>   Fostered alike by beauty and by fear."

Among his father's vines he read Chateaubriand, who
was the imaginative force of the moment, and the author of
Atala was a lover of English literature, which still carried
in France the prestige of independence and romantic
force.   At the age of seventeen Lamartine began to keep
a record of the authors he read, and in 1808 the name of
Pope occurs in it for the first time.   Next year his curri-
culum widened, and he read Sterne, both in *Tristram
Shandy* and the *Sentimental Journey*.   An English tutor is
mentioned, and at the age of nineteen we find him deep in
the study of our language.   Pope is continued, Fielding
and Richardson are added to the list.   We cannot fail to
see how much there was in *Eloïse to Abélard* and in the
Unfortunate Lady which would attract the happy but
melancholy youth at Milly.   Pope, in my judgment, was
the original source of the elegiacal disposition of Lamartine.

But in 1810 we find a still more powerful lodestone
drawing the mind of Lamartine towards England.   In that
year he met with Young's *Night Thoughts*, and was deeply
impressed by this stately and lugubrious poem, which,

the frivolous reader of to-day should note, still held at that time its domination over the minds of all pious and meditative readers of verse.   French critics have taken for granted that Lamartine only knew Letourneur's prose translation of the *Night Thoughts ;* of this I do not see any evidence, though he may have used Letourneur as a crib to help him with the original.   It would be tedious to cite many examples, but here is one at random.   In the earliest of the *Meditations* Lamartine called upon death—

> " Viens donc, viens détachez mes chaînes corporelles !
> Viens, ouvre ma prison ; viens, prête-moi tes ailes,
> Que tardes-tu ? "

There is nothing like that in Letourneur, but Young had lamented how man :—

> " Prisoner of earth, and pent beneath the moon,
> Here pinions all his wishes ; wing'd by heaven
> To fly at infinite."

The whole of *L'Immortalité* is steeped in the sentiment of *Night Thoughts*, and often in the language, too.   It is, perhaps, not surprising that in 1810 Lamartine succumbed to the spell of Ossian, which was woven so closely around all romantic spirits in that age.   When he was twenty he studied Otway.   No particular play is specified, but we may believe that it was the painful domestic tragedy of *The Orphan* which engaged his melancholy leisure.   In the same year he read Gray's *Elegy in a Country Churchyard*, which must have made a deep impression on his memory, since the form of it is manifest in the technique of the noblest of all Lamartine's poems, *Le Lac*, of August, 1817. I do not remember that this has been observed by any French critic.

The fascination exercised over the early Romantics by the writings of James Macpherson has often been noted. But there was no poet of eminence who succumbed to it more completely than Lamartine.   He attributed the

original impetus of his fancy to the study of two foreign
authors, Tasso and Ossian, who may seem to us to have
remarkably little in common. He met with the ravings of
Temora and Fingal in the early months of 1808, and more
than forty years afterwards he gave a somewhat florid
report of the adventure :—

" Ossian was the Homer of my earliest years ; to him I owe somewhat of my melancholy as a painter. This is the sorrow of the sea.
I very rarely tried to imitate him : but involuntarily I assimilated
the vagueness, the dreaminess, the self-annihilation in reverie, the
eye that contemplates confused apparitions far away. Ossian was
for me an ocean after tempest, on which something was floating
under the light of the moon, where figures of young girls seemed
lifting their white arms and spreading out their wet hair upon the
foam of the waves, where I heard plaintive voices interwoven with
the moaning of the waters upon the reef. Ossian is the unwritten
book of dreams, and the pages of it are covered with enigmatical
characters on which my eye rested as I wrote and re-wrote my own
poems, as a dreamer may compose landscapes out of the motions of
the clouds."

Lamartine was a prodigious reader in his youth, and it
would be an error to exaggerate the effect of English literature upon his mind. But the evidence of that effect is far
too great to be laid aside. In his charming autobiographical
sketch *Des Destinées de la Poésie* (1834), he paid a tribute
to Milton, whose *Paradise Lost* he appears to have met with
when he was twenty. Of Thomson, Addison, and even
Dryden mention is made, and in 1813 he read *Clarissa
Harlowe* again, this time through to the end—a considerable
feat. In all this, however, he does not seem to have
proceeded later than the middle of the eighteenth century,
and the innovations of Wordsworth and Coleridge, which
acutely interested the young Sainte-Beuve, seem to have
been unknown to Lamartine. It is very tempting to
discover a relation between the author of *Stanzas Written
in Dejection near Naples* and of *Le Golfe de Baïa près Naples*,
but it cannot be maintained. The former belongs to
Shelley's later residence in Italy, and is commonly dated

1818. Lamartine, who equalled Pope in sly autobiographical artifices, stated, for reasons of his own, that he wrote *Le Golfe de Baïa* in 1813, but M. Lanson shows that 1816 is the probable date. Sentiments of ecstatic melancholy expressed in these two poems were in the air at that time, and it is impossible to believe that Lamartine and Shelley, who had much in common, had ever heard of one another.

But the revelation of a new spirit in English poetry came upon the French minstrel of the *Méditations* when the fiery planet of Byron swept into his ken. This appears to have been in 1812, when some verses of the English poet were recited to him. Three years later he says that he saw a young man of striking appearance manœuvring his yacht on the Lake of Geneva, between Evian and Thonon, in rough weather. In another connection, he declares that the English poet was on horseback on the shore. Some days later he was informed that this was Milord Byron. In 1818 Louis de Vignet wrote to him from Geneva about a young English lord "whose life is a mystery and his verse a prodigy." In October of that year Lamartine says that he read *Childe Harold* at Milly, and was overwhelmed. " I shall always remember the spot, the season, the day, the room, the hour when this book fell from heaven into my solitude." He burned a packet of his own elegies, which were doubtless tinged with the florid sadness of a writer who now ceased to please him, Harvey of the *Meditations on the Tombs*. He sat down in a frenzy of inspiration and wrote his famous rhapsody *L'Homme*, which was an invocation of Byron by name.

Such is the narrative of Lamartine, but it is strewn with difficulties. For instance, Byron was in England through the whole of 1815, and could not have been seen battling with the elements or riding along Lake Leman. M. Lanson throws cold water on all these ardours. He thinks that

Lamartine had never heard of Byron until he went to Paris
in the autumn of 1818, when he found the English poet a
subject of general curiosity. " *Qu'est-ce que Lord Byron ?* "
everybody was asking : who is this " *esprit mysteriéux—
mortel, ange ou démon ?* " Lamartine probably bought the
new Galignani edition, and internal evidence points to the
conclusion that it was *Manfred*, and not *Childe Harold*,
which created that picturesque perturbation in the soul
of Lamartine, who accepted to the full the popular conception of Byron as the angel-demon of lyrical revolt :—

> " Et toi, Byron semblable à ce brigand [the homicide eagle],
> Les cris du désespoir sont tes plus doux concerts,
> Le mal est ton spectacle, et l'homme est ta victime ;
> Ton œil, comme Satan, a mesuré l'abîme,
> Et ton âme, y plongeant loin du jour et de Dieu,
> A dit à l'espérance un éternal adieu."

By some curious accident, Byron heard of the enthusiasm
of Lamartine, whom he spoke of to Moore as " my laureate
in Paris," and he asks for information about that " most
sanguinary *Epître* against me " of which he had been told
in June 1820. This, of course, was *L'Homme*, but it was a
eulogy, not an attack. The relations of the two poets are
extremely puzzling. It is not even certain that Byron saw
what the Frenchman had written about him until 1823,
when Lamartine sent him his published works. Whether
Byron, nearing his end, read them is unknown, but Lamartine preserved all through his own life a prodigious admiration for the author of *Manfred*, whom he always regarded as
" incontestably the greatest poetical genius of modern
times."

A wonderful book, this collection of *Méditations* of 1820,
which M. Lanson has edited with the last profusion of
learning and care. No one can be surprised, in turning
over its pages, that the splendour and light of such verses,
with their rush of wings and storm of voices, should have
bewitched France at the moment ·when her poetry was

waking from its ancient slumber. Lamartine was the long-awaited link with Racine ; he was the clarion of romance, the herald of a new music. We find it equally comprehensible that, when the first rapture was overpast, the negligences and the hollow places in all this fervid and melancholy improvisation should become apparent. Lamartine had risen like a rocket, and when his first hour was over no one ever fell in such a shower of expiring sparks. Excessive laudation was succeeded by extreme neglect, and for a long time after his death scarcely a note of appreciation was heard. But the critics of 1870 were blind, and I take this occasion to say, with humility, how it hurts me to remember that more than forty years ago I wrote of Lamartine in terms of ignorant and narrow detraction.

That would be impossible to-day, for he has gradually taken his place again as one of the great poets of Europe, and we have all come back to our senses. He himself summed up his claim on our regard when he said, " I was the first man to bring poetry down from Parnassus, and to give to what was called the Muse, not a conventional lyre of seven strings, but the very fibres of a human heart, touched and thrilled by the innumerable vibrations of nature." His faults were a tendency to mistiness and incoherence of thought, an excess of spontaneity laxly voluminous, and a prodigality of ornament not sufficiently under his control. But he could say, with no less truth than did his great English contemporary :—

> " Thanks to the human heart by which we live,
> Thanks to its tenderness, its joys, and fears,
> To me the meanest flower that blows can give
> Thoughts that do often lie too deep for tears."

SECOND THOUGHTS

SECOND THOUGHTS

Mr. George Moore is one of the best living writers of
English prose, and I think he is the most conscientious.
He is never satisfied with the choice of his language and the
structure of his sentences, and he longs, more passionately
than any one else, to achieve the impossible perfection.
So few writers indulge any such longing, or, indeed, have
ever dreamed that perfection in prose can exist as an ideal,
that Mr. Moore's vagaries with regard to revision ought to be
treated tenderly, even respectfully. He, at least, is an
artist through and through, and posterity will bring him his
reward. It is well to be certain of that, since it is to be
feared that the contemporary novel-reading public does
not appreciate and does not even perceive the zeal which

> " always moving as the restless spheres,
> Wills him to wear himself and never rest,
> Until he reach the ripest fruit of all "

in a new strange version of a familiar old story. Some
years ago, under pressure from his admirers, Mr. Moore
took an oath never again to attempt the re-writing of a
novel, but he broke it when he turned the *Drama in Muslin*
of 1886 into the completely reincarnated *Muslin* of 1915.
What he is capable of when he sets his mind on re-composi-
tion may be seen in the various versions of *Evelyn Innes*,
where Mr. Moore did not shrink from " the formidable task
of re-writing 300,000 words." Formidable, indeed; and
is the result of such an experiment ever worth the labour
expended ? Let us see what is to be said for and against
the practice.

In favour of a drastic revision there is, first and foremost, the conscience of the writer. When a man is so profoundly and continuously occupied with the various problems of style as Mr. Moore manifestly is, to remark that it is not worth while for him to take so much trouble is an impertinence. His natural reply is that he does not write to arrest our indolent attention with a tale, but to add to the literature of the country another durable ornament. That being the case, he is haunted by the fear lest, as it has been given to the public, it may contain " disgraceful "—by which he means awkward and inharmonious—pages, and he re-reads it with that suspicion. His taste, trained to an extreme delicacy, prevails upon him to conceive that this fear is indeed well founded.

Given this scruple of the disinterested artist, and it is difficult to see how Mr. Moore can be expected to resist the impulse to re-write. His variations of his early text are inevitable ; the only alternative would be for him to moon around in silence nursing an afflicted conscience. In the latest instance, now before me, he says that while he was writing some portions of *Héloïse and Abélard*, his " inspiration died suddenly without his perceiving it," so that many of the circumstances and thoughts needful to make the tale perfect " dropped out of his mind."

This is an interesting and plausible way of accounting for inequality of workmanship, but why wait until the work has long been published before picking up these thoughts and bringing inspiration back to life ? Other people suffer from such misfortunes, but are able to redeem them on their proofs, and Mr. Moore would save his future editors a vast amount of worry if he would do the same.

Against the practice of re-writing books already accepted by the public there is a great deal to be said. In the first place, it is a falsification of history. Everybody has reviled Pope for altering and heightening the style of his own

correspondence when he gave it to the booksellers to publish, but if he chose to regard a letter as a piece of literary
art, how does he differ from Mr. George Moore tinkering
The Lake or *Evelyn Innes?* In each case the new text does
not represent the mood of the old time, and must therefore
be in discord with it and with the new time as well.

When Mr. Moore published *A Mummer's Wife*—that is
to say, thirty-seven years ago—he did not write so correctly
as he does now ; indeed (to be brutally frank), he often
wrote very indifferently. But it is of the greatest interest
to observe the growth of Mr. Moore as a writer ; the
imperfections of *A Mummer's Wife* add a peculiar lustre
to the beauty of *The Brook Kerith*. Yet when the author,
to satisfy the craving for uniform perfection, " re-writes "
in the language of 1920 what he composed in 1880, we lose
all indication of development, and the gain is far less than
would be the composition, in the hours so fantastically
spent, of a new work of art, in spirit as well as form, appropriate to the author's maturity.

Another objection is that, however generously the new
wine is poured into the old bottle, there is always some
old wine left in the bottle, and this produces a mixture
of dubious gusto. These " revised " and " re-written "
chapters invariably present a confusion of styles, an
irregularity of tone. The appended pages do not complete
the design of the author, which ought to proceed, if he must
be consistent, until nothing of the old is left. Bacon, who
was on the side of Mr. Moore, confessed that " after my
manner, I alter ever, when I add, so that nothing is finished
till all be finished." The revising author is faced by the
familiar dilemma—if you get your umbrella re-covered
and then introduce a fresh stick and handle, how much of
the old umbrella survives ? Mr. Moore gives us to-day
what is no more than a tassel and a button—namely, a
new chapter and some revised conversations ; but we feel

no certainty that he may not presently rip off the brown silk cover and give us a green bombazine in exchange. He feels the need of some apology, and he treats us to one of his amusing and ingenious prefaces of defiance.

Mr. Moore is an improvisatore, and his divagations into history will give his commentators a great deal of trouble. If he is pursued by tiresome pedantry he is apt to vanish, like the ghost, with a twang of music and a delicate perfume. It seems unkind and almost profane to trouble him with vain inquiries, but his new preface leaves me no choice. By way of defending his practice of revision he gives instances of other celebrated writers who have re-written their works. He asks, with a fine scorn, " Have all you who write in newspapers forgotten that whosoever wrote *Othello* added to it ? " Well, I have to confess that I am one of those who had " forgotten " this very interesting fact. Mr. Moore must produce his evidence, for, so far as I know, none has ever yet been adduced. *Othello* is an unfortunate instance, since it is a play about the composition of which we know absolutely nothing. It appeared first in quarto in 1622, six years after Shakespeare's death, and again immediately afterwards in the First Folio. The latter offered some improvements in the text, but they were very unimportant ; " a compositor or an actor would be competent to have suggested the changes." If Mr. Moore has private information as to the revision of *Othello* by the poet whom he so quaintly calls " Whosoever," we must urge him to make it public. Till then the only evidence of revision is a certain cutting out of words like " sblood " and " zounds " from the quarto. This is not re-writing, dear Mr. Moore !

Our ingenious minstrel does not seem to be more lucky when he reaches the moderns, for he takes Landor as his example of drastic revision. He is probably thinking of the famous lines to Rose Aylmer, which offer, it is true, a

strong argument for the polishing of published verses by
their critical author. Landor wrote, about 1805, an elegy
which is in all the anthologies, and which closed with the
stanza :

> " *Sweet* Aylmer, when these wakeful eyes
>   May weep, but never see,
> A night of *sorrows* and of sighs
>   I consecrate to thee."

Long afterwards the Poet corrected this too :—

> " *Rose* Aylmer . . .
> A night of *memories* and of sighs,"

alterations which justify Mr. Moore to the full in his theory.
No greater improvement was ever made by unsatisfied
genius. It is also true that in reprinting the *Imaginary
Conversations* Landor sent to the press some passages to be
inserted ; Mr. George Moore will doubtless remind me of
the apologue about Truth in the *Marcus and Quinctus
Cicero ;* but I cannot admit that any one of these extensions
constitutes a re-writing of the book in the sense that Mr.
Moore has used it in altering his own novels.

The new chapter which Mr. Moore has inserted into
Héloïse and Abélard will take its place early in Vol. II.
Readers of the romance—and it is fresh in all our memories
—will recollect that when the lovers arrived by ship from
Orléans to Tours, they met the famous Trouvère, the Comte
de Rodebœuf. But when Héloïse went into hiding with her
friends in Brittany, Abélard rode off alone to Blois. Mr.
Moore has felt that at this point of the story he has dwelt
fully on the metrical stimulus given by Rodebœuf, but has
not said enough about the effect on Abélard's spirit of
separation from Héloïse. As he puts it : " There were
no meditations, which, in my opinion, was a great loss to
the book." The pages which he now inserts correct this
omission and show that the image of the man's dear lady
was constantly before him. He revives old memories of

the stealthy life they lived together under the Canon's roof in Paris before the dread of exposure and scandal drove them to their westward flight. That Mr. Moore has never written more admirably, an extract from these " meditations " will show :

" He rambled on, thinking of Héloïse, for now nothing else seemed worth thinking about. Realism and Nominalism songs and lute-playing, were forgotten in remembrances of the light as it fell upon her clear brown face, of her laughter with a touch of sorrow in it always, of her fragrant fingers, of the lighting up of her face as a thought came into her mind—such thoughts came into a woman's mind before. In the woods of Franchard she was so near to him that he often looked up, almost expecting to see her ; nearer, he continued, than when we were together in the false world that we call reality ; to reveal her to me a few leagues were needed, and he vowed that when they met his love would be more worthy of her than it was in the past. And his thoughts, breaking away suddenly, he asked himself if death would reveal the significance of our life to us. For the past being a mirror, he continued, death may be a greater mirror. The sound of water gurgling through the reeds accompanied his thoughts."

The other and slighter corrections deal with the talk of the child Astrolabe, who was made, the author thinks, to talk like a boy of eleven, instead of like a child of eight and a half. A further puerility and inconsequence, therefore, have now been added to the speech of Astrolabe. Perhaps Mr. Moore, with his passion for reconstruction, may feel himself obliged to overhaul this character still more drastically in a future edition. For my own part, I was quite satisfied with Héloïse's precocious little son as I first met with him.

HOW TO READ THE BIBLE

HOW TO READ THE BIBLE

In the course of an earnest and sober appeal for a revision of our attitude of mind towards the Sacred Books, I meet with this statement of fact : " No scholar now holds the old doctrine of the verbal inspiration and inerrancy of the Scriptures." Such a pronouncement, coming from no revolutionary source, but from the pen of Professor A. Seth Pringle-Pattison, who is one of the most conservative and responsible thinkers of our age, is calculated to set in action a memory like mine, which goes back to a period when the uniform inspiration of all portions of the Bible was practically unquestioned in the religious world.

Opinion glides along in the rapid evolution of our time, and we hardly realise how completely our views change within the course of a couple of generations. Fifty years ago *The Duty of Candour in Religious Teaching* would have shocked the sensibility of most educated persons, and would have seemed to be the work of what the seventeenth century called a " libertine," that is to say, a man for whom moral and religious responsibility had no existence. Yet it is written by a philosopher whose admirable book, *The Idea of God*, revealed a tender and pious conscience regulated by a reverent intellect. What Dr. Pringle-Pattison has to say on matters of such moment as the widening and deepening of our attitude to Biblical study must be worthy of our grave attention.

The conviction of most people half a century ago may be summed up in words which were constantly repeated in my ears as a child. The Bible, in its English-translation, was regarded, from Genesis to Malachi, from Matthew to Revelation, as dictated to its so-called authors, but more properly transcribers, by the Holy Ghost. It was definitely affirmed that not merely the doctrine, but the actual language, was Divine, incapable of error, superior to all the frailties which accompany human literature. " The words are as much the Spirit's as the ideas." It is difficult to credit, but it is the fact, that the Authorised Version of 1611 was very widely held to enjoy this immunity from criticism, as though, without any previous Greek or Hebrew text, the English of Lancelot Andrewes and his colleagues had descended upon them direct from heaven. When it was pointed out that the earlier translators, like Tyndale and Coverdale, had produced versions which differed from that of 1611, the reply was that these were imperfect, and that the Holy Ghost first spoke finally and fully in the Authorised Version.

Among the Evangelicals there were many who could not accept this illogical theory, and they went back to the ancient texts, finding the plenary inspiration there, and trying, by awkward literal translations of their own, to get still nearer to the Sacred Utterance. But all united in believing that God, as they said, had " employed human speech," and that revealed religion was contained in a single volume, written down at various times, but in all its parts preserving the same level and possessing the same literal value.

The earliest definite revolt against this theory of verbal inspiration was made by Robertson Smith in 1875. His famous article on the Bible was received with a howl of horror, and led, after a controversy of unexampled bitterness, to his expulsion from his chair of Biblical Exegesis in Aberdeen. We must not overlook the fact that what gave importance to the arguments of Robertson Smith was that they were not put forward by an outsider, but by an insider. Of course, deists and other pronounced types of infidel had long treated the canon of Scripture with hostility or derision. Two hundred years ago people like Toland and Matthew Tindal had declared " Christianity not mysterious," and had mocked at revelation. They, however, were in the bond of iniquity, and what they gabbled mattered nothing to the elect.

But Robertson Smith was elect himself; he started altogether a new idea, namely, that the language, " the human speech," was a finite thing, and that it was therefore no longer reasonable for those who held the inner fort of orthodoxy to exclude from their weapons of defence such historical and textual criticism of it as is universally applied to the structure of other books. The object of Robertson Smith and of those who supported him in his appeal for a " charter of critical freedom " was not to undermine or reject revealed religion, but to strengthen it by insisting on the moral value of an honest search for truth.

We can very well understand the horror with which this proposition was received among orthodox bibliolaters. It was the steadying by mortal hands of an immortal mystery which was quite capable of supporting itself; it was the sin of Uzzah, who put forth his hand to hold the Ark of God, because the oxen shook it. The unwillingness of the rank and file of believers to accept the new conception, so far from confirming the mystical character of the Bible has weakened it. Mr. Gladstone, who was not averse to an occasional plunge into theology, spoke of " the corporeal perfection " of Scripture, and there were many, for a long time the majority of Christians, who protested that to question whether Moses' rod was turned into a real zoological serpent, or whether the walls of Jericho fell literally flat at the seven-fold blast of Joshua's trumpet, was to abandon everything which the Bible contained, not of history only, but of doctrine as well.

M.B.T.   z

"Am I to believe that the Holy Ghost has set his seal to a lie, simply because phenomena are recorded of which my finite senses can render no explanation?" Thus have I heard the case put by one more formidable in argument than the Numidian lion. "Every jot and tittle of the revealed narrative, or nothing at all!"—such was the logical and daunting alternative. It followed that if we admitted the smallest criticism, there was nothing for it but to reject the Bible altogether, and to abandon the least attempt at its defence.

Dr. Pringle-Pattison faces the dilemma, and discovers a third course. The aim of his eloquent and persuasive plea is to reject what is no longer tenable, but with the express purpose of drawing closer to us and making a more precious part of our intellectual experience what is living and eternal. We are to admit all that careful criticism has alleged with regard to those portions of the Old Testament which are plainly transitory, that is to say, which bear upon their very face the evidence of human agency, and, in fact, of human error. We are to look upon the tribal legends of Genesis as recording the finite, but often pious and beautiful, speculations of men who, in the old phrase, "walked with God," who, in other words, endeavoured, by such light as the morning of the world vouchsafed them, to discover the Divine Purpose in life.

Above all we are to avoid what was the cardinal error of the bibliolaters, namely, their refusal to admit the bare possibility of progress in revelation. The Pentateuch, with all its fables and its folk-lore, was held to be as true in fact and detail, as completely unassailable on all points, as a very careful record of what happened in some English community yesterday would be. That God should have addressed to the infancy of man a message couched in exactly the same terms, and demanding the same experience as that addressed to a full maturity of the ages—this was the absurdity, and if we may say so, actually the impiety of the old theory of verbal inspiration.

The purpose of our philosopher, then, is to commend the Bible to readers of our day, who have so widely abandoned the study of it on account of the chasm conventionality opens between common sense and formal tradition. There is much evidence that the English Scriptures are losing their hold on the attention of the Christian Churches. The Sacred Books are worn with routine, deadened with the familiarity of their use in combination with habits of hackneyed speech. It is not merely that an ever-increasing class is trained to be hostile to the Bible because of the outworn dogmas and " plans of salvation " which are founded upon it, but, as Dr. Pringle-Pattison ably points out, its acceptance as an inspired and complete revelation is more and more felt to be " in flagrant contradiction to the system of our best-established secular beliefs." His suggestion of a remedy is worthy of careful consideration :—

"I believe, he says, that it is the bounden duty, as well as the plain interest, of the Churches at the present time to undertake a campaign of instruction in regard to the Bible, and primarily in regard to the Old Testament. They should, through their most authoritative members, cut themselves loose in the plainest terms from the old doctrine of inspiration and inerrancy. Its manifest falsehood should be frankly and fearlessly expounded. . . . It is ridiculous to read that one of the recurring conundrums of religious debate in the trenches was the question, Who was Cain's wife! . . . In my view the Church should do its own rationalistic criticism, and thereby make its members immune against attacks conducted with such obsolete weapons."

These are courageous words, and without going into any question of theology, which is plainly not my province, I venture to urge in support of Dr. Pringle-Pattison that such action as he recommends would have an immediate effect in re-opening our eyes, which have become dulled to its fascination, to the marvellous beauty and vivacity of the Scripture narrative. It would make the Bible once again a living volume, a fountain of perennial interest.

z 2

These " holy and ghostly books " would become once more
what Cranmer wished them to be, " a better jewel in our
house than either gold or silver."

No one wants " a new Bible " ; what is called for is a
wise and sensible appreciation of that old one which has
been the solace of mankind and the model of pure language
for three hundred years. I know not when the practice of
printing the Testaments in chapters, and still worse in
verses, came into practice, nor what was its original object,
though I suppose the latter to have been connected with
ecclesiastical ritual. That it should be convenient so to
divide the Psalms can easily be understood, but in the
historical narratives it becomes a mere vexation, and has
doubtless had a good deal to do with the neglect of those
portions of the text. It has been remedied in Sir James
Frazer's " Passages of the Bible Chosen for their Literary
Brevity and Interest," than which I am acquainted with
no more delightful bedside companion. This selection,
taken implicitly from the Authorised Version, but arranged
as literature without those distracting ritual divisions,
should be in the hands of every one who joins Dr.
Pringle-Pattison in his campaign of instruction in regard
to the true value of the English Bible.

BLAKE AND GRAY

BLAKE AND GRAY

YEARS have passed since any discovery has been made on the field of English letters so sensational as that which Professor Grierson has the privilege of revealing in a magnificent folio. The history of the precious volume of Blake's designs for Gray's poems is curious, and yet simple. But, in the first place, it must be explained that these drawings have hitherto been, not merely undescribed, but unsuspected. That Blake had an interest in the verse of Gray was unknown, and still less was it imagined that his interest extended to the composition of no fewer than one hundred and one large drawings in colour. It is now observed that in the sale of Flaxman's effects, on July 1, 1828, lot 85 was " A Copy of Gray's Poems, illustrated by W. Blake, with his portrait by Mr. Flaxman." If that entry ever caught a critical eye, it was only to be forgotten, but in the meantime the " Copy of Gray's Poems " was bought, for eight guineas, by a Bond Street bookseller.

How had they come into Flaxman's possession ? Mr. Grierson seems to think that Blake presented them to him when the two artists were particularly intimate in 1800, when the sculptor appeared to the painter-poet " a sublime archangel, my friend and companion from eternity." This may very well be the case, but there seems to exist no reference to Gray in all the correspondence between the friends. I would not pit my opinion against Mr. Grierson's, which is founded on the closest study. But may not the designs have passed into Flaxman's hands at a later date, when he was striving to help forward Blake, who was no

longer quite so gracious as he might have been ? Dates
only further bewilder us, for Blake died after Flaxman, yet
before the Flaxman sale. Yet another conjecture I put
forward for what it is worth. Is it not possible that the
Gray designs never were Flaxman's property at all, but
were put into the Flaxman sale by Mrs. Blake, who in this
summer of 1828 was parting with many of her late husband's unsold works ? Yet a copy of verses addressed to
Mrs. Ann Flaxman, and signed by Blake, follows the
Elegy in a Country Churchyard, and is some evidence to the
contrary.

The further adventures of the Gray designs are hardly
less obscure. We find them presently in the library of
Beckford, who was an early collector of Blake books. But
still no one described them, and after Beckford's death,
in 1844, they passed unnoticed to his daughter, the Duchess
of Hamilton. No mortal eye seems to have seen them
again till Mr. Grierson examined them in a beautiful cedar
book case just before the dismantling of Hamilton Palace.
They had escaped, still unobserved, when the books were
sold in 1882, and were only discovered when everything
came to be moved. They have, therefore, remained to the
present day in the strictest sense unedited, and the warmest
thanks of all lovers of English painting and poetry are due
to the Duke and Duchess of Hamilton for allowing them
to be made public.

The æsthetic and historic value of this momentous relic
is extreme, and it is with emotion that we examine, after
such a prolonged seclusion, these illustrations of the double
art of Gray and Blake, " striking representatives," as Mr.
Grierson felicitously puts it, " of two clearly and deeply
cut periods in the ever-changing history of English imaginative art in poetry and painting." The edition of Gray's
Poems which was used by Blake has no bibliographical
value ; it is that published by John Murray in 1790, and

it simply reproduces the text which was settled by the edition of 1768.

I may dwell for a moment on the portrait of Blake by Flaxman, which is now for the first time reproduced from the pencil drawing—a slight and improvised affair, probably drawn from life in a few minutes. Mr. Grierson, no doubt, has compared it with the finished painting by Linnell, made in 1827. The features are the same, but not the shape of the skull, which in Linnell's portrait is remarkable for its extreme depth. If the portrait was intended to accompany the Gray designs, and if Mr. Grierson's supposition that the latter were made in 1800 is correct, Flaxman's model was forty-three years of age at the time. To me he looks considerably older.

A problem is involved in the sentiment which induced Blake to devote so great a length of time and disinterested care to the illumination of a poet with whom he might seem to have little in common, and with whom he had never come in contact. Under the *Ode on the Spring* he has here written :—

> Around the Springs of Gray my wild root weaves ;
> Traveller, repose and dream among my leaves !

We obey the summons with alacrity. After more than a century of silence, the gates are unlocked, and we tread the corridors of Blake's enchanted palace. In his excellent preface, which demands close attention, Mr. Grierson remarks that to a reader of the age of Blake, who had no Coleridge or Keats to compare him with, " Gray was far more of a romantic than he appears to us." This may happily recall criticism, which has adopted of late a grudging attitude towards the accomplished art of Gray, to a saner and a juster recognition of a poet who displayed exquisite and exalted imagination at a time when the lips of the Muses were locked or only murmured humdrum things.

But the contrast between Gray and Blake is so great that
Blake's now revealed devotion to Gray's poetry must
vividly stimulate our curiosity. The one man was elusive,
reserved, and quintessential, the other profuse, declama-
tory, and prophetic. The one " never spoke out," the
other had a trumpet ever at his lips. What can it have
been that attracted Blake to Gray ?

This is the question which Mr. Grierson discusses in his
prefatory essay. He remarks that there were " two qualities of Gray's poetry which were of a kind to appeal to
Blake's imagination—Gray's imaginative and finished
personifications and his feeling for the romantic element in
older English history, and yet more in the primitive
imaginings of Celtic and Scandinavian myth." He notes
that as early as 1785 Blake had exhibited at the Royal
Academy a tempera painting of " The Bard." This picture
Gilchrist was not able to describe, and Mr. Grierson also
does not write as if he had been it, but the entry shows that
Blake thus early—two years after the publication of his
own wonderful *Poetical Sketches*—had been attracted to
the romantic ardour of Gray's great ode. We may suppose
that he approached the text in the spirit which inspires the
fourteen magnificent designs which are here introduced.

The frontispiece to the poem reveals the Bard, an
apparition in long robes embroidered with stars, who
stands beside a gigantic harp on the sands of a creek
among mountains. A dark sea breaks in foam at his feet,
and storm clouds gather above his head. Winds sway
across his breast the tangled tresses of his long white beard,
while his vast eyes gaze out into infinity. Still more violent
is the next plate, in which a famished eagle shrieks above
the corpses of the murdered bards ; while in the next the
chief minstrel, demented with anguish, sweeps the rope-
like chords of his harp in a delirium. Extraordinarily
grotesque is the coiled figure of " the sweeping whirlwind,"

imagined as a human-headed sea monster, lying in wait on the surface of the sea for the " gilded vessel." The personifications in Gray's third stanza offer Blake an irresistible temptation to create those attenuated sexless graces, those monstrous bearded intensities, that shadowy flight of spectres, which represented to his imagination " pale Grief," " fierce War," " Truth severe, by fairy Fiction drest," and the remainder of them.

Gray, as all readers of his correspondence and of two of his principal poems are well aware, had a great sense of fun. But playful humour was not Blake's strong point, and we therefore turn with curiosity to his illustrations for the *Ode on the Death of a Favourite Cat* and *A Long Story*. He has not shirked his task in either case, but gives us six full-sized plates for the former and twelve for the latter. The designs for the Cat ode are singularly interesting. There were two ways of illustrating this poem, one a realistic representation of a brindled cat gazing down into a china vase while goldfish are swimming below her. This was not Blake's method at all. He chose the other, the purely symbolical and allusive way. In the frontispiece, the Cat is suspended in mid-air above, not a vase, but a limitless ocean, and the goldfish that tempt her are turned by the passion of her longing into human spectres, with toad faces and nude limbs propelled through the water by a prickly webbed armature of wings or fins.

In the next plate, Blake's fancy has shifted again. The " pensive Selina " has now a tiny naked woman squatted between her shoulders, and is not looking down into the vase, where the goldfish, no longer transformed by the intensity of her desire, are sailing in their normal shape. In the third plate, she has become human, with nothing but " her conscious tail " to suggest the Cat, and she gazes into the vase, where " the azure flowers " painted on the porcelain have come to serpentine life and wave their tendrils in the water. A very powerful design then shows Selina, slipping off her female shape, and plunging, a Cat of cats, into the water, while the goldfish, once more turned to spiky phantoms of humanity, dart from her grasp. The last plate displays her, wholly human and swathed in long white draperies, emerging for the eighth time from the flood, while the goldfish, who have ceased to be the object of her longing, have become mere stolid fish again.

Not less curious is the treatment of *A Long Story*, a sort of rambling ballad, founded on the trifling circumstances that two ladies, Lady Schaub and Miss Speed, called at the house in Stoke Poges where Gray resided with his mother and one of his aunts, and nearly caught the poet, who, however, took refuge in the one retreat secure from their curiosity. This seems a subject well suited, let us say, to Chodowiecki or Fragonard, but having the thick of the world between it and the genius of Blake. He has, nevertheless, been undaunted in twelve large drawings full of his peculiar vision. In illustrating the lines

> Full oft within the spacious walls
> When he had fifty winters o'er him,
> My grave Lord-Keeper led the Brawls:
> The Seals and Maces danc'd before him.

Blake, whether out of whimsical defiance of common sense, or from sheer misunderstanding of the poet's text, has made the dancers an actual Seal and Mace, the former a sprightly fairy, the latter a horrible grinning monster of an over-grown schoolboy, brandishing his sign of office, and astonishing the grave Lord-Keeper.

Later on in the ballad, when the two ladies had rummaged the poet's mother, pinched his aunt, and searched for him in vain throughout the house, " out of the window, whisk ! they flew." This line gives Blake his opportunity ; in the midst of forked lightnings and the frenzy of the elements, Lady Schaub and Miss Speed are seen vehemently

projected down into space like rebel angels, or Pestilence
and Famine unchained, yet in unruffled costume at the
height of the fashion, with the hat of one and the bonnet
of the other undisturbed. Blake usually keeps close to
his text, but for this poem he has invented a ghost of
prodigious size and hideousness, terrifying a hapless lady
in the mighty solitude of a gallery.

The general character of these designs is exactly what
long experience has taught us to expect from Blake, but
the drawing is not so emphatic as was the case in most of
the artist's work in the period of *America* and *Jerusalem*.
The style suggests the later period of the illustrations to
Blair's *Grave*, that is to say, between 1805 and 1808.
Between the shapeless dreams of the Prophetic Books and
the more intelligible designs made to adorn the text of
Young and Dante and Job there is a good deal of difference.
The Gray drawings seem to be akin to the last-mentioned,
and this is one reason why I incline to think that Mr.
Grierson may have conjecturally dated them a little too
early. But their date is of no importance. They are of
deep value as revealing the mingled audacity and docility
with which Blake approached a classic text. He accepted
the poetry with gratitude and gusto, but he reserved to his
own fancy the right of interpretation.

The figures appended to Young's *Night Thoughts* are well
known, and perhaps attract more admiration than their
sprawling limbs and vacant vehement faces deserve. The
abstract nature of most of Young's verse tempted Blake
to give way without scruple to his dangerous tendency to
make ideas take the place of images. The drawings for
Young are often majestic, but they are monotonous, and
it has to be an idolater, not an admirer, of Blake who refuses
to find them dull. In illustrating Gray, the more objective
and varied nature of the poetry had a salutary effect.
These drawings are often preposterous, but they are seldom

dull, except those interpreting the *Elegy in a Country Churchyard*, a poem which, strangely enough, seems to have failed to set Blake's vision on fire.

To these highly suggestive and seductive designs, instinct with eccentricity and vehemence, Mr. Grierson has prefixed an essay which is one of the most interesting which he has published. I regret that this finished piece of writing should be reserved for a costly and unhandy publication where few can have a convenient opportunity of reading it, and I hope that the author will not delay to republish it in a more convenient form. By this time Mr. Grierson must have issued, in the form of prefaces and addresses, quite enough critical writing to form a volume. Let him delay no longer to produce it. Mr. Grierson is not merely a professor of recognised erudition, but he is a very lively and charming writer, who has only to be more widely read to be generally recognised. His present essay deals mainly with Gray and the poetical ideas of the eighteenth century. I cannot close without congratulating the Oxford University Press on its enterprise in undertaking so huge a project as the complete reproduction of these designs by Blake, and on the skill with which the task has been conducted.

DOMESDAY BOOK

DOMESDAY BOOK

THE publisher's puff on the cover of this huge poem states that " for startling originality," and for various other things, " it should rank among the masterpieces of the world." This embarrassing violence nearly prevented me from opening the book, and delayed my notice of it for several weeks. But I have conquered my natural repulsion, and, having destroyed the paper cover on which the puff is printed, can face the overlauded prodigy calmly.

Domesday Book, which is as long as *Paradise Lost*, and much longer than *The Excursion*, is a modern story of American provincial life, told in blank verse. That it should be hailed as one of " the masterpieces of the world " is an example of the hysterical tendency of the hour to exaggerate the value of anything which is startling or unusual, and especially of anything which is ugly and depressing. It is also an instance of the inability of current criticism to express itself in terms of moderation. *Domesday Book* is a curious and interesting production ; by the side of great imperfections, it presents some sterling merits. It is very readable, and it indulges to the full the fashionable •pessimism and preference for squalor. It demands careful attention, but it is no more " one of the masterpieces of the world " than is some very handsome system of public sewage.

In 1915, Mr. Edgar Lee Masters, who is an American writer resident, I believe, in Chicago, created a certain sensation by publishing a strange book called *Spoon River Anthology*. The idea of that work was that as all the inscriptions in a provincial cemetery are lies, it would be amusing to tell the real grim truth about the persons buried with so much unction. The scheme was carried out in a spirit of eloquence and daring, and we learned what miserable experiences the late inhabitants of Spoon River had secretly lived through. The revelation was sinister, but rousing; and, although there was too much of it, the *Anthology* was highly entertaining. Mr. Masters has repeated his experiment in slightly different form, and whereas the *Anthology* had no other plan than the arrangement of long epitaphs side by side, we have in *Domesday Book* a systematic construction.

Mr. Masters has a passion for naked reality, and a great power of dissecting that " *pauvre et triste humanité* " which it is most people's instinct to cover up and protect. He tears away not merely the clothes but the bandages, and spares us no horror of the soul. His manner has, very foolishly, been compared with that of Walt Whitman; no two authors are more diametrically contrasted. Whitman is an optimist, full of aspiration and indulgence; if he strips away the raiment of humanity, it is to show the world how beautiful is the body beneath. Everything pleases Whitman, and he exults in his vitality. The author of *Spoon River* and *Domesday Book* is a pessimist of the darkest dye, for whom there is, in that provincial American scene which *Leaves of Grass* so radiantly described, nothing but dullness and concealed wretchedness. The most striking feature of Mr. Master's pictures of life is their extraordinary desolation and mediocrity. One is inclined to ask, if existence in Illinois and Ohio is really like this, why do these poor millions of Americans take the trouble to live at all ?

The nearest parallel to the tone of *Domesday Book* may be found in certain of the poems of Crabbe, especially in *The Parish Register* and in *The Borough*. In 1812, in a

remarkable preface, Crabbe refused to " adopt the notions
of a pastoral simplicity " among the peasants of Suffolk,
and undertook, in harsh and sombre verse, to describe them,
type after type, as they really were.   This is exactly what
Mr. Masters does, and with even more acrimony and con-
tempt, in violent reaction against the sentimentality of the
American literature of the nineteenth century, as exemplified by Howells and Mark Twain.

His gallery of tragic portraits is impressive and surprising.
In telling us the secret history of some fifty persons, all
living in one country community, he hesitates to offer us
a single gleam of light.   All the characters were failures,
most of them were criminals, while all, or almost all, preserved a veneer of respectability until the grim hour when
the death of Elinor Murray led, mechanically, to a general
revelation of their shortcomings.   All of them, the poet
says :—

> " Are gone to dust, now, like the garden things
> That sprout up, fall and rot.   At times it seems
> All waste to me."

There is no sense of a higher life ; all is saturnine and cynical.
It is only fair to say that, like other dreadful spectacles, the
picture is often extremely vivid.

As in *The Ring and the Book*, of which *Domesday Book*
faintly but frequently reminds us, the subject is the death
of Pompilia, and how it moulded the lives of a large number
of persons, so in Mr. Masters' new poem the subject is the
finding of the body of Elinor Murray, and the effect of that
discovery on the hidden existence of a whole chain of her
acquaintances.   First we have an account of the childhood of the heroine, and then, abruptly, the conditions in
which her dead body, with no sign upon it of violence or
disease, was found on the shore of a river.   The remainder
of the poem is occupied by the affidavits of various witnesses
at or in connection with the inquest held by Coroner Merival.

Mr. Masters is fascinated by the phenomenon which

A A 2

Lord Haldane describes in his *Reign of Relativity*, the fact that "in the plane of our lives as human beings in the world of nature, physical and social, we belong to the stream of the events which we experience." The corpse of Elinor Murray is suddenly arrested and exposed, and at once becomes a snag on which the reputations of half a hundred persons are caught and wrecked. The author is a sort of Gaffer Hexham, floating on the stream of society, and watching for corpses with his scull in one hand and a boathook in the other. Nothing excites him so much as to unravel the linked causes of things, and such is the hideous corruption of the provincial life he describes that his sport is endless. His theme is the horror of private life, and he penetrates its selfishness and secrecy with a gusto that is almost shocking.

If there is a moral to be found in *Domesday Book* it is that lives are wasted from lack of sympathy and imagination. There is no reason why any of the characters should have been wretched if they could have spoken frankly and their idiosyncrasies have been openly accepted. The horror is due to a system of universal misunderstanding and hypocritical concealment, acting in a narrow society which is defaced by poverty and mediocrity. Elinor Murray, who is the type of the self-emancipated victim of this bondage, is the daughter of a druggist in the village of Le Roy. Husband and wife have kept up the show of decent relations, but secretly hate one another ; the woman is a sort of vampire. Elinor is clever, earns her own education, leaves her parents' house and disappears, a teacher in a Western state. At the end of three years she comes back, and her father explains to the coroner :—

> " I knew
> By look of her eyes that some one filled her life,
> Had taken her life and body. What if I
> Had failed as father in the way I failed ?
> And what if our home was not home to her ?
> She could have married—why not ? If a girl

> Can fascinate the man—I know she could—
> She can have marriage if she wants to marry,
> Unless she runs to man already married."

Elinor becomes more cultivated in mind and delicate in
taste, and the druggist's store grows intolerable to her.
Nevertheless she strives to be kind and filial, but when the
war breaks out, she takes occasion to go over to France,
and disappears again.   At the armistice she reappears in
New York, but instead of returning to her parents, pays a
visit to an aunt " to rest and get the country air."   During
this visit she goes out for a walk, and is found dead by the
river.   We are led to suppose that she was walking alone,
until near the close of the poem, when we learn that a lover,
hitherto unmentioned, one Barrett Bays of Chicago, was
with her when she had a fainting fit, and holding her up,
when he ought to have laid her down, had the embarrassment of finding that she died in his arms, at which, in a
paroxysm of terror, he left her on the river bank and fled
away to Chicago until conscience forced him to confess.

The multitude of Elinor Murray's lovers, not one of whom
had in her lifetime been more than faintly suspected of
flirtation, is so great as to be almost ludicrous.   They have
to turn up one after another, from all sorts of unlikely
places, to fill Mr. Masters' canvas.   One of them says,
more pointedly than poetically,

> " She had more life than she knew how to use,
> And had not learned her own machine."

The result of this abundance of lovers is to lower our
estimate of the character of Elinor Murray, with which
Mr. Masters desires that we should sympathise.   We do
sympathise ;   her restlessness and longings, her ups and
downs of ecstasy and dejection, the hopelessness of her
emancipation, and the mess that she makes of her whole
conquered independence, appeal to our pity and interest.
Her useless culture, her vague aspirations, her characteristic revolt against any species of family restraint are

intelligible, and the stern picture of them timely. But we cannot help regretting that she had secret affairs with such a very large number of men. They all come, one after another, and confess with great prolixity to Coroner Merival; but how about poor Elinor Murray? Her polyandry, when every excuse has been made for it, continues to seem rather grotesque.

This is not a book which a young girl of the present day would be well advised to lend to her grandmother. It is what is called "outspoken"; in plainer language, it is very coarse. I find no fault with Mr. Masters on this account, since his purpose is serious, and he would doubtless reply that nature is entirely indelicate. I only reflect on the change which has come over America since Mrs. Lydia Sigourney clothed the legs of her chairs and tables in trousers.

With regard to the purely literary aspect of *Domesday Book*, it may be a salutary lesson to compare the account which the State Governor gives his wife of the effect of the murder evidence on his mind with the Pope's soliliquy in *The Ring and the Book*. The parallel is often quite close, and might be used to explain why Browning is a poet and Mr. Masters is not. But the American satirist is a keen thinker and a powerful writer, with an unfortunate tendency (*Spoon River Anthology* betrayed it) to prolixity. His blank verse is plain and unaffected, but such lines as
> " His duties ended, he sat at a window,"

or,
> " By angina pectoris, let it drop,"

or,
> " Gregory Wenner's brother married the mother "

are too frequent. To sum up, this curious volume is a disquisition on a theme which has been commonly ignored or evaded in Anglo-Saxon literature, namely, that the happiness of youth is undermined by having to conceal the tortures and risks of sexual instinct. At all events, it seems to be so in Illinois.

BROWNING IN FRANCE

BROWNING IN FRANCE

ONE morning in the early 'eighties, when I paid my customary visit to Robert Browning, I found a very quiet elderly French gentleman seated with the poet in the breakfast-room at Warwick Crescent. Browning presented me to him with his usual effusion, adding, " This is Joseph Milsand, my earliest interpreter and my best ! " The poet was in high spirits, and talked rapidly and loudly, with those occasional gesticulations which often gave him a certain foreign air. M. Milsand, motionless, watched and listened, with visible affection and pride, but scarcely spoke or stirred. The contrast was amusing—the sturdy Briton so full of vivacity, the frail Latin so silent in his reserve. This was the only occasion on which I had the privilege of meeting a very remarkable man, whose influence on the life of the great English poet ran deeper than that of any other man of letters, but whose work, and even whose name, was scarcely known in this country.

Milsand died on September 4, 1886, and Browning dedicated *Parleyings with Certain People* to his memory, in touching Latin words : " The absent one still hears and sees the absent." Milsand, who was five years junior to Browning, had reached his seventieth year, and their friendship had lasted for a quarter of a century. In his excellent *Life of Robert Browning*, published in 1910, Mr. H. C. Minchin has collected a few contemporary notes regarding Milsand, whose excessive modesty has kept his name unduly in the background.

When the Brownings arrived in Paris on their first visit,

in September, 1851, they were met by the agreeable news
that two articles of considerable length on the poetry of
Robert had appeared in August in the *Revue des Deux
Mondes*. These were signed by Joseph Milsand, a young
artist of Dijon, who, having been obliged to abandon
painting because his eyes had given way, had concentrated
his attention on recent English literature, and had been
commissioned to write for the *Revue* a series of contemporary
studies. The double article was highly agreeable to Robert
Browning, because here, for the first time, his poetry was
treated with seriousness and elaboration. Even his sweetness of nature had become faintly embittered, and his wife
had been made exceedingly angry, by the persistence with
which English people spoke of him as the " husband of the
poet," as though he himself were a negligible appendage.
Milsand was the earliest reviewer to insist on the dominant importance, as an original master, of the author of
Paracelsus and *Pippa Passes* and *Saul*.

Browning was thirty-nine when the articles appeared,
and he had published enough, in quality and quantity, to
give him a foremost place among the writers of the century,
but English criticism resolutely refused to do him bare
justice. This was now bravely done by the French critic
from Dijon, who happily chanced to be in Paris in the following January, when he met the two English poets, perhaps
at the house of Mme. Mohl. Friendship was instantaneous
and lasting. Mrs. Orr has recorded that for the remainder
of their lives Browning submitted all his poems before
publication to the censorship of Milsand, who corrected
even the punctuation. There was no other man from
whom Browning accepted such direction.

It has never been very easy to refer to what Milsand did
say about his friend in the articles of 1851. These were not
reprinted during his lifetime, and have not yet, so far as I
know, been translated into English. They were included

in a semi-private volume printed by the family of Milsand
at Dijon in 1893, but even this is not easily accessible. I
am surprised that at the time when the study of Browning
reached almost excessive proportions, soon after his death,
no one brought out an English version of what Milsand had
written. (Perhaps some one did, for the mass of Browning
literature was a perfect haystack.) The position taken by
Milsand with regard to this poet, then wholly unknown in
France, and the object of no honour in his own country,
is very remarkable. He says himself that he has to adopt
the *rôle* of a prophet—that he guarantees Browning as
a new religion. He analyses the style and the philosophy
of the young poet with as much firmness, as much jubilant
confidence, as did the idolaters of half a century later, but
with more judgment. No wonder that Browning was
pleased, since here, for the first time, was put forward a
deliberate and unflinching claim by a critic of great erudition
in English literature for a place in the forefront of English
poetry.

Milsand's eloquence, however, seems to have fallen upon
deaf ears, for the works of his client have never been comprehended in France. A study of Mme. Duclaux's eloquent
little book has sent me back to Milsand, though she finds
no occasion for mentioning him. I find myself asking two
questions : Why did the elaborate and singularly adequate
criticism of Milsand fail to attract the French public to
Browning, and what effect was made on Browning himself
by the subsequent animadversions of Milsand ? In respect
to the first of these, I own to surprise at the extreme
obscurity of the French critic. Nowadays, such prose
might pass in Paris, but in 1851 it was unusual for a writer
to be so dark and cryptic as Milsand is. He labours with
his thoughts, which almost overpower him ; he is so con-
densed as to evade the readers' comprehension. These
articles are dark with excess of light, like Browning's own

poetry, and it is curious to speculate whether, indeed, it was not the very difficulty of the verse which inspired this intensely alembicated prose. No wonder the Paris of Alfred de Musset and Lamartine could make nothing of these analyses of *Paracelsus*, and allowed Browning, in spite of Milsand, to drop unobserved.

My other question, as I turn the Dijon pages, deals with a more subtle matter—what influence Milsand's private assiduity between 1851 and 1887 may have had on Browning himself. We know that he allowed no other censure than that of Milsand to affect him, and that to this he paid instant attention. The editors of the posthumous volume say plainly that the serried dialectic and the singular abstractedness of Milsand's mind " *effrayait plutôt les esprits légers ou médiocres* " ; in other words, almost every class of readers ; but they violently attracted Browning. I am inclined to think that they encouraged him to devote himself more and more to what have been called his ethical acrostics. In Milsand the English poet found an admirer for whom his expression could never be too cryptic, nor the flood of his intellectual problems too turbid. They were not really turbid or really cryptic, but they gave an impression of obscurity, and I think that Milsand, who evidently liked them to be difficult, discouraged Browning from that lucidity towards which, after his marriage, he had certainly been tending.

This feature of Browning's poetry is one main stumbling-block to its acceptance in France. Mme. Duclaux, whose style is transparent and simple, acknowledges the " stupor " with which the French mind receives such poetry as *Pacchiarotto*. She does not repeat the mistake of her predecessor, who, like a Diogenes, met the pride of the poet with a greater pride than his. Mme. Duclaux, with genuine and instructed enthusiasm for her theme, never allows herself to forget that her object is to prove to French readers how much beauty and exaltation they miss by remaining ignorant of works like *Pippa Passes* and *Two in the Campagna*. She does not force *Sordello* down their throats. She bravely doubts whether any French reader needs to toil through the whole of *The Ring and the Book*. She recommends the Prologue, the Confession of Pompilia, and the Second Confession of Guido Franceschini. "All this," she says, "is very beautiful and not difficult. I sincerely believe that a French reader will do well to skip the rest." This is wisely put.

For some years after Browning's death there was an exaggerated attention paid to his genius, with the inevitable result that a general fatigue ensued. There were books published about his mission as a Christian teacher, about his philosophy, about his politics—a flood of more or less tiresome sharpening of other people's razors at his hone. This sort of propaganda was most unwelcome to Browning's own simple and virile nature, and so long as he was alive he did not exactly check it—for he enjoyed the attention which it implied—but he kept it in order. When he was once buried, the orgy of emotional commentary broke out unregulated, producing in time a weariness and a silence.

The consequence is that, for the last twenty years, with the exception of Sir Frederick Treves' valuable topography of *The Ring and the Book*, no imposing contribution to Browning literature has been produced. It is to a new generation, as well as to a foreign audience, that Mme. Duclaux offers her excellent little monograph. She had the advantage of knowing the poet well when she was very young and he already old, but she has the possibly still greater advantage of being able to see the facts in perspective. As the poet Mary Robinson, she can estimate the English verse, as the author of the *Vie de Froissart*, and other accomplished studies, she can measure it by French standards, nor has she any need to follow what other admirers or disciples have said. Her point of view is ardently appreciative, but it is entirely independent.

Criticism of poetry is of little use or interest to a foreign reader when it is not accompanied by adequate translations. The occasional versions scattered through Mme. Duclaux's pages are made by herself, and they strike me as often extremely happy. She is daring in paraphrase where the contortion of Browning's language positively refuses to be straightened out into logical French, and she invariably gives the English original as well. The most astonishing of her feats in this way is her version of the celebrated and amazing lyric, called *Popularity*, which might well daunt the most athletic of translators. Mme. Duclaux closes with it, and I think throws it like a perfect Carpentier. " Hobbs, Nobbs, Stokes, and Nokes " she turns into " Dumont, Durand, Dupuy, Duruy," and this is what she does with the final stanza :—

> " Hobbs hints blue—straight he turtle eats ;
> Nobbs prints blue—claret crowns his cup ;
> Nokes outdures Stokes in azure feats
> Both gorge.   Who fished the murex up ?
> What porridge had John Keats ?

"Et Dupuy rivalise avec Duruy, dans l'ardeur de leurs exploits azurés. Ils seront rassasiés. Mais qui, après tout, pêcha la murène? Et quelle bouillie d'avoine mangea John Keats?"

This takes my breath away, though I miss the claret and the turtle. But is Mme. Duclaux quite sure that *murène* is the right word ? I fancy that *murène* is some species of eel-like fish, particularly the lamprey. But what is French for *murex*, the solid white shell, the *purpura*, which is a very different object ?

Mme. Duclaux's biographical and critical monograph is followed by 125 pages of translation by other hands. These, which include the whole of *Sludge, the Medium*, are conscientiously performed, but in a manner much inferior to

Mme. Duclaux's. I find it hard to persuade myself that these supplementary versions can give a French reader, wholly ignorant of our poetry, any definite idea of the intense romantic quality which is diffused through Robert Browning's analysis of his notes of human action. In the careful French what seems to have unfortunately evaporated is exactly what the translator wishes above all things to reproduce. I return, therefore, not I hope ungratefully, to Mme. Duclaux herself, who often retains that intangible perfume. What could be better as a rendering than this :—

" A minuit dans le silence des heures endormies,
    Quand vous libérez vos pensées,
    Iront-elles vers ce lieu bas ou (captif de la mort, pensent
        les insensés),
Il repose, celui qui vous a tant aimé, que vous avez tant aimé ?
    Vous apitoierez-vous sur moi ? "

A VISION OF BURMAH

A VISION OF BURMAH

WHEN Oscar Wilde was in America, forty years ago, he
told his audiences that his thoughts on art and life had
come to him while he meditated in his beautiful home by
the banks of the Thames. His auditors imagined a wood-
land retreat such as might be found by Susquehanna or by
Muskingum. As a matter of fact, Wilde had been living in
London, in lodgings, close to the Strand, where the Thames
bears not the slightest resemblance to the Susquehanna.
The utterance was an example of two master instincts in
this strange being—the constant obligation to mystify
other people and the even stronger need to deceive himself,
He required an atmosphere of fantasy to breathe in, and,
as fortune denied him the real thing, he exhaled from
his inward consciousness a scented illusion. He was the
extreme type of dweller in glass-houses, surrounding himself with light from coloured panes in an enclosure dim
with the perfume of pastilles. Through the iridescence of
the artificial world he lived in, all illusions became possible
to others and to himself, even the illusion that he was
a great creative poet and a philosopher of extraordinary
subtlety.

As a matter of fact, he told the truth when he said to
M. André Gide that he " put all his genius into his life ;
he only put his talent into his writings." This has been
too constantly forgotten. He was great as a personality,
sinister, and even forbidding, in several aspects, but
irresistible in arresting attention and in provoking analysis.
As a person he stands alone ; as a writer he is not exactly

negligible, but second-rate. He will survive in a splendid and dreadful legend long after his last reader has ceased to open *Dorian Gray*.

The insufficiency of Oscar Wilde as a writer arose in large measure from his indolence. He hated the effort of penmanship, and greatly preferred to it the art in which he marvellously excelled—that of conversation. At the height of his fame he liked best of all things to sit in a restaurant, with a few intelligent friends, and talk interminably while he smoked his famous gold-tipped cigarettes. One of his eminent gifts was his voice, which was penetrating, silken, and a little monotonous, but extremely agreeable. He appeared at his best while he was talking ; his verbal gymnastics seemed in the haze of the tobacco smoke more original than later reflection allowed them to be. He alternated his paradoxes with remarks on literature, which were often sound, for he loved it, in spite of his affectations, and with remarks about persons, which were often as shrewd as they were amusing. In opposition to the common opinion, Wilde was not ill-natured ; his sympathies were better than his practice, and he had a genuine admiration of good writing and sincere writers. His phraseology in talk was opulent, but not so vapid as in his books. Much more did he deserve to wear the golden butterfly than Whistler, who was a golden wasp. Wilde's conversation often took the form of stories, short apologues, or parables, which he introduced very artfully and turned topsy-turvy. These tales were intended to amuse, please, or exasperate his listeners, but, above all, to dazzle them. Wilde was like some tropical bird, excited by being whistled to, who walked up and down his perch, preening his plumage and lifting his crest. Perhaps at these moments he reached the highest point of his " genius."

The specimen of Wilde's talent which has just turned up has given its editors a good deal of trouble to define, and they have not been very successful. They describe *For Love of the King* as " a masque or pantomimic play," but it is neither the one nor the other. Wilde himself called it " a fairy play," which it certainly is not. In the first place, with characteristic indolence, the author has not " written " his piece at all ; he has only sketched the outline of it, and expatiated on the ornament. It is a scenario, and that not of a drama, though it is divided into acts and scenes, but of a story, one of those gilded and perfumed apologues of which Wilde had then recently collected a series in *A House of Pomegranates*. The exact date of composition is uncertain, but it was evidently 1893 or early in 1894. The Wildes had a friend, Mrs. Chan Toon, who had married a Burman, and this lady had sent Oscar a volume of tales *Told in the Pagoda*. He also enjoyed " long and luminous talks " with Mr. Chan Toon, and the result was that he exclaimed, " Burmah calls to me." It called to such purpose that it evoked in return this dramatised sketch of an episode in Burmese history. Wilde " was meditating writing a novel as beautiful and as intricate as a Persian praying-rug." This could not be *For Love of the King*, which is surprisingly simple. It has, indeed, nothing to boast of but its trappings, and if these were stripped away it would be seen that, as in Hans Andersen's immortal parable, the King has got no clothes.

The author facetiously desired to see *For Love of the King* acted in an English garden " on some night when the sky is a sheet of violet and the stars like women's eyes." Evidently this was not one of the occasions when he took himself seriously. The gorgeousness of life in Burmah had seized his imagination, and he " let himself go " in a surfeit of goblets of gold and jewel-encrusted bells. He professed to have composed the piece while " bathing his brow in the perfume of water-lilies." The prefatory letter to Mrs. Chan Toon is the best thing in the book ; as a sample of

Oscar Wilde's preposterous prose it well deserved preservation. It is a precious specimen of the time when he wore velvet small clothes and carried a lily, and when George du Maurier advertised the escapades of Bunthorne. We have gone so far " out of that minute " that the pose has ceased to be exasperating, and now amuses the reader no less than it did the author.

When the curtain rises, the Lord of Countless Umbrellas, King Ming Beng, is discovered sitting in a robe of apple-green silk, on a cushion sewn with rubies, while he receives the two ambassadors of the King of Ceylon, who consents that his only daughter shall marry the Lord of a Thousand White Elephants. We are told that " many flowery speeches pass," but Oscar Wilde has been too lazy to write any of them, and, in fact, there is no dialogue at all. He preferred to indicate by description the profuse luxury of the traditional scene, and it is interesting to note that he had not yet developed any of that skill in dialogue which was to mark his comedies a few months later, and was, in fact, to prove the most durable of his literary gifts.

At midnight, after this official reception, the King walks, alone and unrecognised, through the crowd assembled in the Pagoda of Golden Flowers, among " charming Burmese girls, with huge cigars, and handsome Burmese men smoking cheroots and wearing flowers in their ears." A lovely maiden, Mah Phru, throws herself at his feet and implores his love, which he grants her without a moment's hesitation. They retire to her hut in the jungle. But in two years' time the Cinghalese princess will arrive to be the Queen of Burmah. What then ? The lovers have two years before them, and " After two years ? " she asks. " Death," he answers, but whose death is not explained. Two lovely sons are born in the hut in the jungle, and then the Princess of Ceylon's ship is sighted. Ming Beng is " terribly distressed," and " the melancholy cry of the peacocks fills the silence," but there is no help for it, the King has to marry his bride.

For seven years Mah Phru waits in her hut, constantly surprised that Ming Beng does not return, but ignorant of the cause of his absence. A bevy of horsemen arrive to tell her that the Queen is dead. " What queen ? " she asks, for this is the first she has heard of Ming Beng's marriage. The boys are to proceed to court, but their mother is to remain in the jungle. Mah Phru is " a model of restraint and dignity, blent with colour and beauty and infinite grace," but she is not going to put up with such treatment as that. She determines to make trouble, and she goes to visit a Chinese wizard. The description of the wizard's home is a specimen of Oscar Wilde at his best :—

" Buddhas of gigantic size fashioned of priceless metals, with heads that move ; swinging banners with fringes of many-coloured stones ; lanterns with glass sides, on which are painted grotesque figures. The air is full of the scent of joss sticks. The wizard reclines on a divan, inhaling opium slowly, clothed with the subdued gorgeousness of China—blue and tomato-red predominate. He has the appearance of a wrinkled walnut. His forehead is a lattice-work of wrinkles. His pig-tail, braided with red, is twisted round his head. His hands are as claws. . . . Only the eyes of the dragons move, and the heads of the Buddhas go slowly like pendulums."

The wizard obligingly turns Mah Phru into a large white peacock, and meanwhile the King is smitten with mortal disease. Mah Phru approaches the palace, but stays in the garden, where colonnades of roses stretch away on every side, and perfumed fountains spray water-lilies " of a monstrous size." She hears the court physicians say that the King cannot live beyond the night, and, hopping upon the wall, she indulges in a melancholy scream. Her young sons approach her, and offer her, in her peacock form, a handful of food, but she will not eat. All seems very distressing, but Mah Phru, by help of the wizard, exercises some magical recovery, and the King starts from what was judged to be his death-bed in perfect health. " Jewels

glitter," and the curtain falls. Unkind critics will say that
it is all tinsel which glitters, and it is hard to meet their
objections. But there is something to be said on the other
side.

In the first place, *For Love of the King* is almost certainly
an intentional burlesque of the author's favourite man-
nerisms. He is only partly the dupe of his own magnificence.
His attitude in this respect was not unlike that of
Disraeli in *Lothair*, with its luscious description of Muriel
Towers, where, among the fountains and the statues, there
were "perhaps too many temples." Oscar Wilde liked
to encourage his fancy to feed on incomparable splendours
such as never existed in real life or even on the stage. But
he was preserved from actual fatuity by his consciousness—
or dim sub-consciousness—of the ridiculous side of the
whole thing. Among his jewelled betel-nut boxes and his
vases fashioned like the lotus he was always on the point
of tottering into a peal of laughter. But he liked the
splendour and sonority of words, which, indeed, are sensitive
and fantastic things, possessing a charm that is not to be
denied. In such pieces as *The Sphinx* we see Wilde absolutely abandoned to the worship of beautiful words, chosen
not for their meaning, but for their sound and colour. He
liked to write about a creature—

> "Whose wings, like strange, transparent talc,
>   Rose high above his hawk-faced head,
>   Painted with silver and with red,
>   And ribbed with rods of orichalch."

It was great fun to write like that, and so it was to
imagine the scene in the garden of the Burmese King, where
Mah Phru, turned into a large white peacock, sits and
screams on the burnished balustrade. Nor is it within the
capacity of many writers to achieve this kind of solemn
and absurd magnificence. It required a special gift,
which now begins to have a sort of historic attractiveness.

But it must be admitted that *For Love of the King* is too slight a peg on which to hang a general estimate of the value of Oscar Wilde's compositions. He was what the Nonconformist lady at Reigate called "no serious seeker after truth."

MATTHEW ARNOLD

MATTHEW ARNOLD

ON Christmas Eve, 1822, one of the most beautiful and fruitful minds which adorned the nineteenth century was born into the world. Matthew Arnold first saw the light at Laleham on the Thames, the " shy " and " sparkling Thames," which he was always to love best of all the rivers of the world. His father, Thomas Arnold, although only twenty-seven years of age, was already famous for his " manner of awful reverence when speaking of God or of the Scriptures," for his profound classical learning, and for views with regard to education which naturally led the trustees of Rugby, soon after the birth of his eldest son, to appoint him headmaster of that school.

If the brilliant fame of Dr. Thomas Arnold had become somewhat tarnished, it has recently been furbished up by the brilliant little portrait of him contributed by Mr. Lytton Strachey to his *Eminent Victorians*. That portrait, although enlivened by touches of satirical merriment, may be taken as a serious introduction to any sketch of his eldest son, since it is obvious that to comprehend Matthew aright it is necessary to observe the difficulties which beset the opening of his career.

Dr. Arnold was a prodigious fellow ; he was one of those men whose vigour of character and pertinacity of effort are apt either completely to alienate a youthful mind or to crush it into passivity. In the case of Matthew they did neither, although they collided against an intelligence and a will not second to themselves, because, along certain lines, the son was glad to accept and to extend the views of the father. But it is quite plain that for a long while the strenuous orthodoxy and limited æsthetics of Thomas Arnold hampered and even frustrated the development of Matthew. They did him no ultimate harm, but they delayed him ; probably, however, the loyal struggle of his conscience against these parental forces gave his mind a muscular strength which it might otherwise have lacked. John Nichol, after hearing Matthew Arnold at Oxford, is said to have styled him " David, the son of Goliath." But this David had one smooth pebble in his pouch which Goliath could not match, since Thomas Arnold was totally devoid of humour.

It is reported, I know not on what authority, that Matthew Arnold, but how or to whom is not stated, forbade the preparation of any " Life " of himself. Perhaps eminent men would be well advised to leave this matter open to posterity. The embargo on a biography has, in the case of Arnold, made it difficult, and perhaps impossible, to trace the development of his mind and character during the years when we should find most instruction from following it.

The case is a strange one. Here is a man of marked urbanity and social charm of manner, who was born into an intellectual circle, surrounded from childhood by observant and gifted friends, and about whom we yet practically know nothing till he reaches his twenty-eighth year. None of his early letters seem to be preserved ; none of his contemporaries in Oxford or Keswick or London is found to remember anything about him ; in a society much exercised about verse, no one seems to have noted the fact that here was a young college don writing some of the most beautiful poetry of the age. The child and youth spends his holidays close to Rydal, and one chance phrase in a letter of Clough reveals that he was the *protégé* of Wordsworth, and his juvenile associate off and on for twenty years.

Matthew Arnold travelled frequently in his youth, and in Switzerland the shadowy Marguerite becomes *Marguerite Revisited*. But who was she, and what were the young poet's relations with her ? We do not know. In 1848 he announces that he perceives " a wave of vulgarity, moral, intellectual, and social," about to break over Europe ; that is the earliest definite statement attributed to him, until next year he comes before us as a poet at the mature age of twenty-seven.

The reception of his first book, the slim green treasure called *The Strayed Reveller and Other Poems, by A.*, of 1849, adds to our bewilderment. It was a desperate failure. The mid-Victorians were singularly unappreciative of the stars as they rose on the horizon—*Pauline* and *The Queen Mother and Rosamond*, and the Meredith of 1851—but their unbroken silence around *The Strayed Reveller* is the strangest phenomenon of all. Surely in " the home of lost causes, and forsaken beliefs, and unpopul . names, and impossible loyalties," somebody might have had wit enough to perceive the pure beauty of *Resignation*, the attitude of him " who saw life steadily and saw it whole," the melodious passion of *The Forsaken Merman*, the dignity of *Mycerinus*, the composure of Wordsworth orientalised in *The Sick King of Bokhara ?* No one in Oxford recognised any of these qualities—no one but a single precocious undergraduate, Algernon Charles Swinburne.

The author of all those lovely things plaintively expressed his wonder that " nobody took pleasure in this or that poem." Well he might ! And when, three years later, he repeated the shy experiment in another slim green volume, *Empedocles on Etna*, the same thing happened, or a worse thing, since, if *The Strayed Reveller* had been ignored, *Empedocles* was positively attacked and ridiculed. So scornful were the critics that before fifty copies had been sold the volume was withdrawn from circulation. Arnold's own family thought his poems " silly " ; his familiar friend, Clough, desirous of being just, was " in suspense " about *Sohrab and Rustum*, the most adequate effort at majesty in narrative verse which the world had seen since *Hyperion*. J. D. Coleridge, another familiar friend, was positively " vicious." But this time help came from a quarter wholly unexpected, for the young Fascisti, who called themselves " Pre-Raphaelites," happened on one of the fifty copies, and nailed it to their banner. The reputation of Matthew Arnold as a poet had started in *The Germ*.

When recognition came at last, it came rapidly. In his thirtieth year Matthew Arnold was appointed by Lord Lansdowne to be an inspector of schools, and he began to devote himself to the development of elementary education. This drew him into the study of politics, though he was never tempted to take part in what he called the " Thyestean banquet of clap-trap " in the House of Commons. He began to reflect on the dogma of orthodox Christianity, and to form views of which a whisper would have made the hair of Thomas Arnold stand on end. He evolved the doctrine of " sweetness and light," he pronounced in favour of a force which he called " sweet reasonableness," he began to polish shining arrows of philosophic irony which were to transfix all manner of shams and fallacies in our social, religious, and scholastic polity. He did not do all this at once, of course, but from 1852 onwards this Whig philosophy continued to inspire his active and lambent mind. Yet he might have explored all these paths and have pierced with the lantern of his wit into their darkest recesses, and yet hardly occupy our attention very actively to-day. We think of him not as a school inspector nor as an exegesist nor as an opponent of the Burials Bill, but as a writer exquisite alike in verse and prose.

Of his art as a prose writer, Matthew Arnold showed no

evidence until 1853, when he prefixed to the first collected
volume of his *Poems* a long essay, which should be better
known than it is, since, while there is no effort in it after
novelty of style, the thought is so sound, the emotion so
genuine, the vision so stately and luminous, that it would
suffice, if it stood alone, to proclaim its author one of the
foremost of English critics. It is signed from Fox How,
October 1, 1853.

The friends who surrounded and hampered him had
desired him to devote himself in poetry to modern subjects,
which were in the taste of that day; he was told by the
reviewers to leave " the exhausted past," and to write no
more about Empedocles and Mycerinus and the Sirens.
He rejected this advice as " completely false," and he
announced his loyalty to the ancients and to " the Grand
Style," of which he was afterwards to say so much. This
preface of 1853 contains all his critical principles in germ,
a later study of Sainte-Beuve having only confirmed and
regulated his judgment. More persons began to accept
him now as a critic than as a poet, and he was induced to
compete for the Professorship of Poetry at Oxford. His
opponent was a certain Reverend Mr. Bode, a Bampton
lecturer. It was what is called " a near thing "; the
clerical satyr ran neck by neck and almost beat Hyperion,
since Oxford was still deficient in " sweetness and light ";
but Arnold was elected, and forthwith became a famous
figure, not yet, indeed, as a poet, but as a lecturer whose
reading-lamp shot its rays through the civilised world.

Matthew Arnold was, in the Baconian sense, such a
" full man " that to speak of him at all in so rapid a survey
as this seems almost futile. No justice can be done here
to the controversialist of *On Translating Homer*, to the
sparkling harlequin of *Friendship's Garland*, to the sincere
and earnest philosopher of *Culture and Anarchy*. None of
these books enjoyed a large sale—Matthew Arnold was

never a " best " or even a " good " seller—but they made
themselves deeply felt by the flower of the cultivated
classes. They penetrated the best opinion, they led a
revulsion against the deadness of obscurantism and the
fever of excess. He who called out against the " incredible
scantiness of vocabulary " among the lower classes in our
country was no less stringent in condemning the equally
incredible poverty of thought in the upper classes.

As a critic of life and literature his attitude has outlived
the substance of his strictures. In literature, particularly,
his views on the work of individual authors have ceased
to carry authority ; many of them were delusive from the
outset. Matthew Arnold was curiously led into error
about particular writers ; he was oddly and obviously
wrong in his estimate of Shelley and Coleridge and Racine.
We do not apply to him for specific but for generic criticism ;
he is with Goethe, not, after all, with Sainte-Beuve.

His merits and his limitations are well marked in the
remarkable essay which he prefixed to his rock-built
drama of *Merope* in 1858, an essay inspired by the purest
enthusiasm, and by " a passion for the great masters."
Even here, however, in Arnold's admirable survey of the
principles of Greek tragedy, we may discern his far greater
sureness in handling broad principles than in citing individual
examples.

A generation which knew not the prophet whom we
loved and almost worshipped governs us to-day. It may
not be impertinent to offer a few words addressed to those
who had not the opportunity of judging him except in the
light of his books. To such readers I would say that Mr.
Matthew Arnold was better fitted for the study or for a
dinner-party—where, indeed, I remember his saying that a
glass of champagne invariably disposed him to conversation—than in the lecturing desk. When I returned from
a tour in the United States in 1886, Mr. Arnold, who had

preceded me there, asked me to come and talk to him about
America. " Did you make them hear you ? " he asked,
and continued : " I couldn't. They did not like my manner.
The Chicago newspapers said that I resembled an elderly
macaw pecking at a trellis of grapes. How lively journalistic
fancy is among the Americans ! But they were very kind."
In fact, his voice and elocution were hardly suited to large
democratic audiences. His eyeglass, his Oxford intonation,
a certain air which seemed supercilious, in combination
with a weak voice and a see-saw utterance, were obstacles
to complete enjoyment.

But in private intercourse he was perfect. His manner
was suave, sympathetic, a little reserved and remote, but
not cold ; his smile was enchanting. The peculiarity of
blue eyes, combined with black hair and black Victorian
whiskers, gave his tall, upright figure a noticeable character.
In these days of ours, when behaviour is so very lax and
unbuttoned, his elaborate politeness would seem, perhaps,
a little alarming, though he habitually unbent in easy,
familiar talk about people and things—more fluently, I
think, than about books, the discussion of which in conversation was apt to bore him. Perhaps the most charming
of the great men whom it was my privilege to look up to
in the years of my youth, I remember him with reverence
and affection. Matthew Arnold offered himself to us, in
private no less than in public, as a specimen of the modern
world created and moulded by the Greek imagination.
He was a marvellous example of the paradox that the
most composite of minds may at the same time be profoundly original.

INDEX

INDEX